KEATS AND HIS POETRY

KEATS AND HIS POETRY

A Study in Development

Morris Dickstein

THE UNIVERSITY OF CHICAGO PRESS
CHICAGO AND LONDON

International Standard Book Number: 0–226–14795–9
Library of Congress Catalog Card Number: 74–136019
The University of Chicago Press, Chicago 60637
The University of Chicago Press, Ltd., London
© *1971 by The University of Chicago*
Published 1971
Printed in the United States of America

To my parents

Contents

Preface

> Reality is so complex, history is so fragmentary
> and so simplified, that an omniscient observer
> could write an indefinite, and almost infinite,
> number of biographies of a man, each of which
> would emphasize different facts; we would have
> to read many of them before we realized that the
> protagonist was the same man. . . . A history of a
> man's dreams is not inconceivable; or of the or-
> gans of his body; or of the mistakes he has made;
> or of all the moments when he imagined the
> pyramids; or of his traffic with night and with
> dawn.
>
> Jorge Luis Borges

> Give me this credit—do you not think I strive
> —to know myself?
>
> Keats

THE appearance of a new book on Keats so soon after several
major biographies requires an explanation. The following
pages constitute a critical study of the poems themselves, but
one which does not wholly renounce biography for interpretation. I have tried to trace the inner history of Keats' imagination, more on the model of John Middleton Murry's *Keats
and Shakespeare* than any more recent account. Murry's
book, first published in 1925, is not much remembered today,
at least in America, but it deserves to be, for it conveys the
shape of Keats' poetic life with a discriminating clarity and
inwardness that has yet to be matched.

The present book does not often follow Murry's account of
specific poems, but it is much akin to his concerns as well as
his example. It proposes a reading of Keats' development in
terms of his changing attitudes toward "consciousness," what
Keats calls "the thinking principle," by which he means not
pure intellection so much as self-awareness and awareness of

the world that surrounds, nurtures, and conditions the self. Often in Keats' poetry such consciousness has not only a painful but even a tragic quality. But the odes affirm "the wakeful anguish of the soul," which the "Ode on Melancholy" opposes to drowsiness, death, and Lethe (the classical symbol of *un*consciousness, forgetfulness).

Keats' conflicting attitudes in these poems bring into focus the whole problem of Romantic subjectivity. He himself was not obviously an introspective or autobiographical writer—he recoiled from Wordsworth in this respect, and like some of his greatest contemporaries, who envied his *Hyperion,* he sometimes perversely aspired to classical distance and elevation. But even if his work were more consistently personal, it would be difficult to study his growth toward self-awareness, or even toward *ideas* of subjectivity, which are undoubtedly bound up with unconscious and divided motives (witness Rousseau, the most self-revealing and most elusive of all writers). Nevertheless, such problems must be explored for they are crucial not only to Keats' poetic imagination but for the understanding of Romanticism in general.

The central significance of self-consciousness for the Romantic poets has only recently begun to receive adequate attention. Murry's work, which touches on this problem in various ways, found little echo in later criticism. Older writers had taken due note of the emergence of the autobiographical impulse and the lyrical mode during the period and, depending on their degree of sympathy, had described the results as self-expression, subjectivism, emotionalism, or even exhibitionism (in Byron's case), ineffectual immaturity (Shelley), and egotism (the standard charge against Wordsworth, at one time endorsed by Keats himself). Keats, though classified by the Victorians with Shelley as a "subjective" poet, a connoisseur of feeling, has found favor in our own century as the most objective and disinterested of all these writers. The

classicistic taste of the New Criticism found much to admire
not only in the dense imagistic and moral texture of the odes
but also in Keats' ideas of negative capability and the poetical
character, which seemed to foreshadow the doctrine of impersonality proclaimed by Eliot in "Tradition and the Individual Talent." But the formalism of Eliot's separation of
"the man who suffers and the mind which creates" has little
to do with Keats' praise of Shakespearean empathy, *Ein-
fühlung*. Where Keats can say, with almost sensual relish,
that the poetical character "enjoys light and shade," "lives in
gusto," and "has as much delight in conceiving an Iago as an
Imogen," Eliot, with typical spiritual dryness, affirms that
poetry is "an escape from emotion . . . an escape from personality." Moreover, Keats went on from this notion of the
poetical character that "has no self" (which he expounded,
significantly, while writing *Hyperion*) to a very different
stress on a process of "soul-making," by which individuals
"acquire identities, till each one is personally itself" (an idea
contemporary with the odes).

The subjectivity of the Romantic poets cannot be confined
to self-expression, cannot be reduced to what Eliot calls "a
turning loose of emotion" and "the expression of personality,"
nor can it properly be opposed to objectivity and knowledge.
To do so is to fall into the conventional kind of dualism or
self-alienation that the Romantics tried to overcome. Geoffrey
Hartman has defined the traditional error succinctly in a
recent essay on Wordsworth, whom he describes as "truly a
subjective thinker":

> *A subjective thinker:* the phrase comes from Kierkegaard.
> But what does subjectivity, that much abused word, mean?
> Especially when qualified by "Romantic" it conjures up a
> world in schism: here objects, there subjects, here idiosyn-
> crasy (calculated oddities, unpredictable sublimities), there
> normative behavior. This understanding of subjectivity is in

error. Subjectivity means that the starting point for authentic reflection is placed in the individual consciousness.[1]

The present study attempts to explore Keats' own mode of subjective reflection (of thinking and feeling and knowing), which has too often been displaced into biography and aesthetics by the understandable fascination of his life and the incomparable greatness of his letters.

A large part of our culture has now entered an aggressively Romantic new phase. In literature the constraints of Eliot's classicism and New Critical formalism have weakened or lapsed entirely.[2] Critics have gradually recognized the continuity of Romantic and modern literature. Recent work on the Romantic poets has proceeded well beyond Eliot's categories, beyond all the parricidal polemics that aided the triumph of modernism. But we have not yet come to terms with the special character of Romantic self-knowledge.

On the one hand certain critics since Northrop Frye have stressed the visionary tendencies of the Romantics, their prophetic independence not only from received wisdom moral or theological, but from the dross of the empirical world. To these critics Romanticism is more a new confrontation with literature than with reality: a revival of the myth-making power and imaginative freedom of Spenser and Milton and a "modern" renewal of the archetypes of pastoral and romance.[3] They see self-consciousness not as an end in itself

1. Geoffrey Hartman, "Wordsworth," *Yale Review* 58 (1969): 515.

2. I have tried to sketch some of the dimensions of the new Romanticism in "Allen Ginsberg and the 60's," *Commentary* 49 (January 1970): 64–70.

3. Frye, for example, appropriates Schiller's term "sentimental" to describe "a later recreation of an earlier mode," and adds, by way of illustration, that "Romanticism is a 'sentimental' form of romance." *Anatomy of Criticism: Four Essays* (Princeton, 1957), p. 35. See also his later books *Romanticism Reconsidered* (New York, 1963) and *A Study of English Romanticism* (New York, 1968), where he continues

for the Romantics but only as a necessary and temporary burden, the negative moment that demands the higher harmony and reintegration of the autonomous imagination. Keats, with his recurrent skepticism about the imagination, does not fit well into this pattern, but at least Professor Wasserman, in his influential book *The Finer Tone,* has contrived to see his whole *oeuvre* as tending toward some condition of self-transcendence, a "realm of pure spirit," from which the mortal poet, mired in "a sense of real things," is unfortunately always falling away.

The most consistent opposition to such a view, at least as it concerns Keats, has come from a distinguished group of present or former Harvard scholars, who have emphasized Keats' skepticism and moral growth. These writers have little patience with the purely sensuous or incipiently visionary elements in his poetry, especially in the earlier poems. One of them, Professor Stillinger, has brilliantly ransacked even Keats' romances for undermining notes of irony and realism, and has gone so far as to find in the very arrangement of the 1820 volume "a progressive abandonment of the ideal and acceptance of the natural world"[4] (this despite the fact the book opens with *Lamia,* which is rife with skepticism, and closes with *Hyperion,* a highly abstract work). But such excesses of local zeal are unusual. With their great editions and extensive writings the Harvard Keatsians have taught us an immense amount about Keats and his circle; their image of

---

to stress the kinship with romance, the importance of mythopoeia, and a vaguely Blakean conception of "the awakened imagination." For a more subtle and original account of Romanticism and romance see Harold Bloom, "The Internalization of Quest Romance," *Yale Review* 58 (1969): 526–36, and (in a fuller version) in *Romanticism and Consciousness* (New York, 1970).

4. Jack Stillinger, ed., *Twentieth Century Interpretations of Keats's Odes: A Collection of Critical Essays* (Englewood Cliffs, N.J., 1968), p. 14.

the poet is far more accurate than Wasserman's, and they have firmly and finally interred the nineteenth-century view of him as a sensitive aesthete. But in presenting Keats (very persuasively) as a tragic humanist, they have also tended to reduce him to a realist and naturalist, as if, after a great deal of early self-indulgence, he had gone on to become a sort of Crabbe, to create the poetry of actuality which he often seemed to promise. Like the New Critics they have tended to rescue Keats by separating him from the other Romantics: they find in him qualities which (in Stillinger's words) "make him a saner if in some ways less romantic poet than his contemporaries" and which should therefore "qualify him as the Romantic poet most likely to survive in the modern world."[5]

This Goethean contrast between the sane and the romantic, with the modern world enlisted on the side of health, simply will not do. It salvages Keats while leaving the clichés about Romanticism standing, instead of exploring the contrary Romantic strains which Keats' career beautifully sums up and which his own conflicting impulses crystallize. The true schism in Romantic poetry is not between the real and the ideal but between self-consciousness and vision, between nakedness (in Yeats' sense) and myth, between existential anguish and imaginative self-transcendence. The true poetry of actuality for the Romantics is not a poetry of naturalism and "process" but a poetry of personal quest or crisis, a poetry of self-confrontation. What makes the "Ode to a Nightingale" so central, not only for Keats but for all of Romantic litera-ture, is the way it dramatizes these contrary strains, the way it charts a circuitous but definitive course through visionary

5. Jack Stillinger, "The Hoodwinking of Madeline: Scepticism in *The Eve of St. Agnes*," reprinted in *Keats: A Collection of Critical Essays,* ed. W. J. Bate (Englewood Cliffs, N.J., 1964), p. 90.

and naturalistic aspiration to tragic self-definition and self-knowledge.[6]

Between these two modes of Romantic awareness my own sympathies are clear enough throughout this book, but I have tried to give a fair and extensive account of Keats' earlier poetry up through *Endymion,* without which no understanding of his transformation and his major work can be complete. My first four chapters concentrate on poems prior to the "living year" of 1819, which have not been granted much close critical scrutiny. The first chapter introduces the problem of consciousness as a thematic pivot of Keats' work. The five remaining chapters are chronological: first the early poems, then a large-scale commentary on the slippery *Endymion,* where, at my peril, I chose not to heed Professor Bate's warning that the poem "does not encourage detailed attention." This is followed by a transitional chapter that proceeds somewhat differently from any other. Elsewhere I shy away from life and letters, seductive as they are, and try to trace the growth of a poet's mind from inside the poems. In this fourth chapter, however, to explore a crisis which made poetry itself problematic for Keats, I marshal a mass of minor poems, letters, and biographical events and treat them like the scattered parts of a single puzzle, fragments of a large poem. These diverse elements seemed necessary, not only as evidence but also to convey the pervasive and obsessive character of the poet's special feelings during this period. In the fifth and sixth chapters I look at some of Keats' major poems, principally the odes and *The Fall of Hyperion,* in the light of Keats' whole development, which they retrospectively sum

6. Cf. Stillinger, for whom the odes culminate in the "unambiguously affirmative" lines of "To Autumn," in which (he says) "the imagination is now devoted not to visionary flights but to a detailed examining of every natural sight and sound at hand." *Keats's Odes,* p. 9.

up and subsume. Thus, though the book does not aim to be inclusive it does attempt to trace the whole arc of Keats' development—its inner form, so to speak—and to focus on those of the major poems which represent the most significant stages and also speak most clearly to our own time.

I leave it to the argument as a whole to justify my choices, for judgments, especially in the matter of modernity and relevance, are precarious and subjective. My own feeling is that the Romantic period was dominated by the experience of cultural break in such areas as theology, politics, morals and aesthetics—an experience which proved both disorienting and exhilarating to those most attuned to it, such as the poets—and that we ourselves are heirs to a continuity of discontinuity, a veritable tradition of crisis. The Romantic sensibility is many sided, but I think the poets still speak to us in what was also their own major mode, first as crisis poets and then as orphaned but autonomous seekers and makers—witnesses to human brokenness and healing dreamers of possible redemptions. In short, the exemplary maladies of the Romantics and their extraordinarily vital therapies remain meaningful for our own problems of self and society.

Keats himself, I am convinced, can now rejoin the other Romantics, can now be rescued from our need for his supposed health and sanity as he was once rescued from an earlier need for aestheticism and decadence. He need no longer be our refuge from the negative emotions of modern literature, from its violence and desperation and apocalyptic longings. Keats too had within him an intransigent and threatening negativity, what Baudelaire calls "the sensation of an abyss" —a "violence of . . . temperament continually smothered down," as he once said.[7] To say this is not to impress Keats into the service of modernism or nihilism but only to insist

7. *The Letters of John Keats, 1814–1821,* ed. H. E. Rollins, 2 vols. (Cambridge, Mass., 1958), 2:81.

that he achieved health and selfhood through intense inner conflict, and that this conflict has much to teach us.

There is a positive side to the Romantic experience of crisis: a creative autonomy of self, a conquest of new territory for the spirit. "That which is creative must create itself," Keats wrote.[8] "By our own spirits are we deified," said Wordsworth in "Resolution and Independence." "I see, and sing, by my own eyes inspir'd," Keats proclaimed to Psyche. But both poets knew of the contingency and peril, the deep inner stress, that attended such godlike freedom and presumption. Wordsworth eventually gave it up, perhaps to forestall an even more drastic fate. As he adds to the line I just quoted,

> We poets in our youth begin in gladness;
> But thereof come in the end despondency and madness.

Romantic self-consciousness is always a double consciousness: innocence and experience, joy and terror, creativity and madness. Romantic poetry improves the quality of our own self-knowledge by recalling us to this double vision.

8. Ibid., 1:374.

Acknowledgments

KEATS has received so much intelligent critical attention that I can scarcely enumerate debts of this kind, but I wish to single out the work of J. M. Murry, Lionel Trilling, Harold Bloom, F. R. Leavis, Geoffrey Hartman (on Wordsworth and on Romanticism), Paul de Man, and Stuart M. Sperry, Jr. (on *Endymion*). Walter Jackson Bate's magisterial biography set a high standard for all succeeding work on Keats. Earl Wasserman's account of the odes proved invaluably provocative. Two admirable teachers, Steven Marcus at Columbia and Frederick A. Pottle of the Yale Graduate School, taught me much about the Romantic poets in their courses, and later encouraged me to undertake the present study. Harold Bloom provided guidance, criticism, and warm friendship at every stage of the project. My friends Marshall Berman, Richard Locke, and Jerome McGann read the whole of an earlier version and offered welcome advice and encouragement. Mary Bickelhaupt and Evelyn Ledyard deserve thanks for their typing. I owe the greatest debt to my wife Lore, my most gratifying reader and editor, who lent me aid and comfort in many a difficult moment.

KEATS AND HIS POETRY

1

Prologue: "The Feel of Not to Feel It"

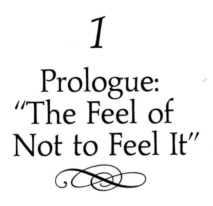

IN HIS essay on the Jewish question Sartre describes anti-Semitism as a "fear of the human condition," a longing to escape from the complexities of consciousness and freedom into "the permanence and impenetrability of stone, the total irresponsibility of the warrior who obeys his leaders."

> The anti-Semite is a man who wishes to be pitiless stone, a furious torrent, a raging thunderbolt—anything except a man.[1]

The Romantic poets were not afraid, but they saw very little theistic or metaphysical consolation for the human condition, and were correspondingly fascinated by man's place in nature, by the fragile line between man and all that is not man. "Attempting to be more than Man We become less," said Blake's Luvah.[2] But Blake's unswerving humanism was complicated by his sense of the phenomenal world as no more than a fallen hint of a possible human wholeness. At times

---

1. Jean-Paul Sartre, *Anti-Semite and Jew,* trans. George J. Becker (New York, 1962), pp. 53, 54.
2. *Poetry and Prose of William Blake,* ed. Geoffrey Keynes, 4th ed. (London, 1939), p. 367.

his difficult vision of an apocalyptic restoration of our full humanity reads very much like an attempt "to be more than Man."

In the probing and unsettling imagination of Wordsworth the difference between "more" and "less" is creatively blurred. Geoffrey Hartman's description of Lucy as a "boundary being"[3] could as easily be applied to many other characters in his poems—children, blighted women, old men—tenacious wanderers on the margins of survival, testing the limits of our humanity and endurance, yet often endowed with a mysterious grace and tranquility that seems to put them beyond our reach. In a famous stanza of "Resolution and Independence" Wordsworth compares the Leech-Gatherer to a huge stone, which in turn he compares to a sea-beast, "for the purpose," he later explained, "of bringing the original image, that of the stone, to a nearer resemblance to the figure and condition of the aged Man; who is divested of so much of the indications of life and motion as to bring him to the point where the two images unite and coalesce in just comparison."[4] (Wordsworth could be a chillingly exact analyst of his own work.) Yet the same Leech-Gatherer, blighted and reduced as he is, can tell his story with surprising if matter-of-fact eloquence and austere dignity. In a narrow sense he proves more articulate than the self-conscious, dejected poet who is the speaker of the poem, and who is mysteriously emboldened by this providential voice, almost an oracle, coming to him from the precarious margins of the human.

Keats is more fascinated by live than inanimate nature. He has little of Wordsworth's grim, stoical attraction to inertia, or desperate concern about the bedrock conditions of survival.

3. Geoffrey H. Hartman, *Wordsworth's Poetry, 1787–1814* (New Haven, 1964), p. 158.
4. Preface to *Poems* (1815), *Wordsworth's Literary Criticism,* ed. Nowell C. Smith (London, 1905), p. 160.

His youthful imagination is less concerned about vital[
about consciousness, the problematic landscapes of the ......
which were also part of the legacy of Wordsworth and
of his own modern temperament. He sought refuge from
these interior regions, often in actual landscapes (or in the
fantasies he could project on them), but in the end he saw
this recoiling impulse as part of the problem and made the
problem his subject.

It was during the writing of *Endymion,* in May 1817,
that Keats complained to his friend the painter Benjamin
Haydon of a "horrid Morbidity of Temperament" which
kept him from working for days at a time.[5] Nine months
later, trying to revise the same poem, he announced to his
publisher the "axiom" that "if Poetry comes not as naturally
as the Leaves to a tree it had better not come at all" (1:238).
With so recalcitrant a temperament it is not surprising that
Keats should envy the natural spontaneity of the tree in preference to the unforeseeable pitfalls of the human mind. In
one sense the composition of *Endymion* imitated that spontaneity: it was a poem mostly without a plan. "It will be a
test, a trial of my Powers of Imagination and chiefly of my
invention which is a rare thing indeed—by which I must
make 4000 Lines of one bare circumstance and fill them with
Poetry" (1:169). By the same token, however, the poem was
forced labor, written to a set length and timetable, a feat of
initiation that would be another kind of triumph over the
vagaries of temperament. By beginning the poem in the
spring and planning to work steadily through autumn, Keats
hoped almost magically to approximate the creative potency

---

5. *The Letters of John Keats, 1814–1821,* ed. Hyder Edward Rollins,
2 vols. (Cambridge, Mass., 1958), 1:142. All quotations from Keats'
letters are from this edition, hereafter cited in parenthesis by volume
and page number. On a few occasions obvious slips of the pen have been
silently corrected.

and sureness of natural fruition. He makes this clear in the lines of self-dedication (34–62) which follow the famous proem, in which he attaches *Endymion* to the rhythm of the natural cycle and resolves to bring it to completion with the year itself, concluding,

> O may no wintry season, bare and hoary,
> See it half finished: but let Autumn bold,
> With universal tinge of sober gold,
> Be all about me when I make an end.
>
> (I, 54–57)

Similarly he defends his decision to "endeavour after a long Poem" (and defends by implication the bizarre, meandering "structure" of the poem) by comparing it to a bower or landscape: "Do not the Lovers of Poetry like to have a little region to wander in where they may pick and choose, and in which the images are so numerous that many are forgotten and found new in a second Reading: which may be food for a Week's stroll in the Summer?" (1:170).

Before autumn was out he had finished the poem. It may have been with a flourish of pride that Keats inscribed the date at the end of the manuscript—"Nov. 28, 1817." Yet there must have been darker feelings as well, for sometime in the next few days Keats wrote a brief lyric whose three stanzas are like a sinister footnote to those four thousand achieved lines. In this poem the natural analogy important to *Endymion* appears only to be brought into question.[6]

---

6. I quote in this case from the Oxford Standard Authors edition, *The Poetical Works of John Keats,* ed. H. W. Garrod (London, 1956), pp. 436–37. This is the only edition in which Garrod followed the autograph discovered in 1951 (see my discussion below). In 1958 he reverted to the obsolete readings of his 1939 edition.

Hereafter, unless otherwise noted, all quotations from Keats' poetry will be from that later edition, *The Poetical Works of John Keats,* ed. H. W. Garrod, 2d ed. (Oxford, 1958).

In drear-nighted December,
   Too happy, happy tree,
Thy Branches ne'er remember
   Their green felicity:
  The north cannot undo them,
  With a sleety whistle through them;
  Nor frozen thawings glue them
    From budding at the prime.

In drear-nighted December,
   Too happy, happy Brook,
Thy bubblings ne'er remember
   Apollo's summer look;
  But with a sweet forgetting,
  They stay their crystal fretting,
  Never, never petting
    About the frozen time.

Ah! would 'twere so with many
   A gentle girl and boy!
But were there ever any
   Writh'd not of passed joy?
  The feel of not to feel it,
  Where there is none to heal it,
  Nor numbed sense to steel it,
    Was never said in rhyme.

This is not the nature of spring budding, of summer ripening, or autumn harvesting "with universal tingle of sober gold." It is the "wintry season, bare and hoary" that Keats had foreseen but not really imagined in its fierce actuality. To describe it Keats uses a powerful epithet that undoubtedly echoed in his mind from the last lines of *Endymion:* "Drear, drear / Has our delaying been," says Cynthia when she finally offers Endymion his consummation. Keats borrows a light, almost tripping meter from Dryden which, because it borders perilously on the comic, forces him to a Blakean concentration of phrasing. Adjectives and nouns are juxtaposed in a startling way. Coleridge (in "Frost at Midnight") had been impressed by the silent and invisible "ministry" of frost unaccompanied by wind, but Keats' "sleety whistle," with its combination of tactile, visual, and aural sensations, evokes the capacity of the frosty wind for direct physical attack. The concise "frozen thawings" tells of something even more cruel, a false spring followed by a renewed onslaught of winter. And the verb "glue" is as unexpected and physically vivid as the sudden frost it describes so pithily.

The crucial phrase in the first two stanzas is "green felicity," which is a neat synecdoche for the juxtaposition of nature and human life that is at the center of the poem. The best gloss on the phrase comes in a late letter of Keats, in which, arguing against optimistic notions of human "perfectability," he supposes a similar parallel:

> The point at which Man may arrive is as far as the paralel state in inanimate nature and no further—For instance suppose a rose to have sensation, it blooms on a beautiful morning it enjoys itself—but there comes a cold wind, a hot sun—it can not escape it, it cannot destroy its annoyances—they are as native to the world as itself: no more can man be happy in spite, the world[l]y elements will prey upon his nature. (2:101)

In the poem too Keats projects sensations upon inanimate nature, and "green felicity" signifies the same sensation: "it blooms on a beautiful morning it enjoys itself." (In "Lines Written in Early Spring" Wordsworth had asserted his "faith" that "every flower / Enjoys the air it breathes.") But the poem, unlike the letter, is not primarily about the destructive elements native to the world. It evokes them with great force, but only incidentally. Its subject is not adversity but our mental dealings with adversity. Here the analogy between human life and natural process, so hopefully and joyously invoked at the beginning of *Endymion,* becomes a desperate and unattainable longing, poignant but lame ("Ah! would 'twere so . . ."). In "In drear-nighted December" Keats invokes nature out of an awareness of separation, and that awareness is the poem's painful theme. It is a poem about consciousness written from what was to become a characteristic modern point of view—that consciousness is a torment and an anguish. The "sweet forgetting" which Keats envies and projects on nature is a complex thing. It involves a privileged relation to the future as well as the past. The branches have no need to worry about the summer to come just as they are happily unable to mourn the summer that has passed. Mankind, however, "writhes" at the loss of the past, and Keats is silent about its relation to the future.

All this is summed up in the most celebrated and controversial line of the poem, "The feel of not to feel it," only recently established as the correct reading. Until 1951, most editors followed the earliest posthumously printed versions of the poem, which had read "To know the change and feel it." In that year an autograph manuscript came to light, establishing the present text and offering the traditional version scrawled in as a variant in a hand other than Keats'.[7] The difference is important. " 'To know the change and feel it,' " writes Alvin Whitley, "links better the third stanza with the two preceding, perhaps, but the result is only a pretty, sentimental lyric of the pains-of-memory, 'passed joy' vs. present

7. Alvin Whitley, "The Autograph of Keats's 'In Drear Nighted December,' " *Harvard Library Bulletin* 5 (1951): 116–22. See also Garrod's discussions, *Poetical Works* (1956), pp. 470–71; *Poetical Works* (1958), pp. lv–lvii.

sorrow type."[8] In addition, "The feel of not to feel it," as hostile critics especially have recognized, has a much more problematic relation to the lines that immediately precede it, and to the whole poem.[9] To what does "it" refer? In the traditional version it clearly refers to "passed joy," but in the present version "The feel of not to feel it" may just as easily refer to the entire preceding line: the feel of not to feel the "writhing" that *is* human consciousness, that is to say, the feel of not to feel *anything,* the feel of insentience itself.

It is remarkable that even critics like Sidney Colvin and J. M. Murry, who have insisted on "The feel of not to feel it," have followed earlier readers in taking it as a lament for absent joy. Murry, with his customary breadth and subtlety, sees in the line an evocation of a state of affectlessness similar

---

8. Keats' friend Richard Woodhouse, who so objected to the third stanza, even went to the length of rewriting it entirely, to make just that sentimentality more obvious and saccharine:

> But in the soul's December
> The Fancy backward strays,
> And sadly doth remember
> The hue of golden days:
> In woe, the thought appalling
> Of bliss—gone past recalling,
> Brings o'er the heart a falling
> Not to be told in Rhyme.

Quoted by Whitley, p. 121. See also Garrod (1958), p. 552 n.

9. Woodhouse was the first to perceive this. "The great objection of the 3d stanza is that the 4 last lines are an excrescence—and ought to have had some connection with the 4 first which are an application of or rather antithesis to 1 & [?] 2 Stanzas." *The Keats Circle: Letters and Papers, 1816–1878,* ed. H. E. Rollins (Cambridge, Mass., 1948), 1:64. Cited by Whitley, p. 120. Garrod, who says that "To know the change and feel it" is "both better poetry and better logic," cites and agrees with Woodhouse, *Poetical Works* (1958), p. lvi. Whitley, though he strongly urges the present version, agrees that "the insolubly loose grammatical structure of the third stanza forms a maddening barrier to any neat or absolute resolution of the meaning or unity of the whole poem" (p. 121).

to Coleridge's in the Dejection ode, and relates it to recurrent moods of spiritual torpor that afflicted Keats, especially on the Scottish tour of the summer of 1818.[10] But this "unpleasant numbness" which "does not take away the pain of existence" (1:287), while an important part of Keats' temperament and crucial to the minor but significant poems of the Scottish tour, is not characteristic of the poems of the winter that preceded that journey. In these poems Keats reaches out to natural models for positive alternatives to the pangs of human self-consciousness. The thrush tells him,

> O fret not after knowledge—I have none,
>   And yet my song comes native with the warmth.
> O fret not after knowledge—I have none,
>   And yet the evening listens.

Even some of the smallest poems of the period are touched by this sense of nature:

> Shed no tear—O shed no tear!
> The flower will bloom another year.
> Weep no more! O weep no more!
> Young buds sleep in the root's white core.
>   ("Fairy's Song," 1–4)

He deals even more explicitly with the theme in the "Epistle to Reynolds," in which, echoing "Tintern Abbey," he contrasts the pains of consciousness with this benign aspect of nature:

> O that our dreamings all of sleep or wake
> Would all their colours from the Sunset take:
> From something of material sublime,
> Rather than shadow our own Soul's day-time
> In the dark void of Night.
>   (67–71)

10. John Middleton Murry, " 'The Feel of *Not* to Feel It,' " in *Keats* (New York, 1955), pp. 199–209. This remains the best account.

In the light of these poems, each with its own nuance, in the light of the whole of "In drear-nighted December," it is difficult to see how commentators can continue describing "the feel of not to feel it" as merely a negative state. The phrase is a capital motto for the whole quest for unconsciousness, for numbness that *will* "take away the pain of existence," which is a central and continuing element in Keats' poetry. This was never said in rhyme not because it is too painful, but rather because it is too unreachable and ambiguous an aspiration, beyond (yet, it may turn out, beneath) human possibility.

But the lines of "What the Thrush Said" and the "Fairy's Song" also suggest a more crucial contrast between human life and nature, pertaining not simply to consciousness but to survival itself. That which belongs to the natural cycle, Keats says, is assured of a permanence or recurrence to which man can scarcely aspire. The song of the thrush "comes *native* with the warmth" for it is both born with the warmth and belongs to it. Its existence is as assured as the coming of spring and warm weather. Similar native certainties are granted to the "young buds" that "sleep in the root's white core," a promise of survival that echoes the first stanza of "In drear-nighted December":

> Nor frozen thawings glue them
> From budding at the prime.

But Keats, out of indecision or bad faith, fails to persist with this theme in the second and third stanzas of the December poem. Through the strict parallelism of the stanzas, especially the first quatrains, Keats asserts that the "passed joy" of man is analogous to the "green felicity" of the tree and the "summer look" of Apollo, once enjoyed by the brook. Only man's memory of joy, his awareness of loss, spoils his happiness. But lines 7–8 imply that the whole analogy is more problematic, perhaps even fallacious. For the tree, Keats tells us, the coming summer is as certain as the past one (not perhaps for this tree, but for the natural cycle in general). "Green felicity" is as much a part of its future as of its past. Can the same be said of man's "passed joy"? Keats remains silent on this point. Professor Bate is ultimately right in seeing this "too happy, happy tree" as an anticipation of the "happy, happy boughs" on the Grecian urn.[11] At first glance they are radically dissimilar. The boughs of the urn cannot shed their leaves; they live in an eternal spring. The December branches here are "barren of leaves,"[12] seeming to suffer with man the seasons' difference. But the branches' participation in a world of temporality and change is an illusion. If their past and future are identical, then the words "past" and "future" are inappropriate. They imply linear progression, which the circularity of the natural cycle excludes.

The bad faith of this poem, then, is that it resolves on a psychological level what we can only call, on the evidence of the first stanza, an ontological difference between the human and the natural.[13] It is not simply in man's mind that his relation to "passed joy" is different from that of the tree or the brook; it is in his whole mode of being. Keats retreats in a comparable way in the "Epistle to Reynolds" when he begins to see nature under a more appalling aspect. He peers "into the core / Of an eternal fierce destruction" but berates himself for seeing "too far," characterizes the vision as a mood of

11. Walter Jackson Bate, *John Keats* (Cambridge, Mass., 1963), pp. 231–32, 584.

12. A few days earlier Keats had quoted to Reynolds from Shakespeare's twelfth sonnet, "When lofty trees I see barren of leaves / Which erst from heat did canopy the herd" (1:188).

13. See Paul de Man, "Structure intentionelle de l'Image romantique," *Revue Internationale de Philosophie* 14 (1960): 68–84, especially 69–72. An English version of de Man's essay can now be found in *Romanticism and Consciousness,* ed. Harold Bloom (New York, 1970).

his mind, by implication associating it with the mere subjectivism that he sometimes imputed to Wordsworth.[14]

This uncertainty helps to account for the difficulty we may feel in reading a related poem of this period, the sonnet that is sometimes called "The Human Seasons":

> Four seasons fill the measure of the year;
>   There are four seasons in the mind of man:
> He has his lusty Spring, when fancy clear
>   Takes in all beauty with an easy span:
> He has his Summer, when luxuriously
>   Spring's honied cud of youthful thought he loves
> To ruminate, and by such dreaming nigh
>   His nearest unto heaven: quiet coves
> His soul has in its Autumn, when his wings
>   He furleth close; contented so to look
> On mists in idleness—to let fair things
>   Pass by unheeded as a threshold brook.
> He has his Winter too of pale misfeature,
> Or else he would forego his mortal nature.

Here again Keats tries to build an analogy between man's life and nature, but without real success. In spite of their quiet beauty the first twelve lines seems a little empty and hollow. This is partly because the three stages they describe lack content. The first two merely adapt and simplify Wordsworth's account of his own growth from an unreflective to a more contemplative response to natural beauty (though the

14. Keats' phrase "Away, ye horrid moods! / Moods of one's mind" recalls "Moods of my own mind," one of the subdivisions of Wordsworth's *Poems in Two Volumes* (1807). Elsewhere Keats addresses to Reynolds a long attack on both Wordsworth and Leigh Hunt—"every man has his speculations, but every man does not brook and peacock over them till he makes a false coinage and deceives himself" (1:223–24). Later in the year he will distinguish his own more self-abeyant view of the poetical character from "the wordsworthian or egotistical sublime" (1:387).

"dreaming" that takes one "nearest unto heaven" is a distinctively Keatsian note). A bit of extrinsic evidence of the hollowness of these lines is that in an earlier version included in a letter to Bailey, they read quite differently:

> He hath his Summer, when luxuriously
> He chews the honied cud of fair spring thoughts,
> Till, in his Soul dissolv'd they come to be
> Part of himself.[15]

The sense of disparity that we feel in the first twelve lines of either version is explained by the fine closing couplet. Keats is yoking together by violence the cyclical phenomenon of the seasons and a fundamentally linear ages-of-man conception of human life. He runs this through twelve lines only by making analogies that lack specificity and by trying to limit the comparison to the "*mind* of man" rather than the life of man. (The mental character of the subject is emphasized even more in the letter to Bailey, where the poem is brought in as "somewhat collateral" to certain arguments about "every mental pursuit" and about the nature of perception. The unrevised lines cited above and the unrevised fourteenth line, which read "forget" instead of "forego," also imply a strictly psychological rather than ontological process.) But in the final couplet the thought of winter leads Keats not simply to its analogous mood or temper. It makes him think of man's "mortal nature"—the mental fact becomes a kind of *figura* of the end to come, of the reality that already is. At this point the poem breaks apart on the rocks of its own honesty. Unlike the "passed joy" of the earlier poem, steeped in ambiguity, the "lusty Spring" of youth with its "fancy clear" can have little promise of cyclical renewal.

Again, as in "In drear-nighted December," the all-too-human poet reaches out wishfully toward the natural process

15. 13 March 1818. *Letters*, 1:243.

as a healing balm, an antidote, for the pains of his humanity. In the end these pains, for being resisted, become all the more his subject—consciousness in "In drear-nighted December," mortality in "The Human Seasons." But the two are inseparably linked: mortality, as we have seen, is the latent theme of the first poem, and it is consciousness, the mind in the very act of creation, that finally betrays Keats in the second. "Poetry," says Wallace Stevens in *Adagia,* "must resist the intelligence almost successfully."[16] For Keats that resistance, though fail it must, is more than an aesthetic dictum. It is a deep inner necessity. Between the harsh truth of the intelligence and the recalcitrant fictions of will and desire lies his mind's dialectic.

Keats returned to these themes in two important sonnets the following year just before writing the great odes. One of them, "On Fame," he composed directly into a long journal-letter to America:

> How fever'd is the man, who cannot look
>   Upon his mortal days with temperate blood,
> Who vexes all the leaves of his life's book,
>   And robs his fair name of its maidenhood;
> It is as if the rose should pluck herself,
>   Or the ripe plum finger its misty bloom,
> As if a clear Lake meddling with itself,
>   Should cloud its pureness with a muddy gloom.[17]

16. Wallace Stevens, *Opus Posthumous* (New York, 1957), p. 171.
17. Later, forgetting the repetition of "lake" in line 12, Keats changed these lines to

> As if a Naiad, like a meddling elf,
> Should darken her pure grot with muddy gloom:

The mythological personification heightens the psychological theme but is otherwise gratuitous, and the verisimilitude of the poem is gravely weakened. Therefore, for these two lines alone, I follow the letter readings, which, as Rollins says, "seem preferable." *Letters,* 2:104.

> But the rose leaves herself upon the briar,
>> For winds to kiss and grateful bees to feed,
> And the ripe plum still wears its dim attire,
>> The undisturbed lake has crystal space;
>> Why then should man, teasing the world for grace,
> Spoil his salvation for a fierce miscreed?

Keats had just written another sonnet describing Fame as a "wayward girl" who is "coy" to those who woo her too actively, "But makes surrender to some thoughtless boy, / And dotes the more upon a heart at ease." As he improvises the second poem, however, those categories (activity, thoughtlessness, the passive "heart at ease") unexpectedly take on larger meaning. He writes a poem not about servitude to fame but about the human mind itself. The desire for fame, he realizes, is not simply a vanity (as he had treated it, with fine wit, in the first sonnet); this wish for secular "grace" through art arises from the passionate human desire for permanence, the inability of the mind to reconcile itself to mortality. Again Keats turns to nature as a model of passive unselfconscious participation in the rhythms of the life process. This time nature is not, as in "In drear-nighted December," full of the same terrors that afflict man, but marked by sensuous reciprocity:

> the rose leaves herself upon the briar,
> For winds to kiss and grateful bees to feed.

It is, moreover, sensuous enjoyment of a peculiarly feminine kind, set off against the masculine activity of the too self-conscious mind. Keats even implies that that mental activity is diseased ("fever'd") and perhaps even partakes of a kind of perverted sexuality. The autoerotic overtone of the rose "pluck[ing] herself," the plum "finger[ing] its misty bloom," and the lake "meddling with itself" is unmistakable, and well supports the primary sense of "unnatural."

The whole passage, especially the lines quoted above,

echoes one of Keats' most important letters, the one in which he included "What the Thrush Said" (with its message of "O fret not after knowledge"):

> It has been an old Comparison for our urging on—the Bee hive—however it seems to me that we should rather be the flower than the Bee—for it is a false notion that more is gained by receiving than giving—no the receiver and the giver are equal in their benefits—The f[l]ower I doubt not receives a fair guerdon from the Bee—its leaves blush deeper in the next spring—and who shall say between Man and Woman which is the most delighted? Now it is more noble to sit like Jove than to fly like Mercury—let us not therefore go hurrying about and collecting honey-bee like, buzzing here and there impatiently from a knowledge of what is to be arrived at: but let us open our leaves like a flower and be passive and receptive—budding patiently under the eye of Apollo and taking hints from every noble insect that favors us with a visit—sap will be given us for Meat and dew for drink. (1:232)

This is not the place to interpret the many implications of this letter. It will suffice if we take note of the recommendation of "passive and receptive" feminine sexuality of the flower, "budding patiently under the eye of Apollo," against the active and masculine bee, "buzzing here and there impatiently from a knowledge of what is to be arrived at."

But there is a darker side to Keats' "wise passiveness," for it partakes not only of sex but of extinction. Our primary text is the sonnet "To Sleep," which Keats wrote just before the sonnets on fame and included in the same journal-letter to George and Georgiana Keats:

> O soft embalmer of the still midnight,
>   Shutting, with careful fingers and benign,
> Our gloom-pleas'd eyes, embower'd from the light,
>   Enshaded in forgetfulness divine;
> O soothest Sleep! if so it please thee, close,

In midst of this thine hymn, my willing eyes,
Or wait the amen, ere thy poppy throws
   Around my bed its lulling charities.
   Then save me, or the passed day will shine
Upon my pillow, breeding many woes;
   Save me from curious conscience, that still lords
Its strength for darkness, burrowing like a mole;
   Turn the key deftly in the oiled wards,
And seal the hushed casket of my soul.

Here Keats replaces the "sweet forgetting" of the natural process with the "forgetfulness divine" of Sleep, but the longing for "the feel of not to feel it" is only the more intense. The passiveness that Keats exalts does not here connote, as in the beehive letter, openness and receptivity. Nor does it imply merely, as in the sonnet on fame, an unfevered acceptance of mortality. Though "casket" has never been a standard word for coffin in England, as it has long been in America, the last two lines nevertheless make clear that the quest for unconsciousness has become a quest for death. In fact in an earlier draft[18] the casket image is directly preceded by a hopeful vision of Sleep's "poppy" casting "its sweet-d[e]ath dews[19] o'er every pulse and limb." In the poem itself the process is more definitive and hardly luxurious. The turning of the key in the lock has a frightening finality, soon confirmed by the verb "seal" (changed from "shut" in the draft), and the smoothness of the oiled wards emphasizes the speaker's collusion. The attendant hush accentuates an already funereal atmosphere.

The twelve-line draft provides further evidence that Keats intended this emphasis. There these last two lines appear, transposed, as lines 9 and 10, followed by two lines which

18. See Garrod (1956), pp. 466–67.
19. Keats wrote "sweet-dath dews" but probably intended "sweet death-dews."

describe the coming of morning. This development is consistent with the invocations to sleep in early Keats, in "Sleep and Poetry" and *Endymion* (I, 453–65), where some weight is given to sleep's restorative power. In the final version of "To Sleep" this recall to life is eliminated and the hushed and sealed casket is brought down to the last line as an emblem of dark closure and a radical extinction of consciousness.

The poem ought not to be taken in isolation however. Along with Novalis' *Hymnen an die Nacht* and Shelley's lyric "To Night" it belongs to the genre of the Romantic night-poem, where the cultural and moral values traditionally attributed to light and dark, life and death, reason and the irrational are audaciously inverted. At times this aims at little more than satanism and shock—"Evil be thou my Good"—and not without a guilty conscience, or a desire merely to titillate; elsewhere, more ambitiously, the Romantics anticipate a Nietzschean "revaluation of all values." The famous comments of Blake and Shelley on *Paradise Lost,* like their poetry itself, go far beyond the satanic reversal of orthodox values. To Blake "Energy is the only life," which explains why Milton "wrote in fetters when he wrote of Angels & God, and at liberty when of Devils & Hell," thus proving himself "a true Poet and of the Devil's party without knowing it." The devil's party is the party of Energy, both sensual energy and the power of unfettered imaginative creation, but Blake strikes something of a balance by insisting that "without Contraries is no progression": *both* Reason and Energy "are necessary to Human existence."[20] Keats makes a similar dialectical qualification when he says of the poetical character that it relishes both "the dark side of things" *and the bright.* But he makes it no less clear that the poetical char-

20. *The Marriage of Heaven and Hell,* in Keynes, *Poetry and Prose,* pp. 182, 181.

acter involves the assumption of forbidden roles and identities: "it enjoys light and shade; it lives in gusto, be it
foul or fair, high or low, rich or poor, mean or elevated—It
has as much delight in conceiving an Iago as an Imogen.
What shocks the virtuous philosopher, delights the camelion
Poet" (1:387). It would be portentous to invoke German
formulations here, such as the aesthetic transcendence of the
ethical, beyond good and evil, and so forth, though they are
more to the point than the cliché of Romantic satanism or a
narrowly aesthetic notion of Negative Capability. What is
involved here, as in the night-poem, is the freeing of the
imagination from moral censorship, a quest beyond rational
enlightenment and common perception toward a recovery
of the night-side of experience.

Shelley's poem instances this very well. "To Night" is built
upon an almost parodistic inversion of a hymn to the sun or
to Apollo. Shelley implores the Spirit of Night to arise and
move west out of its "misty eastern cave." Outside the pale of
civilization and rational clarity Night has been weaving
"dreams of joy and fear" which make it "terrible and dear."
These dreams represent the furthest reach of the imagination,
whose materials are the passions and whose sources are in the
chthonic and the unconscious. In the third stanza, Shelley
describes the daytime,

> When light rode high, and the dew was gone,
> And noon lay heavy on flower and tree.

He turns the carriage of the sun into an arrogant, despotic
chariot and makes day stifling by rendering the sheer physical
weight of the noon heat, its desiccating power, its near enmity
to nature and to life.[21] But the "plot" of the poem takes a
different turn from that of Keats' "To Sleep." Keats follows

21. Cf. Harold Bloom, *Shelley's Mythmaking* (New Haven, 1959),
pp. 5–8.

out the logic of his own desire for passive insentience by concluding in a wish for easeful death. But Shelley, for whom Night and the imagination have from the start of the poem been intensely active principles, goes on to distinguish between Night and its "brother Death" and "sweet child Sleep." The activity of the imagination will require of him above all life and wakeful consciousness.

> Death will come when thou art dead,
> Soon, too soon—

He is addressing Night, but it seems to be directed to his own human self as well, and to the perilous death wish within it (which is also the death wish latent within the whole genre). The result is not a tautology but rather a brilliant juxtaposition. Shelley moves from the painlessly distant and abstract "death will come" to its critique, the concrete and personal "when thou art dead." The "when," which confronts the abstraction with a temporal context, leads directly to the decisive "soon, too soon." Even the sounds are in pointed contrast, for the abstract noun "death," from which the breath escapes, is replaced by the predicate adjective "dead," which is closed at both ends and has a dull, lumpish sound of finality. (Keats himself uses the same effect for like purpose in the Nightingale ode: "To thy high requiem become a sod.") It is conventional today to contrast Shelley's supposed decadence and death worship with Keats' robust health. The evidence at least of these two poems suggests that we might invert that comparison.

Before we too quickly label Keats decadent, however, we must take a closer look at "To Sleep," especially at what we have until now ignored, its structure. The first eight lines of the poem form a natural unit. The rhyme scheme is conventional, a Shakespearean octave, and the poem substantially follows the earlier draft. Each quatrain begins with an invocation to Sleep, and the lines limit themselves to a description of sleep itself. Their unity was enhanced by changes that Keats made from the draft. Originally, after "light" at the end of line 3, he wrote "Of sun or teasing candles," which he recognized as a false start and erased. Instead, still trying to describe the light, he wrote, "As wearisome as darkness is divine." In the final version Keats rejected this too obvious and schematic inversion of light and darkness, and also left all description of the daylight to a later part of the poem. Another unifying change came in line 8 where, as I have noted, Keats originally had Sleep throwing "its sweet-d[e]ath dews o'er every pulse and limb" (which led directly to "the hushed Casket of my soul" in line 9). In the final version he eliminated this early and too facile reference to the luxury of easeful death and confined these lines to sleep alone. But although Keats changed these two particularly self-indulgent lines, the first eight lines remain conventional and facile enough. "Forgetfulness divine" is unearned, and "gloom-pleas'd eyes" echoes the Graveyard melancholists of the mid-eighteenth century. The whole personification is less original and successful than Shelley's in "To Night" and depends heavily on traditional apostrophes to Morpheus.

It is only in the last six lines that the poem achieves greatness. Keats earns his escapism by being more than an escapist. He turns his quest for unconsciousness into a dialectic with consciousness. Lines 9 to 12 form the poem's second unit (though the rhyme scheme sunders them). They form the only section that has no verbal or structural precedent in the draft. They are linked by the repeated "save me," as Keats addresses Sleep and night but turns then at last to a description of their contraries, consciousness and the daylight that is associated with it. Keats offers three fierce images to convince us of the torments of "curious conscience." The first is no more than a suggestion.

> Then save me, or the passed day will shine
> Upon my pillow, breeding many woes.

This, and the two lines that follow it, are a reminiscence of the lines partly quoted earlier, from the "Epistle to Reynolds," in which Keats laments that our "dreamings . . . shadow our own Soul's day-time / In the dark void of Night. For in the world / We jostle—." Here Keats breaks off, but the meaning is clear enough. It is the reverse of what Freud described. We have no dark monsters of the unconscious invading the conscious mind. The fault here is in the world rather than in the self, it is the light of common day that is darkness.

In the sonnet the operative word is "breeding." It is the only natural image in the poem, and it suggests a reciprocity which is ferocious and parodistic. The passed day that will "shine" upon the pillow reminds us of the benign, life-giving sun that shines on the earth in so many other Keats poems. Here it breeds pain and suffering. The image is parallel to Shelley's "And noon lay heavy on flower and tree." What Keats has in mind perhaps is the hot sun of Egypt that breeds monsters out of the slime of the Nile, an image that he knew from Shakespeare. This reciprocity is the opposite of "budding patiently under the eye of Apollo." It is also the negation of Wordsworthian reciprocity, not only because it shows nature at a moment of destructive interplay, but because it inverts Wordsworth's assertion of salvation-by-memory, by which some experiences achieve a healing, consoling permanence in the mind.[22] But here, as in "In drear-nighted December," it is precisely by memory that Keats is wracked. He yearns instead for salvation-by-forgetfulness.

The two other images that Keats uses are even more forceful:

22. See Hartman's exposition of the Wordsworthian "after-image," *Wordsworth's Poetry*, pp. 269–72.

> Save me from curious conscience, that still lords
> Its strength for darkness, burrowing like a mole;

The martial image of consciousness lording its large and almost public strength, is strikingly combined with the image of a power that is no less fierce for being insidious, private, and inward. "Burrowing like a mole," in addition, offers muted overtones of blindness and sinister sexuality. This leads directly to the parallel image of the key in the oiled wards of the lock, in which the gnawing secret sexuality of this "invisible worm" is countered by a desire to be fully possessed—"deftly" suggests a cavalier, almost mechanical facility—and thereby annihilated. In these last two lines Keats turns to Sleep again, not in the naive and conventional way of the first eight lines, but rather after having burned through its fierce dispute with the waking world. It is as if the mental energy that had been generated in the recollection of the "passed day" and "curious conscience" had infused new imaginative power into Keats' vision of their opposite, Sleep. In this dialectical tension the death wish justifies itself.

In the end, though this poem only makes intimations, Keats' escapism is validated by the nature of the world which he seeks to flee, and his quest for unconsciousness is made meaningful by the intensity and pain with which he experiences consciousness itself. The death wish becomes significant when it ceases to be a fanciful self-indulgence ("sweet-d[e]ath dews") and becomes a passionate witness to the life it negates, the world it accuses, the self it can no longer bear.

2

The World of the
Early Poems

> . . . to somewhere
> Virginal perhaps, less fragmentary, cool.
>
> Hart Crane, "For the Marriage of Faustus and Helen"

No PART of Keats' work is more vulnerable to the charge of escapism than the early poems. Dr. Leavis summed up his case against Shelley by attacking his "weak grasp upon the actual,"[1] but in so much of the 1817 *Poems* and *Endymion* Keats like Shelley is in explicit flight from the actual. He seeks out "places of nestling green for poets made," womblike enclosures "sequestered, wild, romantic," far away from the world and all its troubles. Or he longs to "burst our mortal bars" by receiving "shapes from the invisible world, unearthly singing / From out the middle air." He envisions the death of a poet as a kind of transcendental junket beyond this "dull, and earthly mould," to become "enskyed" like Endymion:

> "Fair world, adieu!
> Thy dales, and hills, are fading from my view:
> Swiftly I mount, upon wide spreading pinions,
> Far from the narrow bounds of thy dominions."
>
> ("To My Brother George," 103–6)

1. F. R. Leavis, *Revaluation: Tradition and Development in English Poetry* (New York, 1947), p. 206.

Corresponding to these motifs is a conception of poetry which in its refusal to take any account of the darker side of experience, as Lionel Trilling says half ironically, "puzzles and embarrasses us," for it seems "the essence of Philistinism."[2] In "Sleep and Poetry" Keats attacks poetry that "feeds upon the burrs / And thorns of life." Poetry, he tells us, should provide "trains of peaceful images," should "sooth the cares, and lift the thoughts of man" (244–47, 340):

> And they shall be accounted poet kings
> Who simply tell the most heart-easing things.
> (267–68)

This is inept verse, but the problems it raises are more substantive than technical. Many critics have pinpointed the vulgarities of diction and chastized Keats' models, secure in the knowledge that he was shortly to find better ones. It is less easy to deal with the substance of these poems. In this respect "To Sleep" and "In drear-nighted December" are less troublesome for they are not escapist poems so much as poems about the desire or compulsion to escape. They are born of anguish and mental division, highly self-conscious in their very attack on self-consciousness.

The divisions of Keats in his early poems do not pertain to self-consciousness. The troubled, almost desperate tone of the sonnet "To Sleep" places it firmly in the period that produced the "Ode to a Nightingale" and the "Ode on Melancholy." But if "Sleep and Poetry" and "I stoop tip-toe" are troubled by anything, it is the pain of youth and inexperience, and Keats' sense of not yet having written great verse. They are poems of celebration, and are mainly about poetry itself, the "end and aim" of which, in the perspective of youthful ardor,

2. Lionel Trilling, *Beyond Culture: Essays on Literature and Learning* (New York, 1965), p. 68.

seems clear enough. The complexity of awareness that is the glory and the torment of the later Keats is absent from these poems. Yet in a naive and spontaneous way they undertake many of the strategies that we have seen to be characteristic of Keats at a later, more sophisticated period.

I have previously argued that sleep and death in "To Sleep" and the natural cycle in "In drear-nighted December" are envied not for their own sake but have rather a special meaning for Keats. He appeals to them as antidotes to consciousness, modes of self-transcendence, even to the point of self-annihilation, which the all-too-conscious poet seizes upon. Yet such forms of self-transcendence are no sudden discovery that Keats makes late in his career. They have always been important, particularly to the poet of the 1817 volume and the more complex *Endymion*.

Earlier generations, that took more pleasure in descriptive verse, could be indulgent toward Keats' first volume for what Leigh Hunt in his still interesting review called the young poet's "close observation of nature."[3] But Hunt's sensitive illustration of their descriptive accuracy provided authority for a distortion of critical emphasis. Hunt takes it for granted that the reader will find evidence of sufficient (and probably excessive) imaginative liberty, exquisite proof of a "most luxuriant fancy." Therefore, starting on the first page of the book, he sets out to show that it "presents us with a fancy, founded, as all beautiful fancies are, on a strong sense of what really exists or occurs." Yet this delicate polarity is lost when Graham Hough says of the same volume that

> Keats, like Gautier, was "un homme pour qui le monde visi-
> ble existe." And the visible world meant chiefly the world of
> nature; not nature with all the mystical and moral overtones

3. Hunt's three-part review appeared in *The Examiner,* 1 June, 6 July, and 13 July, 1817, pp. 345, 428–29, 443–44. All my references are to his discussion of "I stood tip-toe," 6 July, p. 429.

that Wordsworth found in it, but simply the unanalysed de-
lightfulness of living and growing things.

Citing several passages from the opening poem, he goes on
to say that "there is nothing here that could not be seen in a
summer afternoon on Hampstead Heath."[14]

A close look at that first poem proves Keats to be less than
satisfied with "le monde visible." The very first line—"I stood
tip-toe upon a little hill"—puts a double emphasis on upward
movement, hinting at the higher flights that the poem will
later undertake. The "natural description" that follows tends
to break away from nature, to make mental constructions
upon it. Line after line yields extreme examples of the pathetic
fallacy. The sweet buds pull in their stems "with a modest
pride" (3). The dew on the buds forms "starry diadems /
Caught from the early sobbing of the morn." The clouds are
likened to "flocks new shorn" sleeping "on the blue fields of
heaven" (8–10),

> and then there crept
> A little noiseless noise among the leaves,
> Born of the very sigh that silence heaves.
> (10–12)

Personification is here bolstered by oxymoron with such effect
that the literal object ("a gentle air in solitude," Leigh Hunt
tells us) is almost obliterated by the power of the formulation.
We have Hunt's assurance that the poem originated with an
actual morning on Hampstead Heath, but as it progresses the
poet seems less and less content with the natural scene. The
"greediest eye" extends itself farther and farther, moves
toward the horizon, and beyond it:

> Far round the horizon's crystal air to skim,
> And trace the dwindled edgings of its brim;
> (17–18)

4. Graham Hough, *The Romantic Poets* (New York, 1964), p. 159.

Gradually, the natural landscape turns into an imagined one, food for speculation.

> To picture out the quaint, and curious bending
> Of a fresh woodland alley, never ending;
> Or by the bowery clefts, and leafy shelves,
> Guess where the jaunty streams refresh themselves.
>
> (19–22)

The visual (to use Geoffrey Hartman's terms) gives way to the visionary. The mind, which began by observing nature, proceeds to contemplate it and be liberated from it.

> I gazed awhile, and felt as light, and free
> As though the fanning wings of Mercury
> Had play'd upon my heels: I was light-hearted,
> And many pleasures to my vision started.
>
> (23–26)

"The 'posey' of luxuries that he then proceeds to pluck," J. R. Caldwell says, "that is the images of beauty which he jumbles out, are items not present to his actual sense, but mere ideas floating across his inward eye as he gazes on the generative scene around him."[5] The seemingly random lines that follow are not primarily objective or descriptive. As Caldwell has shown, they are structured only by a loose process of association in the mind of the living subject.

But Keats' contemplation of nature is not indiscriminate. One motif which recurs so frequently that it seems the epitome of his sense of nature is the bower—the enclosed, sheltered nook, the place of nestling green. Behind this "little space, with boughs all woven round," stands Hunt, but more importantly the poet whom Keats considered Hunt's master and for a time his own, Spenser. In *The Faerie Queene* the

5. James R. Caldwell, *John Keats' Fancy: The Effect on Keats of the Psychology of His Day* (Ithaca, 1945), p. 19. Caldwell's whole study is valuable for both background and criticism of these early poems.

bower, especially the famous Bower of Bliss, is dialectically linked to an opposing motif, that of the traveler or the quest, and both embody values that are important for the poem as a whole. The quest in Spenser connotes growth and moral development, what the Germans call *Bildung,* and no matter how fantastic or allegorical the landscape it always supposes a world of time, toil, and change. The Bower of Bliss, on the other hand, embodies a timeless world of desire, the instinctual life that seems impervious to change and development. For the moral traveler it represents the dangerous temptation of shelter and rest. Just before reaching the Bower of Bliss, the boat of Guyon and the Palmer passes "a still / And calmy bay," sheltered on both sides to make a "plesaunt port." Here Siren-like mermaids call out to Guyon:

> O turne thy rudder hither-ward awhile:
> Here may thy storme-bet Vessell safely ryde;
> This is the Port of rest from troublous toyle,
> The worlds sweet In, from paine and wearisome turmoyle.
> (II, xii, 32)

The Bower itself passes before the moving Guyon as a series of static scenes, and it is largely the firmness of purpose of the Palmer, his moral Virgil, that keeps the knight from stopping or turning aside from his course. At the risk of schematic simplification, we can see the same dichotomy reflected in Spenser's style. From the bower, or the principle of pleasure, springs the famous lushness and sensuousness that so appealed to the Romantics. From the quest, or the principle of *Bildung,* proceeds the complex structure of the poem, its Arthurian epic material, and allegorical method.

The Bower of Bliss well illustrates one of the fundamental ambiguities of the bower motif. Both in pastoral poetry and in the Genesis story the enclosed, sheltered *locus amoenus* usually symbolizes some kind of innocence, the imagined innocence of nature itself, or of our childhood, or of some prelapsarian sexual paradise, free of shame, guilt, and domineering lust. Sometimes all these fantasies are combined, fed as they are by common memories of a lost paradise of total infantile gratification; after all, Freud's announcement of infantile sexuality, like his theory of the unconscious, has many mythic, poetic, and religious antecedents. In any case, the sexual significance of the bower is highly variable, especially in relation to our notions of human innocence, of human nature and purpose. But to the quest-hero of Spenserian epic, who must accomplish his mission in the world of experience, the pleasures of innocence are as regressive and dangerous as the pleasures of sex. Spenser at once exploits the bower tradition and moralizes it when he turns the emblem of innocence into a myth of sexual temptation for the ascetic hero.

In the Romantic period the duality of the bower motif is preserved and developed. Wordsworth's beautiful fragment "Nutting" describes a scene which seems to combine unspoiled innocence and sexual temptation:

> The hazels rose
> Tall and erect, with tempting clusters hung,
> A virgin scene!—A little while I stood,
> Breathing with such suppression of the heart
> As joy delights in; and, with wise restraint
> Voluptuous, fearless of a rival, eyed
> The banquet.
>
> (19–25)

In this poem Wordsworth's boy reenacts Sir Guyon's destruction of the Bower of Bliss, but with an important difference. No one is more deeply concerned with, and committed to, the idea of *Bildung* than Wordsworth. The Immortality ode, as Lionel Trilling has told us, is a poem about "growing up";[6] in fact his whole treatment of time, memory, and childhood reveals a careful avoidance of the dangers of nostalgia. "Nutting" was originally intended as part of his autobiographical poem on the growth of a poet's mind, and Wordsworth, like Spenser, apparently sees the boy's destruction of the bower as a necessary step in that growth.[7] The Bower of Bliss, however, is wholly inimical to the knight's mission: its destruction is a positive moral gesture. But the boy's act, detailed with striking narrative restraint and neutrality, is shot through with moral ambiguity. As he turns away, his exultation is mingled with "a sense of pain" as he observes the "deformed and sullied" being that lies before him. Wordsworth seeks to overcome the crude antithesis that the episode in Spenser proposes between the exigencies of moral development and the turbid claims of the instinctual life. Wordsworth is often accused of being the most asexual of the English poets, but nothing is more important to his sense of nature than the "vital feelings of delight" that animate it. In "Lines Written in Early Spring" he contrasts the idyllic bower with the evil of "what man has made of man":

> Through primrose tufts, in that green bower,
> The periwinkle trailed its wreaths;
> And 'tis my faith that every flower
> Enjoys the air it breathes.

> The birds around me hopped and played,
> Their thoughts I cannot measure:—
> But the least motion which they made,
> It seemed a thrill of pleasure.

6. Lionel Trilling, *The Liberal Imagination: Essays on Literature and Society* (Garden City, N.Y., 1957), p. 127.

7. Hartman, with explicit reference to Keats, devotes some fine pages to the "mutilated bower" of "Nutting." See *Wordsworth's Poetry,* pp. 73–75.

> The budding twigs spread out their fan,
> To catch the breezy air;
> And I must think, do all I can,
> That there was pleasure there.
>
> (9–20)

The emphasis of these lines, like the "thousand blended notes" of the opening of the poem, is on a harmonious reciprocity so great that Wordsworth in the end associates it with the "holy" and unfallen sexuality of Eden, the first of the bowers. In a closely connected poem ("To My Sister") he turns this perception into a virtual manifesto; he promises to restore this natural joy and harmony to the life of man:

> No joyless forms shall regulate
> Our living calendar:
> We from to-day, my Friend, will date
> The opening of the year.
>
> Love, now a universal birth,
> From heart to heart is stealing,
> From earth to man, from man to earth:
> —It is the hour of feeling.
>
> (17–24)

The act of the boy in "Nutting" has none of this utopian simplicity and fervor. It is a violent rather than harmonious intercourse, and it takes place in a post-Edenic world of experience and consciousness, a world in which "a sense of pain" may be attendant on pleasure. But Wordsworth is careful not to moralize or condemn it. It is a necessary initiation, and a sexual one, that brings the boy into contact with the vital spirit of nature.

Keats, too, as early as "Sleep and Poetry," foresaw the need to go beyond the bower, to bid farewell to "the realm . . . of Flora, and old Pan." But unlike Wordsworth he shows a truly Spenserian tendency to linger a while, even at the risk of inconsistency. Keats' early poems remain deeply committed to the bower; yet his use of the motif is strikingly rich and picks up many of the varied strands of meaning that had become attached to it. Like Wordsworth he reads Spenser in his diabolical sense (as Blake and Shelley read Milton) and ignores the Spenserian moral. Wordsworth rejects the Spenserian dichotomy of pleasure and *Bildung:* he emphasizes experiences of pleasure that are also integral to human growth. He tries to free the bower of its regressive element and integrate it into a richer conception of the moral life. The early Keats does nothing so complex. He accepts the Spenserian dichotomy but inverts it. The bower remains regressive and inimical to moral growth, but he embraces it nonetheless. For the Keats of "Sleep and Poetry" a bowery nook is indeed elysium, and the "nobler life, / Where I may find the agonies, the strife / Of human hearts" is no more than a pious intention.

The bower is the central image of all Keats' early poems, but it is no longer necessarily a literal *locus amoenus,* the beautiful spot in nature. Sleep, which shelters and refreshes, is itself a bower "more healthful than the leafiness of dales." The heroes of liberty that appear in the early poems are not treated politically at all. The "patriotic lore" of Milton and Sidney delights Keats' soul only after he finds "with easy quest, / A fragrant wild, with Nature's beauty drest." The name of Kosciusko or Alfred is itself a bower, "a full harvest whence to reap high feeling." The recurrent natural imagery here is more important than the separate objects that evoke it. The work of art is another bower. Keats calls the Chaucerian poem *The Floure and the Lefe* "a little copse: / The honied lines do freshly interlace / To keep the reader in so sweet a place. . . ." In Hunt's *Story of Rimini,* says Keats, the reader

will find "a region of his own, / A bower for his spirit."[8]
This generalizing tendency culminates in the opening lines
of *Endymion,* in which any "thing of beauty" becomes a
bower for the spirit:

> it will never
> Pass into nothingness; but still will keep
> A bower quiet for us, and a sleep
> Full of sweet dreams, and health, and quiet breathing.

The list that follows mixes examples from nature, art, and
history ("the grandeur of the dooms / We have imagined
for the mighty dead"). Keats culminates by transforming the
bower completely from a spatial concept to a temporal and
psychological one, akin to Wordsworth's "spots of time":

> Nor do we merely feel these essences
> For one short hour;

but rather they

> Haunt us till they become a cheering light
> Unto our souls.

We can mostly readily characterize the bower by borrow-
ing the adjectives that Keats applies to Sleep at the beginning
of "Sleep and Poetry": gentle, soothing, tranquil, healthful,
secret, serene, and full of visions. In the lines describing the
realm of Flora and old Pan it is also overtly erotic, though
with an innocence that recalls, as Wordsworth does, the un-
differentiated instinctual fulfillment of childhood. We are
reminded of the explicitly sexual account of the flower and
the bee, which is much more suggestive and general in its
reference. After defending the passive feminine pleasure of

8. I have quoted from "Sleep and Poetry" and from four early
sonnets, "Oh! how I love," "To Kosciusko," "Written on a Blank
Space at the End of Chaucer's Tale 'The Floure and the Lefe,'" and
"On 'The Story of Rimini.'"

the flower against the active exertions of the bee ("and who shall say between Man and Woman which is the most delighted?"), Keats goes on to attach a moral:

> let us not therefore go hurrying about and collecting honey-bee like, buzzing here and there impatiently from a knowledge of what is to be arrived at: but let us open our leaves like a flower and be passive and receptive—budding patiently under the eye of Apollo and taking hints from every noble insect that favors us with a visit—sap will be given us for Meat and dew for drink. (1:232)

In this letter of 1818, Keats is making explicit what remained only a large implication in his "regressive" early poems. He is attacking what has been called the main tendency of all of Western culture—the Faustian impulse. It was Goethe who grasped the modern expression of this spirit when at the end of *Faust* he turned the medieval necromancer into an engineer. He saw that the direction of man's quest to subdue nature had shifted from magic to technology. It is no accident then that the terms that Keats chooses for his attack are partly economic and social. The bee is the epitome of the modern *homo economicus,* "collecting honey-bee like, buzzing here and there impatiently from a knowledge of what is to be arrived at." The bee's activity is not really pleasurable at all, but rather utilitarian: teleologically oriented toward economically useful ends.[9] Keats justifies the passive and feminine against the active and masculine not out of a decadent refinement of sensibility or simple preference for inertia. He is defending enjoyment against productivity and consumption, pleasure against utility. Against the rationality of the *telos* or end, Keats opposes that mode of being which, though economically irresponsible ("sap will be given us for Meat

9. Compare the "irritable reaching after fact & reason" of one who lacks Negative Capability, who is "incapable of remaining content with half knowledge" (1:193–94).

and dew for drink"), needs no further justification, for it is an end in itself. It is not simply out of inexperience or a sense of propriety that the erotic activity in Keats' early poems often shades off into harmless and innocent play, such as biting the white shoulders of nymphs. Keats can combine innocence and erotic activity not because he has a theory of infantile sexuality (though on one level both he and Wordsworth here anticipate Freud), or even because, like Wordsworth in "Lines Written in Early Spring," like Blake, like many of the mystics, he does not accept the Christian association of the Fall with sexuality. It is rather because play for the child, like love-making for the adult, is an irresponsible end in itself, and thus when forbidden by utilitarian rationality from every other area of adult life, it can retain its sway in sexual activity. Keats' mature masculinity, Trilling suggests, "grew easily and gently out of his happy relation with his infant appetites."[10]

It would be a mistake to make too much of the moral orig-inality of Keats' early poems, or to impute to them any direct social consciousness. But the Romantic poets rarely expressed their social values as the novelist did, by dealing directly with historical or social conflicts. Instead their poetry responds to a nascent urban and industrial society by withdrawing from it, by cultivating much that it denies and negates. The almost untroubled sensuality of Keats' early poems, their "exquisite sense of the luxurious" (1:271), does not announce itself polemically as the abolition of repression, or the end of sub-limation, nor does it even reveal many marks of internal con-flict. It nevertheless remains a sharp though implicit attack on the reality principle and on the utilitarian ideal of produc-tivity, which Herbert Marcuse in *Eros and Civilization* calls "one of the most strictly protected values of modern culture." By this standard, he says,

10. Lionel Trilling, *The Opposing Self: Nine Essays in Criticism* (New York, 1955), p. 24.

man is evaluated according to his ability to make, augment, and improve socially useful things. Productivity thus designates the degree of the mastery and transformation of nature: the progressive replacement of an uncontrolled natural environment by a controlled technological environment. However, the more the division of labor was geared to utility for the established productive apparatus rather than for the individuals—in other words the more the social need deviated from the individual need—the more productivity tended to contradict the pleasure principle and to become an end-in-itself. The very word came to smack of repression or its philistine glorification: it connotes the resentful defamation of rest, indulgence, receptivity—the triumph over the "lower depths" of the mind and body, the taming of the instincts by exploitative reason.[11]

"Rest, indulgence, receptivity": these are almost Keats' very words.[12] "Let us open our leaves like a flower and be passive and receptive—budding patiently under the eye of Apollo." Not to master nature but to be mastered by it, almost to become a part of it and participate in its rhythms.

This immersion in the natural process may be an escape but it is not born of despair or envy as in "In drear-nighted December." In the early poems it is a sheer fanciful act of exuberance. Keats even constructs an only half-serious aesthetic upon it:

> For what has made the sage or poet write
> But the fair paradise of Nature's light?
> In the calm grandeur of a sober line,

11. Herbert Marcuse, *Eros and Civilization: A Philosophical Inquiry into Freud* (New York, 1962), p. 141.

12. Marcuse's language as a whole is of course alien to Keats, not only because it is abstract and polemical but because it is political. But the dialectic of withdrawal in the poems has much authentic, albeit negative, political significance. In *Endymion* Keats will explicitly attack the political and historical world which he finds alien to his deepest impulses: "the silver flow / Of Hero's tears, the swoon of Imogen, / Fair Pastorella in the bandit's den, / Are things to brood on with more ardency / Than the death-day of empires" (II, 30–34). I shall deal with this more fully in the next chapter.

We see the waving of the mountain pine;
And when a tale is beautifully staid,
We feel the safety of a hawthorn glade:
When it is moving on luxurious wings,
The soul is lost in pleasant smotherings.
                    ("I stood tip-toe," 125–32)

With the "fair paradise" and the "hawthorn glade" we are at the heart of the bower world. Keats can celebrate the identity of the aesthetics of nature and the aesthetics of poetry only because nature and poetry are both bowers for the spirit. But although the passage begins and continues in simple celebration, a darker undertone gradually can be heard. The motif of shelter and safety so important to Keats' bowers brings to mind the threatening world without. Even the motif of sensuous delight suddenly implies the promise of escape: "the soul is lost in pleasant smotherings." This culminates when

at our feet, the voice of crystal bubbles
Charms us at once away from all our troubles:
So that we feel uplifted from the world . . .
                    (137–39)

Between this poem and the similar gestures of escape in "In drear-nighted December" or "To Sleep" lies a chasm of self-consciousness. Yet here we find the early promptings of their tragic view of the world and the self, both seen as troublesome burdens to be sloughed off. In their rudimentary way these poems, so transparent at first glance, are as dialectical as the later ones; they seem facile only because Keats hardly seems to *earn* his yearnings for the annihilation of self. The soul that is lost in "pleasant smotherings" is being trivialized as well as lost, and could not have been much to begin with.[13]

---

13. As Blake says in another context, "those who restrain desire, do so because theirs is weak enough to be restrained." *The Marriage of Heaven and Hell,* in Keynes, p. 182.

We do not recognize in this the poet who was to call the world "the vale of Soul-making" (2:102). Yet this yearning is so rooted in his mind that we find it expressed in one of the first poems he ever wrote:

> Fill for me a brimming bowl
> And let me in it drown my soul
>
> . . . .
> . . . I want not the stream inspiring
> That fills the mind with fond desiring,
> But I want as deep a draught
> As e'er from Lethe's wave was quaff'd.
>> ("Fill for me a brimming bowl,"
>> 1–2, 5–8)

This is the first gesture toward "the feel of not to feel it," the first expression of that desire for insentience as an antidote to consciousness. But in the 1817 volume and *Endymion* the characteristic means of annihilating self is not insentience but pleasure,

> Richer entanglements, enthralments far
> More self-destroying, leading, by degrees,
> To the chief intensity. . . .
>> (*End.*, I, 798–800)

In his address to Poesy in "Sleep and Poetry" he offers himself up for a hedonistic ritual of self-sacrifice:

> . . . to my ardent prayer,
> Yield from thy sanctuary some clear air,
> Smoothed for intoxication by the breath
> Of flowering bays, that I may die a death
> Of luxury, and my young spirit follow
> The morning sun-beams to the great Apollo
> Like a fresh sacrifice.
>> (55–61)

The common Elizabethan pun on "die" testifies that there is nothing novel in Keats' association of loss of self with an intensity of pleasure. Yet in the lines that follow, Keats begins to recognize that poetic creation is an active process, that only if he resists the loss of self can he become a poet. Only if he "can bear / The o'erwhelming sweets" rather than be sacrificed will he be granted "fair / Visions of all places."

To resist loss of self is not yet to have a complex or mature awareness of self. Similarly, to surmise an active notion of the creative process is not yet to have an adequate theory of the imagination. When Wordsworth in *The Prelude* discovers within himself a "plastic power," a force that rises from the mind's abyss, which he names Imagination, there is no more talk of "wise passiveness." What makes "Sleep and Poetry" so exciting as a transitional poem (along with the almost simultaneously written last part of "I stood tip-toe") is Keats' incipient discovery of Imagination as a creative agency. For the early Keats "vision" amounts to no more than reverie or musings: "I was light-hearted / And many pleasures to my vision started." Sleep is "more full of visions than a high romance." The "fair / Visions of all places" that Poesy offers amount to "an eternal book / Whence I may copy many a lovely saying / About the leaves, and flowers." Here he goes no further than a trivialized version of eighteenth-century neoclassic theory. The poet is a copyist rather than an original creator. The "sayings" preexist him. Instead of Imagination we get "imaginings," which hover round and need only be plucked out of the air: "Also imaginings will hover / Round my fire-side, and haply there discover / Vistas of solemn beauty" ("Sleep and Poetry," 62–73). But this is not the final word of the younger Keats on poetic creation.

Keats never gives himself up entirely to the languorous passivity of sleep and the bower. Even in the meandering catalogue of "Nature's gentle doings" (early in "I stood tip-toe") a contrary principle begins forcibly to assert itself.

> What next? A tuft of evening primroses,
> O'er which the mind may hover till it dozes;
> O'er which it well might take a pleasant sleep,
> But that 'tis ever startled by the leap
> Of buds into ripe flowers; or by the flitting
> Of diverse moths, that aye their rest are quitting;
> Or by the moon lifting her silver rim
> Above a cloud, and with a gradual swim
> Coming into the blue with all her light.
>
> (107–15)

Keats suddenly realizes that nature can be seen as a locus of energy as well as rest, of self-assertion as well as unconscious process. The emergence of flowers from buds, which elsewhere epitomizes the untroubled progress of the organic cycle, here strikes the sleep-prone observer as a startling "leap," with a violence that almost denotes volition. The same quality of self-determining strength is present in Keats' description of the moon, forcefully coming into her own, with a remarkable balance of languorous restraint and energy (e.g., "a gradual swim").[14] Most significant, however, in view of the long

---

14. Such a balance is the key to Keats' famous pronouncement about the nature of poetry in "Sleep and Poetry":

> A drainless shower
> Of light is poesy; 'tis the supreme of power;
> 'Tis might half slumb'ring on its own right arm.
> The very archings of her eye-lids charm
> A thousand willing agents to obey,
> And still she governs with the mildest sway.
>
> (235–40)

Professor Bate, unsympathetic to the early poems, calls this ideal "sculpturesque," thereby annexing it to Keats' later style. But it is difficult to follow him when he says that it does not "have anything to do with escapism, sleep, or revery" (*John Keats,* p. 128). The key phrase, after all, is "half slumb'ring."

poem soon to follow, is Keats' choice of the moon as a focus for these energies.

At the beginning of our discussion we discerned in "I stood tip-toe" an important upward movement by which Keats seemed to resist assimilation into empirical and objective nature. In the moon this movement finds a high symbolic goal. Running through all of Keats' early poems is a persistent theory of visionary inspiration and a desire for transcendental flight. Often, in earlier poems, this motif is conventional enough, as Keats exuberantly imitates the external trappings of romance:

> A sudden glow comes on them, naught they see
> In water, earth, or air, but poesy.
> . . . .
> . . . when a Poet is in such a trance,
> In air he sees white coursers paw, and prance,
> Bestridden of gay knights, in gay apparel,
> Who at each other tilt in playful quarrel.
> ("To My Brother George," 21–22, 25–28)

Later in the poem we have that horrendous apotheosis of the dead poet, which I quoted at the start of this chapter. But when in the same poem the moon makes a brief appearance, it seems to offer a much more genuine and enchanting enticement:

> Ah, yes! much more would start into his sight—
> The revelries, and mysteries of night.
>
> (63–64)

Here Keats approaches the vein of the true Romantic night-poem. Mystery and enchantment are not ornamental details of romance machinery but offer visionary access to new realities, occasions for original creation.

The real breakthrough does not come until the second half of "I stood tip-toe," where Keats, as Leigh Hunt first pointed out, echoes Wordsworth's discussion of mythology in the fourth book of *The Excursion*. In a passage that Hazlitt had singled out for special praise in his review, Wordsworth, who with Coleridge had long sought to prune English poetic diction of the dead wood of personification and mythological reference, gave a sympathetic account of ancient mythology and the pagan gods, as an anthropomorphic product of man's own imagination.[15] Blake, with pithy brilliance, had developed a similar notion in *The Marriage of Heaven and Hell,* concluding that "All deities reside in the human breast."[16] Wordsworth has no such heterodox intentions, nor does he seem interested like Blake in mythology as a manifestation of the visionary power of the poetic genius. He uses mythology, as Keats sometimes will, as part of a polemic against analytic modes of thought, the tendency to view "all objects unremittingly / In disconnection dead and spiritless; / And still dividing, and dividing still, / Break down all grandeur" (*Excursion,* IV, 961–64). He exalts the opposite tendency of man in an otherwise alien and inhuman world to find "a spiritual presence," which links pagan misconceptions to Christian verities. Wordsworth, growing steadily more orthodox and more suspicious of the free imagination, sees this consoling presence not as a life granted to nature by man's perception, but as a true intuition of the divine.[17] In "I stood

15. The passage quoted by Hazlitt was IV, 851–87, probably the most effective section in Wordsworth's long disquisition. Also quoted was the explicit contrast Wordsworth draws with what Hazlitt calls "the cold, narrow, lifeless spirit of modern philosophy" (IV, 941–92). Hazlitt, *The Round Table* (1817), in *The Collected Works of William Hazlitt,* ed. A. R. Waller and Arnold Glover (London, 1902), 1:114–16.

16. Keynes, *Poetry and Prose,* p. 185.

17. Even the early Wordsworth (and some of the fourth book of *The Excursion* was written as early as 1797–1800) could not accept this testimony to the imagination. It was here that Coleridge differed with him: "O Lady," he wrote to Wordsworth's future sister-in-law, "we receive but what we give, / And in our life alone does Nature live"

tip-toe" Keats, though liberated by Wordsworth, stands closer to Blake. The myth-making poet whom he conceives inventing the story of Narcissus or Endymion (out of his humanizing perception of the flower or the moon) is not in search of consolation, nor do his findings confirm any creative power but his own.[18] ("That which is creative must create itself," Keats was to write [1:374] apropos of the composition of his later Endymion poem.)

> Where had he been, from whose warm head out-flew
> That sweetest of all songs, that ever new,
> That aye refreshing, pure deliciousness,
> Coming ever to bless
> The wanderer by moonlight? to him bringing
> Shapes from the invisible world, unearthly singing
> From out the middle air, from flowery nests,
> And from the pillowy silkiness that rests
> Full in the speculation of the stars.
> Ah! surely he had burst our mortal bars;
> Into some wond'rous region he had gone,
> To search for thee, divine Endymion!
>
> ("I stood tip-toe," 181–92)

Here the short upward flight of the beginning of the poem, a mild release from nature into reverie, gives way to a notion of the creative imagination that involves higher visionary flight, even transcendence. The poet seeks not merely a "spiritual presence" in the external world; if Wordsworth aims to "see into the life of things," then Keats in this poem stands closer to Coleridge, who insists in "Dejection" that the

("Dejection: An Ode," 47–48). Coleridge responded to *The Prelude* by writing that "power streamed from thee, and thy soul received / The light reflected, as a light bestowed" ("To William Wordsworth," 18–19).

18. On the contrary, it is the flower and the moon which seem to be languishing and which are consoled by the myths invented by the sympathetic poet.

"fountains are within." Within his own spirit, yet for Keats also involving escape toward another place, a refuge for the spirit, possession almost. "Into what Regions was his spirit gone / When he first thought of thee Endymion?" Keats wrote in an earlier variant.[19] But this expanse of spirit does not make for an experience narrowly spiritual: it is sensuous to the height of synaesthetic intensity. Criticism halts in alarm and wonder at such lines as "the pillowy silkiness that rests / Full in the speculation of the stars." One can take note with Professor Fogle of Keats' juxtaposition of a lush tactile image with an abstract visual one,[20] or admire with Professor Trilling Keats' ability to move "from the sensual to the transcendent, from pleasure to knowledge, and knowledge of an ultimate kind."[21] Yet one is not sure of what that knowledge is, and it seems that some blatant, peculiarly Keatsian excess has been perpetrated in order to achieve it.

Yet this moment is not exceptional, for "flowery nests" indicates that we have come upon another bower. The opposition between the enclosed place and the upward flight is only an apparent one, because the bower and the visionary "middle air" are cities of refuge from the tyranny of what Keats in *Endymion* calls "habitual self" (II, 276). But here the element of escape and self-transcendence, while present and significant ("Ah! surely he had burst our mortal bars"), is subordinate to the achievement of a new creative consciousness. One element of the bower in Keats is always that it offers "fair / Visions of all places," but here Keats goes beyond this sort of reverie. Just as he seeks escape not merely from the phenomenal world but from our mortal condition itself, so his vision will involve not random imaginings but a genuinely original

19. Garrod (1958), p. 10 n.
20. Richard Harter Fogle, *The Imagery of Keats and Shelley: A Comparative Study* (Chapel Hill, 1949), p. 108.
21. *Beyond Culture,* p. 65.

myth-making, one that will offer access to new modes of being, that will encompass spiritual experience without denying physical, that will, in Blake's terms, approach and perceive the infinite through "an improvement of sensual enjoyment."[22] For the early Keats, as for Blake, the autonomy of the poetic imagination will be established by cleansing the doors of perception.

Keats' main attempt in the 1817 volume to find a concrete symbol to represent his new sense of the visionary power of the imagination is a disappointment. The passage in "Sleep and Poetry" in which a mysterious airborne chariot appears has been little understood and even less admired. It follows the well-known lines in which Keats promises to bid farewell to the joys of Flora and old Pan, to "pass them for a nobler life, / Where I may find the agonies, the strife /Of human hearts." Miss Lowell, taking this for a renunciation of the pleasure principle and an embrace of reality, was distressed to see it followed not by a full-fledged manifesto for a new humanist poetry but by an obscure vision.[23] Keats, as almost all critics of "Sleep and Poetry" have noted, was indeed deeply influenced by Wordsworth's account of the stages of human growth, especially by his belief that the human bonds and responsibilities of maturity could provide compensation for loss of the prereflective natural pleasures of childhood. There was a strong tendency on Keats' part, particularly later in his career, to see his own development in terms of stages of growth, and like Donne to provide himself with little imaginative autobiographies. And he was later, on one such occasion, to commend Wordsworth for having "martyr[ed] himself to the human heart" (1:278–79). But in "Sleep and Poetry" Keats is not yet prepared to present himself for martyrdom. The acute Wordsworthian sense of time is absent

22. *The Marriage of Heaven and Hell,* in Keynes, p. 187.
23. Amy Lowell, *John Keats* (Boston, 1925), 1:223.

here; Keats longs somehow to possess all the stages of growth simultaneously.

In some respects Keats is describing aesthetic choices rather than life-choices, not a passage from selfish pleasure to social conscience—the context partly belies this—but the traditional Virgilian progress from pastoral to epic,[24] which for Keats here means from nature to vision. But even these are not exclusive alternatives for him. In the succeeding lines that help us interpret the appearance of the car and charioteer Keats wonders whether

> the high
> Imagination cannot freely fly
> As she was wont of old? prepare her steeds,
> Paw up against the light, and do strange deeds
> Upon the clouds? Has she not shown us all?
> From the clear space of ether, to the small
> Breath of new buds unfolding? From the meaning
> Of Jove's large eye-brow, to the tender greening
> Of April meadows?
>
> (163–71)

The important fact about the car then, which we now know to represent "the high / Imagination," is its upward flight— to the epic realm of the gods, Jove, and "the clear space of ether."[25] These lines introduce the polemic against the school of Pope, which in measured couplets "sway'd about upon a

24. Since writing this I find happily that this was Woodhouse's interpretation (perhaps on the authority of Keats himself) as transcribed in his important annotations to the 1817 volume, only recently brought to light. See Stuart M. Sperry, Jr., "Richard Woodhouse's Interleaved and Annotated Copy of Keats's *Poems* (1817)," in *Literary Monographs*, vol. 1, ed. Eric Rothstein and Thomas K. Dunseath (Madison, Wisc., 1967), pp. 124–25, 153–54.

25. Woodhouse, helpfully if reductively, calls the charioteer a "Personification of the Epic poet, when the enthusiasm of inspiration is upon him" (Ibid., p. 154).

rocking horse / And thought it Pegasus," a contrast which pointedly recalls the flying steeds of the Imagination. "The small / Breath of buds unfolding" and "the tender greening / Of April meadows," however, refer back to none other than the supposedly abandoned realm of Flora and old Pan. Keats seems to be saying that true imagination can encompass both epic and pastoral, can possess both the visionary ether and the natural pleasures of the bower. Both this higher and lower flight he contrasts, unfairly or not, with the deadly middle range of Augustan *vers de société,* with its technical precision, urbane (and urban) wit, and willing insensitivity to the natural world. Keats' charioteer, on the other hand, is able somehow "with wond'rous gesture" to speak to the natural world, to animate the landscape with the very energy of his response to it (an intercourse which recalls Wordsworth's "Prospectus" to *The Recluse,* with its vision of the marriage of mind and nature). But aside from the "shapes of delight, of mystery, and fear," which recalls motifs often associated in these early poems with the moon, there is unfortunately little that is vivid about Keats' description of the car. He experiences nothing about this vision so intensely as the loss of it, and the lines which describe that loss are perhaps the most important in the whole 1817 volume:

> The visions all are fled—the car is fled
> Into the light of heaven, and in their stead
> A sense of real things comes doubly strong,
> And, like a muddy stream, would bear along
> My soul to nothingness: but I will strive
> Against all doubtings, and will keep alive
> The thought of that same chariot, and the strange
> Journey it went.
>
> (155–62)

In one minor sense the reference of these lines is historical and polemical. The visionary car is the great poetry of the sixteenth and seventeenth centuries, the heir (in Keats' view) to the classical tradition of Homer and Virgil, and the muddy stream is the poetry of the century that followed, trapped in an unimaginative "sense of real things." Keats is dedicating himself to the older tradition and to its sense of the powers of the imagination. This passage and the lines about "the high / Imagination" that follow provide a transition to the attack on the Augustans and the account of the state of poetry in his own time. ("Sleep and Poetry," though associative and uneven, is a more unified poem than anyone has been willing to grant.)

But the important reference of the lines is personal rather than public or discursive. This is the first of many crucial passages of disintoxication or disenchantment—perhaps the German *Entzauberung* describes it best—when Keats, after the largest imaginative projects, is brought suddenly back, in a moment of lonely and naked lucidity, to his sole self. It is not simply that imagination or vision, seen as positive quantities, fail him and leave him bereft. As Keats made the car his first symbol of the power of the imagination, he also made it, perhaps less intentionally, the first symbol of his suspicion of the imagination. Keats' "doubtings" are from within; the "sense of real things comes *doubly* strong" only because it must have remained strong even at the height of vision. Yet he preserves a remarkable balance and tension. The sense of real things can also be a muddy stream, can mean the restoration of the tyranny of the merely external object-world, which would darken the waters of inspiration and annihilate the creative ego. The passage expresses poignant loss as well as lucid self-consciousness, and Keats' final resolution is appropriately Wordsworthian. The visionary gleam, Wordsworth had taught, could yet glimmer in the eye of the philosophic mind, naive vision could survive within the self as memory, could bear the buffets of the world by being raised to thought ("The thought of that same chariot, and the strange / Journey it went").

Nature, pleasure, vision—these mean much to the early Keats; they are more than escapist fantasies. Yet they exhibit a common movement of flight from painful realities and arise out of a common impulse to annihilate the self that is the locus of such realities. But this movement and impulse in themselves imply a tragic awareness, in their very resistance to tragedy. In these lines of "Sleep and Poetry" especially, Keats briefly assumes that burden of selfhood, that divided consciousness, which Matthew Arnold called the characteristic modern predicament: "the dialogue of the mind with itself."[26]

26. Matthew Arnold, Preface to *Poems* (1853), in *The Poetical Works of Matthew Arnold,* ed. C. B. Tinker and H. F. Lowry (London, 1950), p. xvii.

3

Endymion

I

FROM the start *Endymion* is a poem in which the self has already fallen into division. This is true not simply because its hero makes his entrance with "a lurking trouble in his nether lip" (I, 179), striking a discordant, "modern" note in an otherwise joyous and untroubled world of pastoral celebration. Endymion, though lacking in sustained dramatic life or symbolic clarity, is certainly meant to be a figure of large Byronic malaise and aspiration:[1]

> Where soil is men grow,
> Whether to weeds or flowers; but for me,
> There is no depth to strike in: I can see
> Nought earthly worth my compassing.
>
> (II, 159–62)

1. A poet writing in 1817 could hardly escape the influence of Byron, or at least of Byronism, though Keats had come to like him less and less. The third (and best) canto of *Childe Harold's Pilgrimage* had been published the previous year. Other immediate models were Wordsworth's Solitary in *The Excursion* and the hero of Shelley's *Alastor*.

Endymion is at once cut off from nature and, to use Words-worth's phase, "at distance from the Kind," alienated from fellow men whose ordinary, unselfconscious lives proceed with the sureness of natural growth. Endymion is burdened by a consciousness which sets him apart from such organic process and by goals which make frustration recurrent and inevitable. But it is precisely this, he says earlier in the same speech, that makes us truly human:

> But this is human life: the war, the deeds,
> The disappointment, the anxiety,
> Imagination's struggles, far and nigh,
> All human.

$$\text{(II, 153–56)}$$

The dark note that Endymion strikes, so fundamental to his situation, is present in the poem even before he comes on the scene. Keats himself sounds it in the remarkable thirty-three-line proem with which *Endymion* begins. These lines have a rich and problematic relation to the poem. Though they come at the start they are not the poem's actual beginning, but a sort of Argument, not fully comprehensible until we have gone through the whole poem. Without having read the fourth book, what are we to make of the following?

> Therefore, on every morrow, are we wreathing
> A flowery band to bind us to the earth.

$$\text{(I, 6–7)}$$

What are we to make of this poetic wreath which, unlike the traditional laurels of Apollo, binds rather than crowns us? How are we to understand being bound "to the earth" when Endymion himself, fated to be "enskyed," reaches for some heavenly ideal associated with the moon?

In addition to being an Argument, however, the proem is an apologetic assertion about the nature of poetry and about *this* poem's relation to reality. Keats has already hinted at this subject in his epigraph, "The stretched metre of an antique song," from Shakespeare's seventeenth sonnet ("Who will believe my verse in time to come?"). These are the central lines of the sonnet:

> If I could write the beauty of your eyes,
> And in fresh numbers number all your graces,
> The age to come would say: 'This poet lies;
> Such heavenly touches ne'er touched earthly faces.'
> So should my papers, yellow'd with their age,
> Be scorn'd, like old men of less truth than tongue,
> And your true rights be term'd a poet's rage
> And stretched metre of an antique song.
>
> $(5–12)^2$

In the light of the whole sonnet the epigraph signifies more than Keats' revival of an ancient myth, or even his highly subjective and personal ("stretched") appropriation of that myth. In context the line is spoken not by the poet but by a mocking and skeptical posterity that denies the veracity of art, that finds the poet a liar and the poem "of less truth than tongue," a thing of mere words. From this point of view the "stretched metre" of the imagination is a distortion, and "antique," accented on the first syllable, has a strong secondary meaning of antic or fantastic.[3]

Keats knew what he was doing when he chose the line. Shakespeare, he writes to Reynolds,

> overwhelms a genuine Lover of Poesy with all manner of abuse, talking about—
>
> > "a poets rage
> > And stretched metre of an antique song"—
>
> Which by the by will be a capital Motto for my Poem—wont it? (1:189)

2. *Shakespeare's Sonnets,* ed. W. G. Ingram and Theodore Redpath (New York, 1965), p. 43.

3. Ibid., editors' note, p. 42.

Keats is being ironic of course, for the sonnet as a whole defends the poet against such abuse. It asserts that for all his apparent distortion of everyday reality the poet may have access to a finer and more subtle reality, to a beauty that seems fantastic but is exact and true. But Keats, by taking as his motto the terms of abuse, contrives to open *Endymion* with an ironic double perspective. He asserts the claims of imagination and at the same time registers a skepticism about those claims. He asserts the power of the artist to create his own vision and at the same time worries about the relation of that vision to the reality that we all experience. This is also the subject of the proem to *Endymion.*

Memory tends to falsify the opening section of the poem by giving too much prominence to that famous first line. That confident assertion of the power of the aesthetic object to triumph over time overwhelms, in our minds, the context in which it is carefully placed. It fixes the proem as a manifesto for the sort of aestheticism for which Keats was revered in the nineteenth century. The text itself gives a more complex impression:

> A thing of beauty is a joy for ever:
> Its loveliness increases; it will never
> Pass into nothingness; but still will keep
> A bower quiet for us, and a sleep
> Full of sweet dreams, and health, and quiet breathing.
>
> (I, 1-5)

The assertion of permanence takes its force from the context of transience and change. By the third line we are reminded of a world in which things do "pass into nothingness," in which "sweet dreams, and health, and quiet breathing" are not always forthcoming. Here, even more clearly than in the earlier poems of Keats, the ideal world of the bower is a circumscribed refuge, given special significance by the quality

of the world to which it is opposed. The predominant note
of the proem is sombre.

> Therefore, on every morrow, are we wreathing
> A flowery band to bind us to the earth,
> Spite of despondence, of the inhuman dearth
> Of noble natures, of the gloomy days,
> Of all the unhealthy and o'er-darkened ways
> Made for our searching: yes, in spite of all,
> Some shape of beauty moves away the pall
> From our dark spirits.
>
> (I, 6–13)

Of all Keats' critics, only Middleton Murry has attempted to
define the dialectic on which these lines—and by implication
the entire poem—are based: "Essentially, the poem is the
effort to create a thing of beauty before the spirit is darkened;
to make the creation of the poem itself a defence against the
onset of the doubts and miseries and feverous speculations, of
which he had a clear presentiment. It is the poem of maiden
experience and maiden thought, indeed, but they are conscious of their doom."[4] Arnold's "dialogue of the mind with
itself" has truly begun.

The world that we experience, Keats is saying, "is full of
Misery and Heartbreak, Pain, Sickness and oppression"
(1:281), but the poet must resist his experience, must create
an alternative reality. The proem professes a subtler version
of the notion of art as therapy or consolation that Keats had
so unconvincingly offered in "Sleep and Poetry." He had
there attacked some kinds of modern poetry in terms that
seemed to dismiss dark subjects entirely:

> Trees uptorn,
> Darkness, and worms, and shrouds, and sepulchres
> Delight it; for it feeds upon the burrs,

4. Murry, *Keats*, pp. 180–81.

And thorns of life; forgetting the great end
Of poesy, that it should be a friend
To sooth the cares, and lift the thoughts of man.

(242–47)

He had concluded that "they shall be accounted poet kings /
Who simply tell the most heart-easing things" (267–68).
Rather than remind us of "the burrs, / And thorns of life,"
poetry should offer us at least the illusion of an escape from
them.

In the opening lines of *Endymion,* however, there is no
longer anything fanciful or self-indulgent about adversity.
They evoke not the fashionable melancholy of Graveyard
verse, but the "dark passages" through which all of us must
pass, the passages that lead away from the state of fresh and
innocent consciousness that Keats calls the Chamber of
Maiden Thought. More than any other poet it was Wordsworth who made Keats mindful of these passages, and he
looms large behind the proem of *Endymion.* Keats himself
would later acknowledge Wordsworth's example:

> . . . This Chamber of Maiden Thought becomes gradually
> darken'd and at the same time on all sides of it many doors
> are set open—but all dark—all leading to dark passages—We
> see not the ballance of good and evil. We are in a Mist—
> *We* are now in that state—We feel the "burden of the Mys-
> tery," To this point was Wordsworth come, as far as I can
> conceive when he wrote 'Tintern Abbey' and it seems to me
> that his Genius is explorative of those dark Passages. Now
> if we live, and go on thinking, we too shall explore them.
> (1:281)

But when beginning *Endymion* Keats was not yet ready to
explore them. He turned not to the dark Wordsworth, the
poet of loss, but to the poet of consolation who in "Tintern
Abbey" had found "tranquil restoration" in the "beauteous
forms" of the Wye Valley:

These beauteous forms,
Through a long absence, have not been to me
As is a landscape to a blind man's eye:
But oft, in lonely rooms, and 'mid the din
Of towns and cities, I have owed to them,
In hours of weariness, sensations sweet,
Felt in the blood, and felt along the heart;
And passing even into my purer mind,
With tranquil restoration.

. . . .

Nor less, I trust,
To them I may have owed another gift,
Of aspect more sublime; that blessed mood,
In which the burthen of the mystery,
In which the heavy and the weary weight
Of all this unintelligible world,
Is lightened.

(22–30, 35–41)

Keats' version of this is at once strikingly similar and subtly
different:

Nor do we merely feel these essences
For one short hour; no, even as the trees
That whisper round a temple become soon
Dear as the temple's self, so does the moon,
The passion poesy, glories infinite,
Haunt us till they become a cheering light
Unto our souls, and bound to us so fast,
That, whether there be shine, or gloom o'ercast,
They always must be with us, or we die.

(I, 25–33)

Keats' assertion is a generalized one, and loses the concreteness with which Wordsworth envisions the particular scene.
Wordsworth's "beauteous forms," which sound abstract, have

admirable specificity in the opening lines of the poem.[5] And the process Wordsworth outlines is strictly psychological and aesthetic, a special account of the workings of memory. But Keats' "things of beauty," which seem concrete, instead are abstract "essences." Keats constructs a simplified Wordsworthian psychology but endows the beauteous forms with metaphysical permanence and timelessness. He describes them as

> An endless fountain of immortal drink,
> Pouring unto us from the heaven's brink.
>
> (I, 23–24)

They are transcendental objects which make a joyful appearance in a world of time and change, as God in divine revelation makes a transfiguring incursion into history. And Keats' last line—"They always must be with us, or we die"—has the urgency of a desire for salvation itself. (Similarly, entry into the Cave of Quietude in Book IV of *Endymion* resembles the process of grace or unconscious election: "Enter none / Who strive therefore: on the sudden it is won," IV, 531–32). There is perhaps no better way we can penetrate to the center of *Endymion* than by taking up this transcendental motif.

The theme originates in the earlier poems where it often takes the simple form of an escapist reverie. The poet delights in his ability to lose himself in the bower of romance and ideal nature, the *locus amoenus* in which we are charmed "at once away from all our troubles: / So that we feel uplifted from the world, / Walking upon the white clouds wreath'd and curl'd" ("I stood tip-toe," 138–40). At such moments "the soul is lost in pleasant smotherings" (132), the self is annihilated by enjoyment, and we are transported to utopian

---

5. As Geoffrey Hartman says, "The emphasis is on *these* waters, *these* steep and lofty cliffs, *this* sycamore, *these* plots of cottage-ground, *these* orchard tufts, *these* hedgerows, *these* pastoral farms." *The Unmediated Vision* (New Haven, 1954), p. 4.

"realms of wonderment" (142). At other times the transcendental flight seems to yield imaginative knowledge that
makes it a genuine act of creation. Significantly it is the in-
ventor of the myth of Endymion who is supposed to have
received

> Shapes from the invisible world, unearthly singing
> From out the middle air, from flowery nests,
> And from the pillowy silkiness that rests
> Full in the speculation of the stars.
> Ah! surely he had burst our mortal bars.
>
> ("I stood tip-toe," 186–190)

We have noted the striking conjunction of the sensuous and
the transcendent: enjoyment that is a form of transcendence,
invisible worlds that realize the shadowy hints of ordinary
sensations. "Earthly love," says Endymion, summing up his
important speech on happiness, "has power to make / Men's
being mortal, immortal" (I, 843–44). This is akin to the "favorite speculation" that Keats confided to Bailey while working
on the last book of *Endymion:* "we shall enjoy ourselves here
after by having what we called happiness on Earth repeated
in a finer tone and so repeated—And yet such a fate can only
befall those who delight in sensation rather than hunger as
you do after Truth" (1:185).

It is not surprising then, that in the proem to *Endymion*
Keats should describe the "things of beauty" as "an endless
fountain of immortal drink." One of the germinal ideas of
the poem, realized at the end, is Endymion's simultaneous
quest for a mistress and an apotheosis, to be carried both "past
the scanty bar / To mortal steps" and "into the gentle bosom
of [his] love" (II, 124–25, 127). The paradox of this goal is
embodied in the apparent rivalry of Cynthia and the Indian
maid in the last book. But the two women are at last shown to
be one, and the poem is full of moments which foreshadow

the happy ending by bridging the gap between pleasure and transfiguration. A word that Keats often uses to describe such a transfiguration to the more-than-human is "'ethereal." In a letter of July 1818, that reads like a reminiscence and a troubled recantation of the "boyish" imaginings of *Endymion,* Keats writes:

> I am certain I have not a right feeling towards Women —at this moment I am striving to be just to them but I cannot —Is it because they fall so far beneath my Boyish imagination? When I was a schoolboy I thought a fair Woman a pure Goddess, my mind was a soft nest in which some one of them slept though she knew it not—I have no right to expect more than their reality. I thought them etherial above Men—I find them perhaps equal—great by comparison is very small. (1:341)

The older Keats, like the Endymion of the fourth book, somewhat ruefully settles for "reality"—gives up the "soft nest" in which the imagination etherealizes and transforms it into divinity. But poetry still retains some of the boyish powers of metamorphosis, at least where reality cooperates. In the Lake District, Keats can still hope "to add a mite to that mass of beauty which is harvested from these grand materials, by the finest spirits, and put into etherial existence for the relish of one's fellows" (1:301).

Even tragedy is rooted in such transformations, perhaps more so, because its painful materials cannot be directly "harvested." The anonymous author of a piece long attributed to Keats writes: "The poetry of 'Lear,' 'Othello,' 'Cymbeline,' &c., is the poetry of human passions and affections, made almost ethereal by the power of the poet."[6] This is achieved

6. "On Kean in 'Richard Duke of York,' " in *The Poetical Works and Other Writings of John Keats,* ed. H. Buxton Forman, 2d ed. (London, 1889), 3:8. This review has been attributed to Reynolds by Leonidas Jones (*Keats-Shelley Journal* 3 [1954]: 55–65), and Professor Bate accepts this view (*John Keats,* p. 236 n.). But such things as the

by what Keats, also in reference to *Lear,* calls "intensity," which is "capable of making all disagreeables evaporate" (1:192). By exciting a "momentous depth of speculation" art not only raises bleakness and pain to tragedy, but vaporizes or etherealizes empirical reality in general, into something more vitally real.[7] Characteristically, in the same breath with these abstractions, the Keats of 1817 tends to describe this process in erotic terms. In Benjamin West's painting *Death on the Pale Horse,* he complains, "there is nothing to be intense upon; no women one feels mad to kiss; no face swelling into reality." Erotic experience in *Endymion* is thus another form of passage or transformation. Endymion's most explicit dream vision of Cynthia is prefigured and complicated by the setting itself:

> It was a jasmine bower, all bestrown
> With golden moss. His every sense had grown
> Ethereal for pleasure; 'bove his head
> Flew a delight half-graspable; his tread
> Was Hesperean; to his capable ears
> Silence was music from the holy spheres.
>
> (II, 670–75)

Here the senses attain a level of intensity at which they cease to be merely sensory: they offer an access to some higher reality. The music of the spheres foreshadows the appearance of Cynthia, who is a kind of externalization of Endymion's desire, hovering "half-graspable" just at the upper limit of his reach. Endymion's "capable ears" are hardly ears any longer,

---

distinction between poetry of romance and poetry of "human passions and affections," as well as the idiosyncratic use of "ethereal," are strikingly characteristic of Keats. Jones later included the review in his impressive edition of *Selected Prose of John Hamilton Reynolds* (Cambridge, Mass., 1966), pp. 206–10.

7. For a useful discussion of Keats' use of words like "intensity" and "speculation," see Murry's essay " 'They End in Speculation,' " in *Keats,* pp. 227–37.

attuned as they are to silence and to the sound of the transcendent. Moreover, just as we glimpse the senses at their
moment of self-transcendence, we catch nature becoming
more than nature: Endymion is in a bower, but the exotic
"jasmine" and the suggestive epithet "golden" imply an ideal
or faery paradise. This is confirmed by Keats' allusion to the
garden of the Hesperides,[8] the mythical source of the golden
apples given to Hera on her marriage to Zeus. Later in the
same book Endymion refers to "essences. . . . Meant but to
fertilize my earthly root, / And make my branches lift a
golden fruit / Into the bloom of heaven" (II, 905–9), making
an explicit analogy between his quest and the imagined point
at which a natural organism transcends itself and becomes
mythic.[9]

At times this transfiguration is more than a passage from
one state to another; it is "a new birth," a passage from death
into life. Pan is addressed by the Latmians in their hymn as

> the leaven,
> That spreading in this dull and clodded earth
> Gives it a touch ethereal—a new birth.
>
> (I, 296–98)

A similar power resides in the moon, which bestows its blessing "every where, with silver lip / Kissing dead things to
life":

> O Moon! the oldest shades 'mong oldest trees
> Feel palpitations when thou lookest in:

8. Douglas Bush, ed., *John Keats: Selected Poems and Letters* (Boston, 1959), p. 321.

9. Keats originally wrote "lift their ripen'd fruit" (Garrod, 1958, p.
124 n.). Both the change and the phrase "the bloom of heaven" indicate that no merely natural consummation is involved, though we need
not go so far as Bernard Blackstone who invokes alchemy. *The Consecrated Urn: An Interpretation of Keats in Terms of Growth and
Form* (New York, 1959), pp. 144–45. The golden apples reappear later
in the poem (IV, 412).

O Moon! old boughs lisp forth a holier din
The while they feel thine airy fellowship.
Thou dost bless every where, with silver lip
Kissing dead things to life. The sleeping kine,
Couched in thy brightness, dream of fields divine:
Innumerable mountains rise, and rise,
Ambitious for the hallowing of thine eyes.
                                    (III, 52–60)

Pan is the vital principle itself, without which this "dull and clodded earth" is no more than lifeless matter. But the moon seems to provide more than a natural vitality: it offers a visionary existence which gives at least the illusion of over-turning the order of nature. The "oldest shades," not only the oldest trees but even the ghosts of trees that were, feel youthful sexual desire. The sleeping animals are possessed by imagination and receive visionary access to a higher reality. (Sleep in *Endymion* is often a form of traveling.) Even the mountains, by Keats' artful repetition of "rise," seem to be lifting themselves from the floor of the earth in an act of self-transcendence. Yet all of this anti-natural activity is expressed in erotic terms—or, rather, in terms which impudently fuse the erotic and the religious. This is possible only because love in *Endymion* is much more than "the mere commingling of passionate breath." It is rather a mysterious force that, accord-ing to Endymion, may "bless / The world with benefits un-knowingly" and "produce more than our searching wit-nesseth." After making this assertion Endymion, in a memorable fancy, speculates about those unknown benefits:

who, of men, can tell
That flowers would bloom, or that green fruit would swell
To melting pulp, that fish would have bright mail,
The earth its dower of river, wood, and vale,
The meadows runnels, runnels pebble-stones,
The seed its harvest, or the lute its tones,

Tones ravishment, or ravishment its sweet,
If human souls did never kiss and greet?

(I, 835–42)

This lush evocation of a great chain of natural fruition and
sensuous delight should not mislead us. Far from submerging
love in the natural cycle, Keats subtly undermines that cycle
by fancying nature to be contingent upon man. Endymion
makes this super-naturalism explicit in the same passage
when he compares love's power to that of

the nightingale, upperched high,
And cloister'd among cool and bunched leaves—
She sings but to her love, nor e'er conceives
How tiptoe Night holds back her dark-grey hood.

(I, 828–31)

In one respect this is a benign reciprocity between individual
love and the natural order, but it is also true that the love song,
while apparently personal, bewitches a cosmic power and
causes a temporary suspension of the natural order.

Love is only secondarily a natural phenomenon or even a
personal one in *Endymion*. It is more akin to what we have
been describing as transcendence. It is an "elysium" that "has
power to make / Men's being mortal, immortal." It is "an
orbed drop / Of light," whose

influence,
Thrown in our eyes, genders a novel sense,
At which we start and fret; till in the end,
Melting into its radiance, we blend,
Mingle, and so become a part of it.

(I, 806–11)

Those who insist on reducing *Endymion* to the sensuous love
poem of an achingly passionate young man must willfully
ignore the complex meanings attached to love in such a
passage. In a sense the older Neoplatonic critics are closer to

the truth, though we need not follow them in their assumption of a preordained system, in their rigid allegorization, or in their moral embarrassments.[10] *Endymion* is more than a love story. It is about a voyage of the self, a "strange journeying" (III, 93), whose vehicle is misleadingly called "love."

Love in *Endymion* is not simply an "elysium," first of all because it is a transcendence that can be achieved only by way of a fall (the theological analogy remains appropriate, I think, though inexact). The first influence of love, says Endymion, "genders a novel sense, / At which we start and fret." Endymion's first visions of Cynthia alienate him from his people and his way of life and leave him in despair and loneliness. The whole poem is given over more to an account of his frustrations than to the isolated moments of promise or fulfillment. Much of the first book describes a passage from

10. Most of *Endymion's* critical history can be easily summarized, for discussion once centered so narrowly on the question of allegory. Older critics, such as Sir Sidney Colvin, Ernest de Selincourt, and Claude L. Finney, perhaps embarrassed by the poem's overt erotic content, claimed to see an elaborate and ordered Neoplatonic allegory: in Colvin's words, "the parable of the poetic soul in man seeking communion with the spirit of essential Beauty in the world." *John Keats: His Life and Poetry, His Friends, Critics and After-Fame,* 3d ed. (London, 1920), p. 205. This view was effectively challenged by Newell Ford in two essays, "*Endymion*—A Neo-Platonic Allegory?" *ELH* 14 (1947): 64–76, and "The Meaning of 'Fellowship with Essence' in *Endymion,*" *PMLA* 62 (1947): 1,061–76, as well as in a book, *The Prefigurative Imagination of John Keats: A Study of the Beauty-Truth Identification and Its Implications* (Stanford, 1951). Ford's view was supported by E. C. Pettet, *On the Poetry of Keats* (Cambridge, 1957). Ford and Pettet succeed in demolishing the excesses of Neoplatonic schematizing, but become reductive when they try to dispose of all symbolic or allegorical meanings and limit the poem to its sensuous surface and external "plot." A useful summary of this controversy is Jacob D. Wigod, "The Meaning of *Endymion,*" *PMLA* 68 (1953): 779–90. More recently, however, a number of critics have rightly ignored this fruitless issue, and the level of discourse about the poem has risen commensurately.

innocence to radical inner disruption, and a similar fall from innocence is crucial to almost all of the stories that Keats introduces as analogues to Endymion's adventure.

The brief account of Alpheus and Arethusa provides an exemplary description of such a fall. Arethusa, a nymph in the service of Diana, is being pursued by the river-god Alpheus. She complains:

> every sense
> Of mine was once made perfect in these woods.
> Fresh breezes, bowery lawns, and innocent floods,
> Ripe fruits, and lonely couch, contentment gave;
> But ever since I heedlessly did lave
> In thy deceitful stream, a panting glow
> Grew strong within me: wherefore serve me so,
> And call it love?
>
> (II, 965–72)

Keats may have been attracted to the myth in the fifth book of Ovid's *Metamorphoses* not only because of the link with Diana, of which he makes considerable use,[11] but he may also have seen the parallel between Arethusa's troubled account of sexual initiation and Endymion's situation. We know from the remarkably candid preface, as well as from many revealing and embarrassing passages, that this experience of sexual awakening is one of the roots of the poem:

> The imagination of a boy is healthy, and the mature imagination of a man is healthy; but there is a space of life between, in which the soul is in a ferment, the character undecided, the way of life uncertain, the ambition thick-sighted: thence proceeds mawkishness. . . .

11. Arethusa, believing her mistress Diana to be chaste, fears her wrath. Yet her words echo Cynthia's own; Cynthia too has been afraid of discovery. "Dian stands / Severe before me: persecuting fate!" says Arethusa. But Alpheus' guess is closer to the truth: "Dian's self must feel / Sometimes these very pangs."

Endymion takes its origin and to an extent its subject from this "space of life between," this ferment of the soul into which both Arethusa and Endymion are thrust. Biologically this is the experience of puberty and adolescence, but love in *Endymion* is not merely biological, or psychological, though Keats does not ignore these dimensions of his subject.

What Arethusa has lost is an original wholeness, which she depicts as a complete identification with nature. In this condition the self cannot be said to exist: it is continuous with its surroundings, which in turn provide it with perpetual delight and gratification. We recognize here another version of the bower experience so important to the early poems. But in those poems the "bowery nook" seemed always available to "easy quest"; from Arethusa we hear about it in the past tense, as a reminiscence, a retrospective longing for the complete sense satisfaction of infancy or childhood.[12] Into that paradise love intruded as a disruptive force, inimical to both nature and the gratification of the senses. "Not once more did I close my happy eye / Amid the thrushes' song," Arethusa goes on to say (II, 973–74). She is unhappy not because Alpheus has violated her, but because of her new and unsettling desire. ("If thou wast playing on my shady brink, / Thou wouldst bathe once again," he says.) As Plato argued in *The Symposium,* desire is the opposite of completeness for it implies absence and unfulfillment; consciousness of desire is thus the beginning of self-consciousness, for it introduces a division between the self (which needs) and the world (which can gratify). Arethusa now experiences such a division; she is

12. Endymion too puts a quintessential bower experience into the past tense when he describes his childhood relation to the moon, which has also been disrupted by the new experience of love:

> On some bright essence could I lean, and lull
> Myself to immortality: I prest
> Nature's soft pillow in a wakeful rest.
>
> (III, 172–74)

alienated from nature's more innocent pleasures, which can no longer satisfy her, yet too guilt-ridden to accept the new pleasures that Alpheus offers.

This paradigm achieves a larger resonance and complexity in the fall of Endymion himself, which occupies most of the poem's first book. The narrative begins with the description of a natural paradise.

> Upon the sides of Latmos was outspread
> A mighty forest; for the moist earth fed
> So plenteously all weed-hidden roots
> Into o'er-hanging boughs, and precious fruits.
>
> (I, 63–66)

Everything about this land exudes a mythical fruitfulness and richness. A perfect though secret reciprocity exists between the earth and the vegetation. The lambs in their "happy pens" are "bleating with content." The flocks range from atop the mountains to "vallies where the pipe is never dumb." They inhabit "swelling downs, where sweet air stirs / Blue hare-bells lightly, and where prickly furze / Buds lavish gold," or they "nibble their fill at ocean's very marge" (I, 200–204). As the priest of Pan says,

> Are not our lowing heifers sleeker than
> Night-swollen mushrooms? Are not our wide plains
> Speckled with countless fleeces?
>
> (I, 214–16)

Both the timeless continuities and miraculous transformations suggest an archetypal world of ever-ripening natural completeness. In Keats' "To Autumn" such richness will also augur the imminence of death, but here the night is as benign as the earth and the sun. Nor is man excluded from this primal harmony:

> . . . 'twas the morn: Apollo's upward fire
> Made every eastern cloud a silvery pyre

Of brightness so unsullied, that therein
A melancholy spirit well might win
Oblivion, and melt out his essence fine
Into the winds: rain-scented eglantine
Gave temperate sweets to that well-wooing sun;
The lark was lost in him; cold springs had run
To warm their chilliest bubbles in the grass;
Man's voice was on the mountains; and the mass
Of nature's lives and wonders puls'd tenfold,
To feel this sun-rise and its glories old.

(I, 95–106)

Keats' exaltation here admits nothing cloying or gross. It is a wonderful evocation of harmonious reciprocity within nature and between nature and man. But behind the tone of celebration a more ambiguous note is sounded. Along with reciprocity the passage describes a kind of benign destructiveness. Apollo's fire is not simply reflected by the clouds; it enkindles them in a metaphoric conflagration. This in turn is seen as a "pyre" in which "a melancholy spirit" might achieve forgetfulness and self-annihilation. This reference looks both before and after: back to the poet of the proem, seeking refuge from moods of "despondence" and darkness of spirit by creating the poem, and forward to the coming appearance of melancholy Endymion. Yet this motif of self-annihilation is not out of place here; it runs through the whole passage. All the elements of the scene merge in a beneficent fusion. The lark is "lost" in the "well-wooing sun." The cold springs melt out their essence in the warm grass. "Man's voice" is disembodied and becomes a part of the mountain landscape. All is submerged in "the mass / Of nature's lives" which, however glorious, precludes individuation. Nature is a pulsing totality in which the Latmians have their secure place.

Keats further emphasizes the absence of individuation in

the human part of the landscape a few lines later as he begins
to describe the procession of Pan:

> And now, as deep into the woods as we
> Might mark a lynx's eye, there glimmered light
> Fair faces and a rush of garments white,
> Plainer and plainer shewing, till at last
> Into the widest alley they all past . . .
>
> (I, 122–26)

The technique is cinematic. Keats places the perceiving eye
at a fixed point, establishes its distance from the action, and
then brings into its range a medley of gradually cohering im-
pressions.[13] What he implies is a pulsing human mass not
unlike "the mass / Of nature's lives" in which the scene is set.

The Latmians have a secure, undisturbed unity with
nature; yet nature is far from transparent to them. The landscape, in addition to its teeming richness, abounds in darker
areas, "gloomy shades, sequestered deep, / Where no man
went" (I, 67–68), "inmost glens" which swallow up stray
lambs forever. It is a landscape that contains unexplored
abysses, that is mysterious at its very center. In the hymn to
Pan this mystery in nature becomes a dominant motif:

> "O thou, whose mighty palace roof doth hang
> From jagged trunks, and overshadoweth
> Eternal whispers, glooms, the birth, life, death
> Of unseen flowers in heavy peacefulness;
> Who lov'st to see the hamadryads dress
> Their ruffled locks where meeting hazels darken;
> All through whole solemn hours dost sit, and hearken
> The dreary melody of bedded reeds—
> In desolate places, where dank moisture breeds
> The pipy hemlock to strange overgrowth. . . ."
>
> (I, 232–41)

13. Edward S. Lecomte makes a similar technical observation without drawing interpretive inferences. *Endymion in England: The Literary History of a Greek Myth* (New York, 1944), p. 159.

Here the richness of nature becomes strange and exotic, not quite sinister, but pregnant with a significance that seems just beyond human reach. "Where man is not, nature is barren," wrote Blake.[14] But this is precisely that part of nature "where man is not," and to Keats it is the opposite of barren. These "desolate places, where dank moisture breeds / The pipy hemlock to strange overgrowth," seem to embody something of the mystery of life itself. Pan is seen as presiding over the very sources of being, the fundamental rhythms of existence, "eternal whispers, glooms, the birth, life, death / Of unseen flowers in heavy peacefulness." It is significant that Keats sees these essential rhythms as a kind of somnolence, for sleep in *Endymion* is frequently linked with access to transcendent knowledge. Equally significant are the gloom and darkness of the scene, akin to the Night dear to Shelley's imagination, but also connected with loss: we meet Pan here as a disappointed lover, "Bethinking thee, how melancholy loth / Thou wast to lose fair Syrinx," sitting drearily over the reeds into which his love has been transformed.[15]

Here we glimpse a fundamental paradox in Pan and in the Nature he embodies. In addition to being "a symbol of immensity" and the "dread opener of mysterious doors / Leading to universal knowledge," Pan is also a melancholy and disappointed lover (much like Endymion at this point) and a benign household god, "breather round our farms, / To keep off mildews, and all weather harms" (I, 283–84). Pan is at once the most esoteric and the most immediate of the gods, the most transcendent and the most familiar, but ultimately

14. Blake, *The Marriage of Heaven and Hell,* in Keynes, p. 185.
15. The story of Pan and Syrinx, though merely alluded to here, is another pregnant analogue to the main action of the poem. Like Arethusa Syrinx is a nymph of Diana who (as Ovid stresses) intently imitates her mistress' supposed chastity. Her metamorphosis turns Pan into a kind of poet, who makes music on a pipe fashioned out of her reeds, and even (foolishly) challenges Apollo himself. (See Shelley's "Hymn of Pan" and "Hymn of Apollo." Also, see below, n. 20.)

"an element filling the space between" (I, 301).[16] This does not mean that Pan offers any easy reconciliation between the two. If he did, Endymion's quest would be superfluous. The important distinction here, which critics have failed to make, is between Endymion and the Latmians who sing the hymn to Pan. It is only to the Latmians that Pan, as the "opener of the mysterious doors / Leading to universal knowledge," is "dread." They are satisfied to leave him "an unknown," an "*unimaginable* lodge / For solitary thinkings" (my emphasis). The quest of Endymion leads him to explore that unknown, to enter those doors. The Latmians are content with a static, sacramental relation to Pan. They "are come to pay their vows" (I, 291); they seek him through ritual, perform a homage which leaves his mystery and their innocence intact. Endymion's mission, however, will lead him to Glaucus, who has been charged to "explore all forms and substances / Straight homeward to their symbol-essences" (III, 699–700) —which, if obscure,[17] is certainly different from the Latmians' relation to Pan. Endymion's quest leads toward understand-

16. The duality of Pan is part of the traditional iconography. Finney cites as a source the following passage in Sandys' commentary on the fourteenth book of Ovid: "The hornes on his head expressing the rayes of the Sun and Moone . . . the vpper part of his body, like a mans, representing the heavens; not onlie in regard of the beautie thereof, but of his reason and dominion: His goatish nether parts carrying the similitude of the earth; rough, overgrowne with woods and bushes." *The Evolution of Keats's Poetry* (Cambridge, Mass., 1936), 1:266–67. Of course this allegorization, with its heavy Neoplatonic and Christian dualism, includes much that is foreign to Keats. Finney offers a thorough account of the possible sources of the hymn (1:258–72).

In her recent and fascinating book *Pan the Goat-God: His Myth in Modern Times* (Cambridge, Mass., 1969), Patricia Merivale greatly illuminates Pan's duality by separating out the Arcadian and Orphic elements of the myth, both very much present in Keats' hymn.

17. We ought not to slight the obscurity here. *Endymion* is always aspiring to penetrate mysteries that it never adequately succeeds in defining. This side of the poem is very close in spirit to that interesting piece of Keatsian apocrypha, "The Poet," with its central lines: "To his sight / The husk of natural objects opens quite / To the core: and

ing rather than ritual; its end is knowledge and transfiguration, not sacramental homage. Endymion's fall is a fall into
knowledge, which breaks the preconscious unity of man and
and nature that had previously been affirmed through ritual
and myth. Of the Latmians, Keats writes,

> those fair living forms swam heavenly
> To tunes forgotten—out of memory:
> Fair creatures! whose young children's children bred
> Thermopylae its heroes—not yet dead,
> But in old marbles ever beautiful.
> High genitors, unconscious did they cull
> Time's sweet first-fruits.
>
> (I, 315–21)

The Latmians are not so much men as "fair living forms"
upon which old marbles have conferred a timeless immortality. We see them here as stylized fantasy, in slow-motion,
not dancing but, rather, swimming heavenly to tunes forgotten. They represent a mythic "golden age" (II, 896),
"unconscious" of the imminent onset of time and history
(e.g., Thermopylae), yet they are the "genitors" of that
history.

Endymion's fall involves severance from this community.
As he sits and hears the traditional discourse of the "aged
priest" and the "shepherds gone in eld" his mind tries vainly
to combat a "cankering venom" (I, 396). Finally he is lost in
a "fixed trance . . . Like one who on the earth had never stept"
(I, 403–4). It is only his sister Peona who can for a moment
"breathe away the curse" (I, 412). She takes him along a path
where two "streamlets fall, / With mingled bubblings and a
gentle rush, / Into a river, clear, brimful, and flush / With
crystal mocking of the trees and sky" (I, 419–22), and thence
to a "bowery island" that Keats identifies with childhood (I,

every secret essence there / Reveals the elements of good and fair"
(Garrod, 1958, p. 528).

433–35). She takes Endymion to the bower of the 1817 *Poems,* a world of soothing nature and refreshing sleep, which provide antidotes for excessive reflection and under whose influence he is "calm'd to life again" (I, 464). This refuge can only be temporary: it can provide momentary renewal but no resolution, for the bower here represents, as Bernard Blackstone says, "the sphere of unconscious felicity which Endymion must relinquish."[18] Endymion does not know this yet, and for the moment promises to return to his old life as a shepherd and hunter (I, 477–86). But Peona herself senses that he has made a radical break, has eaten of the apple and now knows "of things mysterious, / Immortal, starry" (I, 506–7). He proceeds to give her an account of a fall that seems radical and irrevocable:

> I, who still saw the horizontal sun
> Heave his broad shoulder o'er the edge of the world,
> Out-facing Lucifer, and then had hurl'd
> My spear aloft, as signal for the chace—
> I, who, for very sport of heart, would race
> With my own steed from Araby; pluck down
> A vulture from his towery perching; frown
> A lion into growling, loth retire—
> To lose, at once, all my toil breeding fire,
> And sink thus low!
>
> (I, 529–38)

Endymion had been the epic hero, the embodiment of activity without inwardness. The sun, as personified here, becomes a cosmic analogue for Endymion's heroic stature. It also suggests a world in which man and the cosmos were one, in which the sun could be apprehended personally as a muscular warrior and a muscular warrior could perform feats worthy of the sun-god. Now Endymion can no longer play the hunter's and the hero's part: he has fallen from legend to

18. *The Consecrated Urn,* p. 124.

man, from health to despondency, above all, from activity to self-consciousness.

Later in the first book this transformation will figure in an important debate between Peona and Endymion. Presently, however, Endymion introduces a different motif as he gives Peona an account of his first dream-vision of Cynthia. As is often the case in *Endymion,* the setting is as significant as the vision itself. Endymion first describes a sort of *dérèglement de tous les sens:*

> . . . through the dancing poppies stole
> A breeze, most softly lulling to my soul;
> And shaping visions all about my sight
> Of colours, wings and bursts of spangly light;
> The which became more strange, and strange, and dim,
> And then were gulph'd in a tumultuous swim:
> And then I fell asleep.
>
> (I, 566–72)

Characteristically, Endymion speaks less of passion and desire than of imaginative afflatus. He describes a visionary experience that Keats will repeatedly associate either with sleep and dreams or with the moon. The language of this passage recalls the earlier invocation to Sleep, when Endymion had been brought to the bowery island:

> great key
> To golden palaces, strange minstrelsy,
> Fountains grotesque, new trees, bespangled caves,
> Echoing grottos, full of tumbling waves
> And moonlight; aye, to all the mazy world
> Of silvery enchantment!
>
> (I, 456–61)

G. Wilson Knight describes these as "paradise symbols of the *Kubla Khan* sort."[19] This is an appropriate reference, not only

19. G. Wilson Knight, *The Starlit Dome: Studies in the Poetry of Vision* (New York, 1960), pp. 261–62.

because of the comparable symbols that both poets use for the imagination, but because in the later passage Endymion goes on to make something like the rudimentary distinction between the primary and secondary Imagination that Coleridge makes in his poem. The whole last stanza of the Coleridge poem is about the distance between the poet's original vision and what he recaptures when he tries to articulate that vision. Coleridge tells us of a vision of "a damsel with a dulcimer," and then, balancing question and assertion, says,

> Could I revive within me,
> Her symphony and song,
> To such a deep delight 'twould win me. . . .

Coleridge seems deliberately to build a similar distinction into the structure of the poem by providing the apologetic preface and a subtitle ("A Fragment"). The whole poem, he tells us, must be heard as the partial echo of some much grander symphony and song of which we can only have a faint surmise (whose revival would transfigure the poet into a magical and godlike state). Endymion's distinction is similar:

> Ah, can I tell
> The enchantment that afterwards befel?
> Yet it was but a dream: yet such a dream
> That never tongue, although it overteem
> With mellow utterance, like a cavern spring,
> Could figure out and to conception bring
> All I beheld and felt.

> (I, 572–78)

Later, when Peona responds to Endymion's account, she attacks not so much love as "visions, dreams, / And fitful whims of sleep" (I, 748–49), for he has told the story not so much of his falling in love as of his conversion to the life of imagination.[20] We cannot deny—this is part of the poem's

20. Compare the story of Pan and Syrinx, which also moves, though

drastic unevenness—that many of the scenes with Cynthia
consist of literal, often ludicrous and cloying, loveplay. But
this should not blind us to those numerous moments, sometimes groping and confused, when, as Stuart Sperry says, "the
love-dream . . . is . . . largely an extended metaphor,"[21] or
when love itself takes on a larger meaning and becomes much
more than "a mere commingling of passionate breath." At
times Keats offers us a mixture painful to contemplate and
difficult to disentangle. Of this first vision of Cynthia, Endymion says, for example:

> Whence that completed form of all completeness?
> Whence came that high perfection of all sweetness?
> (I, 606–7)

This is partly the idealizing rhetoric of love, but Endymion
is also trying to describe an experience closer to transcendence
than to ordinary love. He had watched the zenith, for instance,
"until the doors / Of heaven appear'd to open for my flight"
(I, 581–82). Then he describes his "high soaring," in an "airy
trance," upon "imaginary pinions." This is followed by the
sudden, magnificent appearance of the moon, with his
"dazzled soul / Commingling with her argent spheres" (I,
594–95). Even his description of their lovemaking, awkward
as it is, moves almost immediately from the literal gratification of passion toward a heightened intensity of being:

> madly did I kiss
> The wooing arms which held me, and did give
> My eyes at once to death: but 'twas to live,
> To take in draughts of life from the gold fount

in a somewhat different fashion, from love to imagination. Patricia
Merivale quotes Coleridge's enticing but morally conventional note:
"Pan, Syrinx / Disappointment turning sensual into purer pleasures
—disapp: Lust by regret, refining into Love & ending in Harmony."
Pan the Goat-God, p. 61.

21. Stuart M. Sperry, Jr., "The Allegory of *Endymion,*" *Studies in
Romanticism* 2 (Autumn 1962): 49.

> Of kind and passionate looks; to count, and count
> The moments, by some greedy help that seem'd
> A second self, that each might be redeem'd
> And plunder'd of its load of blessedness.
>
> (I, 653–60)

This crude passage deserves notice not only for its pallid anticipations—the "full draught" foreshadows the "domineering potion" that the poet drinks at the outset of *The Fall of Hyperion,* and the whole passage prefigures the theme important in both *Hyperion* poems of life and rebirth achieved through some sort of death. Through the tangled syntax of the last three lines—I take it that the "second self" is the beloved, but "each" refers back to "moments," though it might apply to "self"—we mark one of the characteristic moments of "glut" that occur so frequently in the poem. Here, with the "greedy" (i.e., self-interested) aid of "a second self" (not simply "another person," but also something that provokes us to self-recognition), each moment can be "redeem'd / And plunder'd of its load of blessedness."

A moment later the soaring lovers come to rest in a pastoral paradise, which proves characteristically unstable and short-lived. The appropriate comparison is Arethusa's nostalgic evocation of a different kind of perfection:

> every sense
> Of mine was once made perfect in these woods.
> Fresh breezes, bowery lawns, and innocent floods,
> Ripe fruits, and lonely couch, contentment gave.
>
> (II, 965–68)

Like Wordsworth's Lucy, Arethusa had been Nature's child, but unlike Lucy, who dies into nature, she has been forced to undergo what Geoffrey Hartman calls "the crisis of separation,"[22] which is the crisis of growth, individuation, and

22. Hartman, *Wordsworth's Poetry,* p. 160.

humanization, the crisis of self-consciousness and consciousness of others. But instead of facing this crisis, Arethusa looks back longingly, like Blake's Thel, to her former innocence. Endymion, however, grows toward a different sort of completeness, which does not negate the values of the bower or of the pleasure principle which the bower embodies; it rather transposes the bower from a scene of "lonely . . . contentment" and childlike self-sufficiency to one of tense longing, contingent satisfaction, and ultimately a mutual recognition between two selves. Harold Bloom observes that "Endymion's fate is mostly a series of frustrations, and he ultimately achieves his quest only by abandoning it."[23] This seems fundamental to Keats' project, which involves not so much "an immortality of passion" as an ebb and flow, a transcendent quest, but not without "the disappointment, the anxiety, / Imagination's struggles, far and nigh." Just as the car that represents the imagination in "Sleep and Poetry" disappears and must be kept alive by an act of mind and will, so each of Endymion's dream-visions must fade, as this first one does:

> like a spark
> That needs must die, although its little beam
> Reflects upon a diamond, my sweet dream
> Fell into nothing—into stupid sleep.
>
> (I, 675–78)

Just as sleep can be fertile and creative, the soil of imagination, so too can we fall into the barrenness of "stupid sleep." Keats' image of the spark that reflects upon a diamond finely embodies both the beauty of vision and its fragility and transience. At this point Endymion drops into a despair so total that it seems like a fall from grace. The whole world is transformed in his perception:

23. Harold Bloom, *The Visionary Company: A Reading of English Romantic Poetry* (Garden City, N.Y., 1963), p. 388.

> all the pleasant hues
> Of heaven and earth had faded: deepest shades
> Were deepest dungeons; heaths and sunny glades
> Were full of pestilent light; our taintless rills
> Seem'd sooty, and o'er-spread with upturn'd gills
> Of dying fish. . . .
>
> (I, 691–96)

This is not to be taken as an extreme example of "romantic subjectivism" in which the world is entirely transformed by the eye of the perceiver. It tells us that the consequence of passion for Endymion, as for Arethusa, has been to cut him off completely from nature, from the idealized pastoral world of his youth.

The speech of Peona that follows takes up almost all the important themes of Endymion's narrative and initiates a debate which is central to an understanding of the poem. First, she defends the life of action against the life of sensibility. Instead of playing out a sad "ballad" of love and death, she says, "be rather in the trumpet's mouth" (I, 737):

> it is strange, and sad, alas!
> That one who through this middle earth should pass
> Most like a sojourning demi-god, and leave
> His name upon the harp-string, should achieve
> No higher bard than simple maidenhood.
>
> (I, 722–26)

Not long afterward, Carlyle, in *Sartor Resartus,* was to offer comparable advice to his romantic young man in despair: "Close thy *Byron;* open thy *Goethe*"—a Goethe whose central wisdom is that "Doubt of any sort cannot be removed except by Action."[24] Peona recalls Endymion to the heroic, active life that he himself had so vividly described to her. The issue is joined in terms of different kinds of poetry. She commends

24. Thomas Carlyle, *Sartor Resartus: The Life and Opinions of Herr Teufelsdröckh,* ed. C. F. Harrold (New York, 1937), pp. 192, 196.

to him the traditional bard—and the martial life—of epic.
But Keats himself is trying to write a new kind of epic, "striving to uprear / Love's standard on the battlements of song"
(II, 39–40), portraying the conflicts of the inner life rather
than those of the battlefield. He is writing neither ballad nor
epic but taking his "first step," as he later avowed to his editor,
towards "Drama," in which the "chief Attempt" is "the playing of different Natures with Joy and Sorrow" (1:218–19).

Peona's second target is her brother's quest for transcendence. She would have Endymion be content as "a sojourning
demi-god" on "this middle earth," whereas he ultimately
seeks no less than to be "enskyed." She is content to "dote
upon" the mere "semblance" of natural beauty, satisfied to
see intimations of a deeper beauty, but only as they are reflected in the world around her: "would I so tease / My
pleasant days, because I could not mount / Into those regions?" (I, 745–47). She accepts the gleanings of beauty that
the world affords her but would not seek to make them truth,
to realize them in ways that might shake the ordered reality
on which she depends. This leads directly to her third and
chief target, which is imagination itself, as embodied in
"visions, dreams, / And fitful whims of sleep":

> The Morphean fount
> Of that fine element that visions, dreams,
> And fitful whims of sleep are made of, streams
> Into its airy channels with so subtle,
> So thin a breathing, not the spider's shuttle,
> Circled a million times within the space
> Of a swallow's nest-door, could delay a trace,
> A tinting of its quality: how light
> Must dreams themselves be; seeing they're more slight
> Than the mere nothing that engenders them!
> Then wherefore sully the entrusted gem
> Of high and noble life with thoughts so sick?

> Why pierce high-fronted honour to the quick
> For nothing but a dream?
>
> (I, 747–60)

This conception of imagination, like much else in *Endymion,* owes a great deal to the fairy-plays of Shakespeare, *The Tempest* and *A Midsummer Night's Dream,* Keats' earliest favorites among the plays. It owes a more specific debt to a related scene in *Romeo and Juliet.* Mercutio has just made his Queen Mab speech in which this so-called realist and cynic, setting out to caricature the imagination of dreamers and lovers, does so with such zest that the speech becomes one of the chief imaginative acts of the play. It is a flight beyond the immature, conventionally love-sick Romeo of the first act, who grows impatient and cuts Mercutio off:

Romeo.

> Peace, peace, Mercutio, peace!
> Thou talk'st of nothing.

Mercutio.

> True, I talk of dreams;
> Which are the children of an idle brain,
> Begot of nothing but vain fantasy;
> Which is as thin of substance as the air,
> And more inconstant than the wind, who woos
> Even now the frozen bosom of the North
> And, being anger'd, puffs away from thence,
> Turning his side to the dew-dropping South.

Benvolio.

> This wind you talk of blows us from ourselves.
> Supper is done, and we shall come too late.
>
> (I, iv, 95–105)

It is Romeo and Benvolio who lack imagination here. Mercutio not only provides a striking image of the wind of airy fantasy first wooing the frozen North of reality and then turning to warmer regions of the dew-dropping South, but in the process also gives free play to his own airy fantasy. Peona borrows the language of Mercutio but the attitude of Benvolio: "The wind you talk of blows us from ourselves." Peona, like the chorus in Greek tragedy, defends safety and stability, the traditional wisdom of the community, warning the hero against overreaching his proper sphere. To her only the common duties and traditional roles are healthy and real.

Endymion, in his reply, refuses to consign dream and vision to the world of fiction, refuses to grant honorific reality and health to the daylight world, the world of action. He rejects the dichotomy between imagination and reality, a dichotomy that trivializes the realm of consciousness as it aggrandizes the realm of "fact." His dream visions are "no merely slumberous phantasm" (I, 771); he sees "a hope beyond the shadow of a dream" (I, 857), a reality. As Keats himself was to write, "the Imagination may be compared to Adam's dream —he awoke and found it truth" (1:185).[25] Endymion's speech was singled out by Keats in a letter to his publisher—"My

25. This claim is crucial for Romantic poetry in general. Thus Dr. Leavis, no friend to Shelley, feels impelled to distinguish him from his Victorian heirs, whose poetry "turns its back on the actual world and preoccupies itself with fantasies of an alternative—in a spirit very different from Shelley's, for the Victorian poetic daydream does not suppose itself to have any serious relation to actuality or possibility." *Revaluation,* pp. 255–56. Harold Bloom, working from far different premises, makes a similar distinction between Romantic and Victorian mythmaking. *English Romantic Poetry: An Anthology* (Garden City, N.Y., 1961), pp. 20–21.

As described by Basil Willey, Milton's problem in choosing a subject for his epic presents a striking analogy to this Romantic aspiration. As the growth of a rational scientific mentality consigned poetry more and more to the realm of fiction and fancy, the Bible, in the literal sense in which the seventeenth century could still believe in it, remained genuine history, a unique access to both beauty and truth, a reconciliation of art and reality. See "The Heroic Poem in a Scientific Age," in Willey, *The Seventeenth Century Background* (Garden City, 1953), pp. 206–62.

having written that Argument will perhaps be of the greatest Service to me of any thing I ever did" (1:218)—and has as a result been generally taken as the "key" to *Endymion* and subjected to much debate and interpretation. Perhaps a comparative view could provide us with a new perspective.

Paul de Man, in an illuminating essay on Keats and Friedrich Hölderlin, has suggested what seems to me a profitable comparison between *Endymion* and Hölderlin's early novel *Hyperion* (published 1797–99).[26] Near the beginning of that novel is an abstract passage that makes as central an argument as Endymion's speech. Hyperion writes to Bellarmin:

> O blessed Nature! I know not how it is with me when I raise my eyes to thy beauty, but all the joy of Heaven is in the tears that I weep in thy presence, beloved of beloveds!
>
> My whole being falls silent and listens when the delicate swell of the breeze plays over my breast. Often, lost in the wide blue, I look up into the ether and down into the sacred sea, and I feel as if a kindred spirit were opening its arms to me, as if the pain of solitude were dissolved in the life of the Divinity.
>
> To be one with all—this is the life divine, this is man's heaven.
>
> To be one with all that lives, to return in blessed self-forgetfulness into the All of Nature—this is the pinnacle of thoughts and joys, this the sacred mountain peak, the place of eternal rest, where the noonday loses its oppressive heat and the thunder its voice and the boiling sea is as the heaving field of grain.
>
> To be one with all that lives! At those words Virtue puts off her wrathful armor, the mind of man lays its scepter down, all thoughts vanish before the image of the world in its eternal oneness, even as the striving artist's rules vanish before his Urania; and iron Fate renounces her dominion, and Death vanishes from the confederacy of beings, and indivisibility and eternal youth bless and beautify the world.

26. Paul de Man, "Keats and Hölderlin," *Comparative Literature* 8 (1956): 29–38.

On this height I often stand, my Bellarmin. But an instant of reflection hurls me down. I reflect, and find myself as I was before—alone, with all the griefs of mortality; and my heart's refuge, the world in its eternal oneness, is gone; Nature closes her arms, and I stand like an alien before her and understand her not.[27]

Hyperion's letter is of course written from a perspective different from Endymion's. Endymion's speech is a confident prospectus of stages leading to the "chief intensity." It is a prologue to his quest, rather than an epilogue. Hyperion's letter, though it comes at the beginning of the novel, is written at a point of disillusionment and failure. The structure of the Hölderlin passage is, however, similar to the recurrent pattern of *Endymion* as a whole, which is an alternation of ebb and flow, of elation and despair, vision and solitude. Keats makes little effort at dramatic propriety in Endymion's speech. It contains no trace of the malaise and desperation which, until just a few lines earlier, has been his hero's predominant mood. "On this height I often stand," says Hyperion. Endymion's speech is just such a momentary peak, significant but not definitive; neither the "key" to the poem nor a précis of its action, it expresses an ideal possibility that must be measured against the limiting conditions that so frequently reassert themselves along the way.

What is that "height" to which the two poets aspire? Professor de Man describes the main motif of both works as "a quest for unity."[28] In neither case, in spite of the religious vocabulary, does it seem to be a unity with anything supernatural. Hölderlin's "life of the Divinity" and Keats' "clear religion of heaven" (I, 781) are both open to misunderstanding. Recent commentators on Keats' crucial phrase "fellow-

27. *Hyperion, or The Hermit in Greece,* trans. Willard R. Trask (New York, 1965), pp. 22–23. *Sämtliche Werke,* ed. Friedrich Beissner (Frankfurt am Main, 1961), pp. 492–93.

28. "Keats and Hölderlin," p. 35.

ship divine, / A fellowship with essence" (I, 778–79), have stressed the parallel phrase "feel we these things?" (794), and have cited other significant uses of "essence" in *Endymion* to mean objects or things. These studies have stressed the notion of empathy, so central to Keats' aesthetic theory, rather than the Neoplatonic idea that so many earlier writers attached to the passage.[29] This interpretation brings the speech close to Hölderlin's meaning, "to be one with all that lives."

The stress on unity in both passages is a striking link. There is nothing in Keats equivalent to Hölderlin's apparently pantheistic "All of Nature. . . . the world in its eternal oneness [*ewigeinige Welt*]," but Endymion's speech describes what amounts to a series of mergings, "blendings pleasureable," each of which leads to a higher stage of "fellowship." The first merger is expressed in sexual terms:

> hist, when the airy stress
> Of music's kiss impregnates the free winds,
> And with a sympathetic touch unbinds
> Eolian magic from their lucid wombs.
>
> (I, 783–86)

Next we step "into a sort of oneness" (I, 797), but do not experience true unity until the final stage, which Keats calls love. This he compares to "an orbed drop / Of light,"

> At which we start and fret; till, in the end,
> Melting into its radiance, we blend,
> Mingle, and so become a part of it,—
> Nor with aught else can our souls interknit
> So wingedly: when we combine therewith,
> Life's self is nourished by its proper pith,
> And we are nurtured like a pelican brood.
>
> (I, 809–15)

29. See especially Ford, "The Meaning of 'Fellowship with Essence' in *Endymion*"; also Bate, *John Keats,* pp. 181–83.

In both Keats and Hölderlin the desired unity is not an active self-integration but a passive absorption into some larger whole, in which the self is submerged and annihilated. Hölderin desires "to return in blessed self-forgetfulness into the All of Nature," which he describes as a "place of eternal rest." Similarly, Keats' "fellowship with essence" enables us to "shine / Full achemiz'd, and free of space." When we achieve "a sort of oneness"

> our state
> Is like a floating spirit's. But there are
> Richer entanglements, enthralments far
> More self-destroying, leading, by degrees,
> To the chief intensity.
>
> (I, 797–800)

Finally, with love, we "blend, / Mingle, and so become a part of it." Many commentators have glossed this motif in Keats by referring again to a process of empathy, but the result has often been a taming of the radical force of the idea. It is well known that at several important points in his letters Keats refers to the poet (*qua* poet) as necessarily lacking selfhood and identity. The most explicit statement comes in the important letter on "the poetical Character" that he addressed to Woodhouse (27 October 1818). "It is not itself—it has no self—it is every thing and nothing," Keats wrote.

> A Poet is the most unpoetical of any thing in existence; because he has no Identity—he is continually in for—and filling some other Body—The Sun, the Moon, the Sea and Men and Women who are creatures of impulse are poetical and have about them in an unchangeable attribute—the poet has none.
> (1:387)

In the same spirit Keats added that in a roomful of people, "the identity of every one in the room begins to press upon me that, I am in a very little time annihilated." The experience Keats describes here is both more harmless and more oppressive than the one in *Endymion*. It is no more than the aesthetic openness that Keats imputed to drama and to the greatest poetry, above all (following Hazlitt) to Shakespeare.[30]

Thus Keats reassures us that the poetical character "does no more harm from its relish of the dark side of things any more than from its taste for the bright one; because they both end in speculation."[31] It is also, for a poet like Keats, involuntary and therefore at times oppressive, leading to discomfort rather than to "the chief intensity." As his brother Tom lay dying, Keats wrote that "his identity presses upon me so all day that I am obliged to go out" (1:369). In no case can this be likened to Endymion's "richer entanglements, enthralments far / More self-destroying, leading, by degrees, / To the chief intensity." Endymion is describing a willed and total self-annihilation more serious than what the dramatist undergoes in creating his characters. It is an annihilation of the man as well as the poet, and it leads not to creativity but to stasis, to "ardent listlessness" (I, 825) on the part of those who can willingly "let occasion die" and "sleep in love's elysium." This combination of passivity, self-annihilation, and instinctual gratification, this paradoxical union of intensity and inertia that the phrase "ardent listlessness" expresses so well, this "elysium" beyond the bourne of activity

30. "He seemed scarcely to have an individual existence of his own, but to borrow that of others at will, and to pass successively through 'every variety of untried being,'—to be now *Hamlet,* now *Othello,* now *Lear,* now *Falstaff,* now *Ariel*." "On Posthumous Fame,—Whether Shakespeare was Influenced by the Love of it?" *The Round Table* (1817), in *Collected Works of Hazlitt,* ed. Waller and Glover, 1:23.

31. This sort of empathy is harmless enough to be applied to a billiard ball. Thus Woodhouse writes: "he has affirmed that he can conceive of a billiard Ball that it may have a sense of delight from its own roundness, smoothness, volubility, & the rapidity of its motion." Reprinted in *Letters* (1:389).

and volition—all point to another version of the bower and an eloquent restatement of its values.

This in turn raises serious problems about the nature of Endymion's quest and about the coherence of the poem's overall design. If self-destruction is as important a motif as Endymion is made to say, if it is indeed the *via negativa* toward the "chief intensity," how then does Endymion's goal differ from his starting point? It was among the Latmians that "a melancholy spirit well might win / Oblivion, and melt out his essence fine / Into the winds" (I, 98–100). It is Peona, who represents Endymion's earlier life, who takes him to a bower which grants him sleep, but which is clearly regressive, an impediment to the quest, as Blackstone says, "the sphere of unconscious felicity which Endymion must relinquish." All of Latmos is just such a *locus amoenus,* a bower which Endymion leaves behind. Yet Endymion's visions of Cynthia often take place within bowers too. And what of that remarkable bower in the fourth book of the poem, the Cave of Quietude?

Endymion's quest then, at least as he announces it in the first book, must be seen not as a rejection of Latmos but as an attempt to transform it. Keats wishes to preserve the bower by altering its regressive character. The bower of the 1817 *Poems* is usually a simple return to nature and escape from the world. It embodies a pleasure principle, but only as a dream, a utopia, the return to the innocent and total delight of the child, never as a lived experience involving another being, never as the problematic sexual integration of the adult. The love scenes with Cynthia, bad as they are, seem in their cycle of aspiration and frustration to attempt that harder task; and the conjuring of the Indian maid in the last book is a further and more successful effort to pass beyond the "space between" of turbid adolescence to which Keats refers so eloquently in the preface. The bower of Endymion's speech has little reference to nature, except as perhaps a first stage, and Endymion puts little emphasis on the motif of escape. He desires not simply to be "uplifted from the world" but to progress to a new intensity of being.

Yet the element of escape is undeniably present in Endymion's speech, in his polemic—which Keats himself takes up in the prologues to the second and third books—not only against the active life but against politics and the whole historical process, in the name of "love."

> Aye, so delicious is the unsating food,
> That men, who might have tower'd in the van
> Of all the congregated world, to fan
> And winnow from the coming step of time
> All chaff of custom, wipe away all slime
> Left by men-slugs and human serpentry,
> Have been content to let occasion die,
> Whilst they did sleep in love's elysium.
> And, truly, I would rather be struck dumb,
> Than speak against this ardent listlessness . . .
>
> (I, 816–25)

We are far indeed from the millennial overtones of the passage from Hölderlin's *Hyperion,* in which the self seeks not merely a private elysium but a general one, in which the entire world seems elevated to the "chief intensity" and transformed. This motive leads Hyperion to go to battle to free Greece, after being rebuked by his beloved, Diotima:

> Your heart has at last found peace. I believe it. I understand it. But do you truly think that you have reached the end? Do you mean to shut yourself up in the heaven of your love, and let the world, which needs you, wither and grow cold before you? You must shoot down like the beam of light, you must descend like the all-refreshing rain, into the land of mortal men, you must illuminate like Apollo, shake and

animate like Jupiter, or you are not worthy of your heaven.
I beg you: go back into Athens again. . . .

Hyperion finally agrees that "it cannot be so hard to unite
what is outside of me and the divine within me."[32] Keats, it
is true, implicitly grants the value of the revolutionary
political activity that attacks "the chaff of custom" and the
"slime / Left by men-slugs and human serpentry." Even in
the prologue to Book II, where he is most uncompromising
in his denunciation of "pageant history" and "the universe of
deeds" (II, 14, 15), he seems to be referring more to written
than to lived history, to that false intelligence that passes as
history, against which he opposes the more essential history
that he finds in works of art. In this sense he is repeating
Aristotle's dictum that poetry is more philosophical, because
more universal, than history, for it deals not with the acci-
dental particulars of fact but with the recurrent patterns of
human experience. (In this spirit Keats or Reynolds wrote of
Shakespeare's *Henry VI* that "the poetry is for the most part
ironed and manacled with a chain of facts, and cannot get
free; it cannot escape from the prison house of history, nor
often move without our being disturbed by the clanking of
its fetters."[33]) But Keats goes further than Aristotle when he
attacks history for being spurious as well as confining. It is a
"pageant," a "gilded cheat," a distortion of reality:

> Wide sea, that one continuous murmur breeds
> Along the pebbled shore of memory!
> Many old rotten-timber'd boats there be
> Upon thy vaporous bosom, magnified
> To goodly vessels; many a sail of pride,
> And golden keel'd, is left unlaunch'd and dry.
>
> (II, 16–21)

32. Hölderlin, *Hyperion,* pp. 99, 100.
33. "On Kean in 'Richard Duke of York,' " 3:7.

Keats does more than protest the stress on military and
political events to the detriment of emotional events in history. He attacks history for its very continuity. Thus the
Henry VI plays, according to Keats or Reynolds, are constrained by "regularity": "They are written with infinite
vigour, but their regularity tied the hand of Shakespeare.
Particular facts kept him in the high road, and would not
suffer him to turn down leafy and winding lanes, or to break
wildly and at once into the breathing fields." True history
does not follow a linear course or a regular pace, but an eccentric topography of essential experiences, each of which
has a vital rather than a formal relation to us:

> the silver flow
> Of Hero's tears, the swoon of Imogen,
> Fair Pastorella in the bandit's den,
> Are things to brood on with more ardency
> Than the death-day of empires.
>
> (II, 30–34)

The "leafy and winding lanes" of this topography may help
us to understand, if not excuse, the design of *Endymion*.
These bypaths are bowers, and *Endymion* is partly an endless
succession of bowers. This, we will remember, was the way
Keats defended its structure: "Do not the Lovers of Poetry
like to have a little Region to wander in where they may pick
and choose, and in which the images are so numerous that
many are forgotten and found new in a second Reading:
which may be food for a Week's stroll in the summer?"
(1:170). Such a "Region" is a thoroughgoing denial of history. It makes successiveness an illusion, for it gives primacy
to something like a mystic point of contemplation, an experience on which we can "brood" with "ardency," a moment
that overcomes the illusory barrier of time: "One kiss brings
honey-dew from buried days" (II, 7). We are reminded of

the Wordsworthian "spots of time," which have a permanence that seems to overcome time, and of Keats' version of
them, the "essences" of the opening lines of *Endymion:*

> A thing of beauty is a joy for ever:
> . . . .
>   Nor do we merely feel these essences
> For one short hour. . . .

We are reminded also that the "thing of beauty" will keep
"A bower quiet for us, and a sleep / Full of sweet dreams,
and health, and quiet breathing." The word ardency takes us
back to the "ardent listlessness" of Endymion's speech, and
we can now understand why the paradox of that phrase is
only apparent. For Keats at this stage, "listlessness" is no less
the condition of "ardency." It is that suspension of will that
rebels against the mechanical purposiveness and linear
"progress" of ordinary history; it is the condition of mind
appropriate only to the bowers and "leafy and winding lanes"
of essential experience. It is only then that

> Life's self is nourished by its proper pith,
> And we are nurtured like a pelican brood.
>   (I, 814–15)

The pelican was said to wound itself and feed its young
with its own blood. What Keats has in mind need not be
"something approximately Eucharistic," as Professor Wasserman interestingly suggests,[34] but more a return of experience
to its own vital sources, a breakdown of encrusted layers of
selfhood. It is an overthrow of the conventional in pursuit of
the essential, as Hölderlin says, "even as the striving artist's
rules vanish before his Urania." We are at a midpoint here
between the self-annihilation of the 1817 *Poems,* which is

34. Earl R. Wasserman, *The Finer Tone: Keats' Major Poems*
(Baltimore, 1953), p. 32.

often no more than an escapist flight in which "the soul is lost in pleasant smotherings," and the self-transcendence of Apollo in *Hyperion* and the poet in *The Fall of Hyperion,* which is a process of self-creation and "soul-making." It is significant that in Endymion's speech Keats still emphasizes regression rather than progression; to be in touch with life's "proper pith" is to return to the mother's breast. Still, in seeking to return not simply to the mother but to that ultimate and self-limiting mother who nourishes with her own blood, Keats also expresses a wish to destroy the mother, a wish that he will begin to realize in his portrait of the malicious Circe in Book III.

Yet this ambivalence does not call into question the fundamental principle of "ardency" or "intensity," as Keats' letters amply suggest. Keats in Endymion's speech and in the prologue to Book II does not simply express a "romantic" preference for love over politics and soldiery. What Keats describes as love seems, at its most subtle, to be the distinctively human element of all experience, just as what Wordsworth describes as "poetry" in the preface to the *Lyrical Ballads* is not only verse but rather the distinctively human element in all knowledge. Wordsworth writes that "poetry is the breath and finer spirit of all knowledge; it is the impassioned expression which is in the countenance of all Science." Even the remotest discoveries of science may some day become the province of poetry, he adds, should they become "familiar to us," should they become "manifestly and palpably material to us as enjoying and suffering beings."[35] Admittedly some of the details of Keats' description of love seem more narrowly literal ("Juliet leaning / Amid her window flowers,—sighing, —weaning / Tenderly her fancy from its maiden snow"), but this should not distract us from the larger intention that Keats

35. *Wordsworth's Literary Criticism,* ed. N. C. Smith, pp. 27–28.

intermittently realizes. Keats' attack upon history and activity is a return to inwardness, a rejection of knowledge that cannot be "proved upon our pulses" and experience that has lost touch with our vital energies as "enjoying and suffering beings."

The second book is mostly enmeshed in literal love scenes—the erotic is after all the most immediate and pressing of those energies. But in the last two books the meaning of both love and the moon is insistently generalized. Book III begins with no less than four separate glimpses at a high goal beyond external reality. First, in the prologue Keats rephrases the prologue of Book II, attacking politics in the name not of love but of a politics of the spirit, mysterious "regalities" and "majesties" that underlie the world of appearances and are accessible only to the imagination, which fill "every sense / . . . with spiritual sweets to plenitude, / As bees gorge full their cells" (III, 38–40). Then Keats addresses the moon, which we see "with silver lip / Kissing dead things to life" (III, 56–57). Here the moon, like Pan, becomes the vital principle itself, at once the principle of pleasure and the ground of being. Next, Keats invokes love:

> O Love! how potent hast thou been to teach
> Strange journeyings! Wherever beauty dwells,
> In gulf or aerie, mountains or deep dells,
> In light, in gloom, in star or blazing sun,
> Thou pointest out the way, and straight 'tis won.
> Amid his toil thou gav'st Leander breath;
> Thou leddest Orpheus through the gleams of death;
> Thou madest Pluto bear thin element.
>
> (III, 92–99)

The "strange journeyings" have been the poem itself, and its progress has transformed love from a passive "elysium" of "ardent listlessness" to an active principle of quest and dis-

covery, rivaling the toil of Leander, Orpheus, or Pluto. Soon
afterward Endymion himself addresses the moon as a yet
more general attraction underlying all his passions, an "under-
passion," an element of "every joy and pain" of his boyhood:
"and as I grew in years, still didst thou blend / With all my
ardours" (III, 162–63). By the fourth book we have moved
toward a principle which underlies not only all human experience but upon which (as Endymion's speech in Book I
had implied) the vitality and authenticity of external nature
is dependent. As the Indian Maid says,

> "And thou, old forest, hold ye this for true,
>   There is no lightning, no authentic dew
>   But in the eye of love . . .
>   there's not a breath
>   Will mingle kindly with the meadow air,
>   Till it has panted round, and stolen a share
>   Of passion from the heart!"
>
>   (IV, 77–79, 82–85)

II

None of the last three books of *Endymion* has the coherence
and continuity of the first, and as a result they do not reward
as close a scrutiny. It remains for us to trace the outcome of
Endymion's quest for the light it sheds on Keats' own "strange
journeyings" in the year 1817. One barrier is the insufficiency
of Endymion even as a consistent mask, let alone a convincing
psychological creation. If such a quest is perforce an account
of growth and change, we cannot deny that Endymion lacks
the modicum of personality that could register such growth.
This is related to what Middleton Murry calls the "main
defect" of *Endymion,* "disproportion of structure,"[36] border-

36. *Keats,* p. 171.

ing, one is tempted to add, on complete absence of structure. Consequently a great deal could be asserted, with the help of local citation, that would by no means be borne out by the poem's overall design, or lack of design. It must be for this reason that Professor Bate tells us categorically that *"Endymion* does not encourage detailed attention"[37] and that he gives it so brief a reading in so ample a volume. Nevertheless the journey, though confusing and—as Keats himself admitted—confused, is not random, and has a number of stopping-places which yield significant light on Keats' development.

Of all of the books the second is certainly the least satisfactory as a whole, though it is rich with significant passages. The psychological inadequacy of Endymion is most pressing here, because the book is about the awakening of "maiden thought" within him. It records the first stages of his fall into consciousness, and this helps to explain the rapid, sometimes even ludicrous alternations of moods that the poet thrusts upon him. At one moment he is enchanted by "wonders rare" (II, 621). Then suddenly grisly shapes appear and

> The solitary felt a hurried change
> Working within him into something dreary,—
> Vex'd like a morning eagle, lost, and weary,
> And purblind amid foggy midnight wolds.
> But he revives at once. . . .
>
> (II, 633–37)

At times this is more than mere volatility of mind. Endymion's sudden depressions are part of a regular cycle of elation and despair, an ebb and flow that resembles the structure of Hölderlin's *Hyperion,* and that foreshadows the important developments of Book IV:

37. *John Keats,* p. 185.

> There, when new wonders ceased to float before
> And thoughts of self came on, how crude and sore
> The journey homeward to habitual self!
>
> (II, 274–76)

> He did not rave, he did not stare aghast,
> For all those visions were o'ergone, and past,
> And he in loneliness.
>
> (II, 588–90)

As in "Sleep and Poetry" no less than the "Ode to a Nightingale," the last stage of vision is always its failure or departure, the return to "a sense of real things" or the "sole self." Yet it is just this pattern that Endymion, and Keats through him, is trying to overcome. They both seek "richer entanglements, enthralments far / More self-destroying" than those that lapse into "the journey homeward to habitual self"; they aspire to "an immortality of passion" in which "life's self is nourished by its proper pith." Yet these homeward journeys of disenchantment and naked selfhood do continue to recur, not simply as obstacles on the otherwise triumphant path of the quest, but rather as necessary conditions that gradually become more real to Keats than the quest itself. They are evidence to us, and to the poet himself, of the divided consciousness which he finally acknowledges near the end of the poem (IV, 776–80), where he confesses his divergence from the original significance of the myth and the intended progress of the poem.

Endymion's depressions arise not simply from the lapsing of vision but from a different movement, toward what Keats calls "the goal of consciousness" (II, 282). He begins in Book II with an awareness of his alienation both from nature and from the human community:

> Where soil is men grow,
> Whether to weeds or flowers; but for me,

There is no depth to strike in: I can see
Nought earthly worth my compassing.
(II, 159–62)

He rejects the natural process as a model for human life. At
one of the lowest moments of Book I, "all the pleasant hues /
Of heaven and earth had faded: deepest shades / Were deepest dungeons" (691–93). Now Endymion willingly moves
from nature toward consciousness. He accepts a call into those
"deepest dungeons" to explore "the silent mysteries of earth"
(II, 214) and enters a region in which those extreme shades
of light and dark have been muted and joined, in which finer
distinctions are necessary.

Dark, nor light,
The region; nor bright, nor sombre wholly,
But mingled up; a gleaming melancholy.
(II, 221–23)

The region is mysterious indeed, but it is clearly anti-natural,
more like some product or symbol of the human mind. A
vein of gold "with all its lines abrupt and angular" leads
Endymion along a path

Through winding passages, where sameness breeds
Vexing conceptions of some sudden change.
(II, 235–36)

This region embodies what it also evokes in its explorer: the
instability of consciousness, as well as its frustrating complexity and difficulty. Endymion's descent into the earth is
essentially an inward journey (though Keats only intermittently holds to his purpose). But Endymion, though he
has willingly separated himself from nature soon, like
Wordsworth's Solitary in *The Excursion* or Hölderlin's
Hyperion, is overcome by painful solitude and longing for
nature:

> What misery most drowningly doth sing
> In lone Endymion's ear, now he has raught
> The goal of consciousness? Ah, 'tis the thought,
> The deadly feel of solitude: for lo!
> He cannot see the heavens, nor the flow
> Of rivers, nor hill-flowers running wild
> In pink and purple chequer, nor, up-pil'd,
> The cloudy rack slow journeying in the west,
> Like herded elephants; nor felt, nor prest
> Cool grass, nor tasted the fresh slumberous air.
>
> (II, 281–90)

Endymion longs to return to the bower. The forward step towards consciousness incurs the pain of separation, which leads to nostalgia. Endymion's backward longing finds expression in the most important episode in Book II, the vision of the bower of Adonis, whose story is both a parallel to Endymion's quest and a caricature of it.

Adonis, like Endymion, had roused the love of an immortal (Venus), but had unforgiveably been "content to let her amorous plea / Faint through his careless arms: content to see / An unseiz'd heaven dying at his feet" (II, 462–64). Content with the active masculine life of the hunt, Adonis had, as if in retribution, been killed by the boar—perhaps a sexual wound, though Keats does not tell us, as Ovid does, that he had been pierced in the groin. The tears of Venus, however, had

> Heal'd up the wound, and, with a balmy power,
> Medicined death to a lengthened drowsiness:
> The which she fills with visions, and doth dress
> In all this quiet luxury.
>
> (II, 483–86)

The key terms here—the healing balm, the lengthened drowsiness, the visions, the quiet luxury—indicate that the bower of Adonis is a summation of all the bowers of Keats' early poems. This is why Keats, unlike his immediate sources, puts central emphasis on the sleep of Adonis. This bower is the epitome of that delicious unconsciousness and indolent sensuality that had so attracted Keats in the 1817 volume. But all this passive enjoyment has left Adonis quite unmanned:

> Sideway his face repos'd
> On one white arm, and tenderly unclos'd
> By tenderest pressure, a faint damask mouth
> To slumbery pout; just as the morning south
> Disparts a dew-lipp'd rose.
>
> (II, 403–7)

There is the suggestion, amid the luxury, of something decidedly effeminate—or infantile. It is as if Adonis' "silken couch of rosy pride" were a cradle rather than a bed of love.[38] It is something of a bier as well, for though Adonis has achieved that recurrent dream of early Keats, complete absorption into nature, to be resurrected with the seasons, the ideal now carries with it an overtone of death-in-life. Nature appears to be dressing a corpse:

> Above his head,
> Four lily stalks did their white honours wed
> To make a coronal.
>
> (II, 407–9)

The resurrected Adonis seems little more alive than the sleeping one. It is as if Venus' tears had "medicined death" without really healing it.

I suggest that the bower of Adonis is far from an unambiguous model of the achieved love-quest for Endymion, as it has often been taken,[39] and that this reveals something sig-

38. Sperry, "The Allegory of *Endymion*," p. 50.
39. Northrop Frye's recent essay is a notable exception. He goes so far as to see in Venus an anticipation of Circe. But he denies that this implicates Endymion's "love dream," or Keats' own longings: "The

nificant about Keats' development and about the progress of
the poem. We need not say that Keats deliberately emphasizes
elements of caricature against the predominant tone of sensuous luxury. However, the lush, jaunty, Huntian diction
to which Professor Bate has so strongly objected[40] belongs
largely to one of the Cupids, clearly a spokesman for the
bower, rather than to Keats or Endymion. The thirty-line
descriptive introduction with which Keats begins has a different quality: the verse is more dense and Shakespearean.[41]
Endymion himself, except for one reaction indirectly re-
ported, says nothing; he remains strangely apart from the
scene. And the one passage in which Keats made an effusive

---

love of Venus for Adonis is already much more possessive than the love
of Phoebe for Endymion, much more of a Blakean 'female will' who
keeps the lover bound to a cycle of possession and loss." *A Study of
English Romanticism* (New York, 1968), pp. 139–40.

40. *John Keats,* p. 186.

41. Compare, for example,

> Here is wine,
> Alive with sparkles—never, I aver,
> Since Ariadne was a vintager,
> So cool a purple: taste these juicy pears . . .
> (II, 441–44)

or,

> . . . a bunch of blooming plums
> Ready to melt between an infant's gums,
> (II, 450–51)

both of which are singled out for attack by Mr. Bate, with the following:

> and round him grew
> All tendrils green, of every bloom and hue,
> Together intertwin'd and trammel'd fresh:
> The vine of glossy sprout; the ivy mesh,
> Shading its Ethiop berries; and woodbine,
> Of velvet leaves and bugle-blooms divine;
> Convolvulus in streaked vases flush;
> The creeper, mellowing for an autumn blush.
> (II, 409–16)

and total identification with the scene was almost entirely cut when he made his revisions.[42]

The reorientation of Keats' sympathies is hardly decisive, or even consistent, in Book II; it is little more than a suggestion. Endymion goes on from the bower of Adonis to a bower of his own, which becomes the setting for the most explicit and passionate love-dream in the poem. By the time it has ended, Endymion has become another Adonis:

> O he had swoon'd
> Drunken from Pleasure's nipple; and his love
> Henceforth was dove-like.—Loth was he to move
> From the imprinted couch, and when he did,
> 'Twas with slow, languid paces, and face hid
> In muffling hands.
>
> (II, 868–73)

He too has had his reversion to infancy, but far from providing him with a couch of "quiet luxury," it offers him visions that are strange and terrifying:

> So temper'd, out he stray'd
> Half seeing visions that might have dismay'd
> Alecto's serpents; ravishments more keen
> Than Hermes' pipe, when anxious he did lean
> Over eclipsing eyes.
>
> (II, 873–77)

Alecto was the fiercest of the Furies, but the other allusion is the more pregnant. The "eclipsing eyes" are those of hundred-eyed Argos, when Hermes succeeded in lulling him to sleep in order to cut off his head. In a poem that puts so heavy an emphasis on the visionary delights of sleep and dreams, Keats suddenly sees fit to remind us of their latent power to terrify and even destroy us—a self-destruction that is by no means a stage toward the "chief intensity."

42. See Garrod (1958), p. 112 n. (lines 526 ff.).

But the dark and threatening side of the bower does not appear clearly until the episode of Glaucus and Circe in Book III, in which Keats depicts a bower that is a dialectical counter-statement to the bower of Adonis.[43] The story of Glaucus, like that of Endymion and Arethusa, is an account of a necessary fall. Like them, Glaucus knew a period of idyllic innocence when he was at home in nature:

> I was a fisher once, upon this main,
> And my boat danc'd in every creek and bay;
> Rough billows were my home by night and day,—
> The sea-gulls not more constant; for I had
> No housing from the storm and tempests mad,
> But hollow rocks,—and they were palaces
> Of silent happiness, of slumberous ease.
>
> (III, 318–24)

There is a subtle shift of emphasis here from the earlier stories. This nature, though providing "palaces / Of silent happiness, of slumberous ease," is also full of terror: rough billows, tempests, dread sea-monsters. Yet the pastoral golden world of Latmos is present as well:

43. I am indebted here to Sperry's brief but valuable commentary, pp. 50–51. The older view of the Glaucus episode, almost universally accepted, is expressed by de Selincourt, who says that it was "introduced by Keats in order to develop still further his conception that only after active sympathy with the fate of others could Endymion realise his aspirations." Ernest de Selincourt, ed., *The Poems of John Keats,* 5th ed. (London, 1926), p. 438. The episode of Alpheus and Arethusa is usually similarly interpreted. But Keats' prayer for Alpheus and Arethusa is only an afterthought, not central to the episode at all, and the Glaucus episode also seems more important for the parallels to Endymion's story rather than for the unrealized emotions of sympathy that we may suppose it to have evoked in him. Endymion does, however, overcome his initial self-centered revulsion from Glaucus, and the revival of the drowned lovers may be seen as a parallel to Hyperion's campaign to liberate Greece, as de Man suggests. But the Circe flashback is more significant than either of these.

There blush'd no summer eve but I would steer
My skiff along green shelving coasts, to hear
The shepherd's pipe coming clear from aery steep,
Mingled with ceaseless bleatings of his sheep:
And never was a day of summer shine,
But I beheld its birth upon the brine.

(III, 357–62)

But all this primal harmony and richness must be shattered. Glaucus, like Endymion (and the unwilling Arethusa), feels "distemper'd longings," which Keats explains cryptically— he often leaves the nature of the fall obscure—and he plunges "for life or death" into the sea. In Ovid the plunge is a direct and successful attempt to become a god. But Keats blurs this simple significance: transcendence has by this time become problematic for him, as Book IV will show. (We are surprised two hundred lines later when Circe remarks to Glaucus, "thou hast thews / Immortal, for thou art of heavenly race," 588–89). Instead, Glaucus achieves the special Keatsian version of transcendence, freedom from self-consciousness and access to a wondrous visionary world. At first he dwells

Whole days and days in sheer astonishment;
Forgetful utterly of self-intent;
Moving but with the mighty ebb and flow.

(III, 385–87)

Then he visits "the ceaseless wonders of the ocean bed."

The immersion in the watery medium seems, as with Arethusa, to represent an awakening into sexuality. Glaucus falls in love with a nymph named Scylla, who flees from him, and his feelings quickly heighten into desperation:

My passion grew
The more, the more I saw her dainty hue

Gleam delicately through the azure clear:
Until 'twas too fierce agony to bear.

(III, 407–10)

Glaucus calls upon Circe for assistance, and here Keats makes
the most significant departure from his source. In Ovid, Circe
offers Glaucus her own love, and when he refuses she takes
terrible revenge upon Scylla. Here, instead, she entraps and
deceives him, which allows Keats (with the aid of Book X of
The Odyssey and Spenser's bower of Acrasia) to treat us to
the most revealing of all the bowers thus far. Circe, weaving
"a net whose thraldom was more bliss than all / The range
of flower'd Elysium," offers Glaucus "a long love dream":

Who could resist? Who in this universe?
She did so breathe ambrosia; so immerse
My fine existence in a golden clime.
She took me like a child of suckling time,
And cradled me in roses.

(III, 453–57)

This is a bower to end all bowers, a full return to the complete
sensuous delight of infancy. It is a self-transcendence from
which every thought of pain or conflict is excluded, where
time is marked only by a renewal of pleasure: "every eve, nay
every spendthrift hour / Shed balmy consciousness within
that bower (III, 466–67), which is the opposite of the "consciousness" that in the second book had visited Endymion with
"the thought, / The deadly feel of solitude" (II, 283–84).

Soon this "specious heaven" is transformed into "real hell"
(III, 476). Glaucus awakes one morning to find his love-
goddess unmasked as La Belle Dame. Already he has figura-
tively been transformed by his appetite into an animal, seeking
her lips to slake his "greedy thirst with nectarous camel-
draughts" (III, 479). He finds Circe "seated upon an uptorn
forest root," as if nature itself had suffered a blight: she is

surrounded by grotesque images of deformity. These are men who have been transformed into actual animals, whom she feeds with "clusters of grapes, the which they ravened quick / And roared for more; with many a hungry look / About their shaggy jaws" (III, 511–13). The very fruits of the bower's natural lushness have become the symbols of its degeneration and the bower itself is now a "dark lair of night" (560), one of whose inhabitants pleads eloquently for release into death. Now Circe proceeds, as Stuart Sperry says, "to parody the whole conception of the love-nest":

> "Ha! ha! Sir Dainty! there must be a nurse
> Made of rose leaves and thistledown, express,
> To cradle thee my sweet, and lull thee: yes,
> I am too flinty-hard for thy nice touch:
> My tenderest squeeze is but a giant's clutch.
> So, fairy-thing, it shall have lullabies
> Unheard of yet: and it shall still its cries
> Upon some breast more lily-feminine."
>
> (III, 570–77)

This is a Circe who has read Keats. It is also a Circe who has grasped a central motif of the bower, a key to both its attractiveness and final inadequacy for Keats: the element of infantile regression. Professor Trilling has written of "dialectic of pleasure" in the poems of Keats: he is at once "the poet who made the boldest affirmation of the principle of pleasure and also . . . the poet who brought the principle of pleasure into the greatest and *sincerest* doubt." He had a sense "that there is something perverse and self-negating in the erotic life" and could imagine the country of La Belle Dame, "the scene of an erotic pleasure which leads to devastation, of an erotic fulfillment which implies castration."[44] It is after he "had swoon'd / Drunken from pleasure's nipple" that En-

44. *Beyond Culture,* pp. 66, 67.

dymion had terrifying visions, and Glaucus finds at Circe's breast not a cradling mother, but a vengeful and destructive one, whose very love involves castration:

> ". . . such a love is mine, that here I chase
> Eternally away from thee all bloom
> Of youth, and destine thee towards a tomb."
> (III, 590–92)

Until the sight of Endymion, the image of his younger self, restores his vitality and makes him a "young soul in age's mask," Glaucus is cut off from his "youthful pleasures." He becomes the old man of the sea and undergoes ten centuries of death-in-life.

There are two approaches by which I would venture to explain this "dialectic of pleasure" in *Endymion*. One, the less satisfactory, is psychological, and requires us to deal with Keats' own emotional development and with motives that are to some degree unconscious. To do this we must ponder again Keats' assertion that *Endymion* is the product of that turbulent period of transition that we call adolescence:

> The imagination of a boy is healthy, and the mature imagination of a man is healthy; but there is a space of life between, in which the soul is in a ferment, the character undecided, the way of life uncertain, the ambition thick-sighted. (Preface)

That Keats had, as Trilling says, "a happy relation to his infant appetites,"[45] is clear from the earlier poems, and confirmed in *Endymion*. That Keats also had intense adult appetites no reader would be likely to deny. But in *Endymion* the distinction between the two has not yet been clearly established for Keats. *Endymion* is the product of a soul in ferment, of a tumultuous "space of life between," between two poles of health and stability. In spite of the quest plot he tended to

45. *The Opposing Self*, p. 24.

imagine sexual consummation in terms of passive dependency that will disappear in such later poems as *The Eve of St. Agnes,* terms of infantile gratification that still deeply appealed to him.[46] Thus we may say that lack of sexual experience is responsible for the embarrassing awkwardness of the love-scenes in *Endymion.* We may account for what Keats calls their "mawkishness" by remembering his description of another poem he came to consider mawkish, *Isabella:* "there is too much inexperience of life, and simplicity of knowledge in it" (2:174). We may go further, as Miss Aileen Ward implies we should,[47] and describe the whole quest for "an immortality of passion" as an adolescent pipe dream, a longing for erotic omnipotence.

Finally, the Circe motif of sexual betrayal and entrapment could also lead us to much tenuous psychological speculation about Keats, but this would be of no help in understanding the artistic design of the poem or its realized significance for our own experience. We may feel that ultimately it lacks such design and significance, that its interest lies mainly in its testimony about Keats' emotional growth, but we should not be too quick to concede the point. From another point of view Keats' metaphoric use of infantile sensations in some of the sexual descriptions in *Endymion* may be based upon more

46. I am not sure, in spite of Keats' explicitness, that Freud would find anything extraordinary here. Freud treats the infant's relation to his mother's breast as the first experience—and prototype of all later experiences—of the libido's "finding an object" outside itself. "At the time at which the first beginnings of sexual satisfaction are still linked with the taking of nourishment, the sexual instinct has a sexual object outside the infant's own body in the shape of his mother's breast. . . . There are thus good reasons why a child sucking at his mother's breast has become the prototype of every relation of love. The finding of an object is in fact the refinding of it." *Three Essays on the Theory of Sexuality,* trans. James Strachey (New York, 1965), pp. 124–25.

47. Aileen Ward, *John Keats: The Making of a Poet* (New York, 1963), pp. 142, 143.

than "inexperience of life, and simplicity of knowledge," may be, if not wholly conscious, then at least purposeful. The infantile associations, like the notion of "an immortality of passion," may be Keats' way of presenting a radical sexual demand, an insistence on an erotic ideal that goes beyond culturally defined sexual roles and "mature" modes of gratification. It is such an ideal that has led some recent writers on psychoanalysis to turn to the "polymorphously perverse" sexuality of the infant as an alternative to traditional adult behavior,[48] an inversion which is the latest development of the Romantic discovery of childhood and the Romantic quarrel with culture and traditional morality.

We noted in our discussion of Book I the paradoxical use of the bower motif already evident there. The bower, though idyllic, represents, in Blackstone's words, "the sphere of unconscious felicity which Endymion must relinquish"; yet on the other hand it is the locus of the dream encounters with Cynthia, that is, it also represents the ideal for which he is striving. The same can be said for the motif of sleep and passivity, which belongs both to the bower of Peona and to the "elysium" of "ardent listlessness," itself but a higher bower. Keats' original goal was not to relinquish the unconscious felicity of the bower but to adapt and ultimately preserve it. But by the third and fourth books, such a goal— though Keats will never entirely abandon it—seems less possible and also less desirable. It is this that may have led Keats to portray the Circean parody of the bower.

As I have argued, the meaning of the bower, like the meaning of the whole poem, can not be defined in narrowly sexual

48. See especially Norman O. Brown, *Life Against Death: The Psychoanalytical Meaning of History* (Middletown, Conn., 1959). See also Marcuse, *Eros and Civilization,* and Trilling's defense of "biological *reason*" against the reason of culture, "Freud: Within and Beyond Culture," in *Beyond Culture,* pp. 89–118.

terms. The poem is more than the expression of adolescent erotic longings. Keats manages, though not consistently, to transmute those longings into a larger quest, for what we may call selfhood. Yet, implicitly from the start, increasingly as the poem progresses, Keats is torn between two conflicting ideas of selfhood. The first is symbolized by the bower, which, even in its higher and adapted form in Endymion's speech on happiness, represents a static idea of perfection, outside of time, self-transcendent though not other-worldly, dedicated to dream and vision rather than " a sense of real things," nourished by an ideal of pleasure not much encumbered by a recognition of pain. The second idea sees selfhood in terms of growth and development, what I have referred to in relation to Spenser as the notion of *Bildung*. The self is seen in evolution rather than in ideal perfection, often divided against itself, grappling with the real world, subject to the ultimately tragic laws of time and change, at times suffering a purgatorial ordeal as the price of its salvation.

This second notion of selfhood, while muted, is foreshadowed by many things in the first two books of *Endymion:* the tragic tone of the proem, Endymion's Byronic malaise and his repeated frustrations, the very idea of the quest itself (which had no place in the original myth), the narrative detachment in the bower of Adonis. By the third book, however, a distinct shift is evident. Glaucus goes through a genuine ordeal. The death-in-life to which he is condemned ("Disabled age shall seize thee: and even then / Thou shalt not go the way of aged men; / But live and wither, cripple and still breathe," III, 595–97) anticipates the more powerful and tragic torment of Moneta in *The Fall of Hyperion* ("deathwards progressing / To no death was that visage," I, 260–61). Like Moneta, Glaucus is wise as well as terrible. He is the Urizenic image of frosty death and has lost his youthful lover's body, but he is also the wizard with the book who has learned all the mysteries of the deep, the Prospero who will reunite all the drowned and shipwrecked lovers. He has fallen into knowledge, not only magical knowledge but the knowledge of Circe and her bower, which Endymion, his redeemer, will take upon himself. By acknowledging his kinship with Glaucus and hearing his story, Endymion vicariously undergoes his whole ordeal, just as the poet in *The Fall of Hyperion* receives from Moneta her terrible knowledge of the fall and suffering of Saturn.

Circe's bower, like Spenser's Bower of Bliss, turns out to have been not the reward of the quest but an impediment to it, or at best a stage on the negative way toward selfhood and identity. The poem's new and more sombre direction must have jolted Keats, for the remainder of the third book is a strained effort to restore the world of faery, romance, and sensuous intoxication. Endymion stands, "'mid the sound / Of flutes and viols, ravishing his heart" (771–72), as the lovers are revived ("Death felt it to his inwards; 'twas too much: / Death fell a weeping in his charnel-house," 787–88):

> Enchantment
> Grew drunken, and would have its head and bent.
> Delicious symphonies, like airy flowers,
> Budded, and swell'd, and, full-blown, shed full showers
> Of light, soft, unseen leaves of sound divine.
> The two deliverers tasted a pure wine
> Of happiness, from fairy-press ooz'd out.
> Speechless they eyed each other, and about
> The fair assembly wander'd to and fro,
> Distracted with the richest overflow
> Of joy that ever pour'd from heaven.
>
> (III, 796–806)

It is as if Circe must be exorcised at all costs, and a dream-world restored from which every strain of conflict and danger has been eliminated. This is only the beginning. The pageant in the hall of Neptune which follows (probably the dullest scene in *Endymion*) represents a complete reversion to the picturesque mode of Keats' earliest daydreaming attempts at romance.[49] The repeated emphasis on the dreamlike and fairy-tale quality of this consummation serves but to heighten its falseness and unreality.[50]

The real transformation occurs in the fourth book, which not only adds a new dimension to the poem but also comes close to destroying what original design Keats might have had. A new tone is evident in the prologue, which comes as a shock after the strained fairy-tale apotheosis which has just passed:

> Great Muse, thou know'st what prison
> Of flesh and bone curbs, and confines, and frets
> Our spirit's wings: despondency besets
> Our pillows; and the fresh tomorrow-morn
> Seems to give forth its light in very scorn
> Of our dull, uninspired, snail-paced lives.
>
> (IV, 20–25)

A moment earlier Keats had celebrated the work of the great English poets, without which "these our latter days had risen / On barren souls" (19–20). But "the thing is done"; it has been "a full accomplishment." There seems little more that we can do, and somehow our barrenness of soul persists. Keats is brooding about his problem as a modern poet, his difficulty in completing *this* poem, which is so caught be-

49. The revival of the lovers comes directly from the 1817 volume, from Keats' earlier Endymion attempt, "I stood tip-toe" (lines 221 ff.). Even so inveterate an allegorizer as Sir Sidney Colvin is frustrated by the intractable meaninglessness of the Neptune procession: "The book closes with a submarine pageant imagined, it would seem, almost singly for the pageant's sake." *John Keats: Life . . . and After-Fame* p. 196.

50. See, for example, lines 809, 843–44, 857, 861, 884–85, 887.

tween classical *cum* visionary aspiration and a modern sense
of existential limits. The tone turns tragic, and the details
allude pregnantly to some of the poem's central motifs, to
sleep and to winged spiritual flight. Against these are set the
hard realities of "despondency" and of this "prison / Of flesh
and bone," which take us back to the "despondence" of the
proem to Book I and to Endymion's many moments of
despair and disappointment.

But there is an important difference in this prologue. The
proem had expressed a dialectic upon which *Endymion* was
to be based: though our experience is tragic the imagination
is not, though our life is transient the imagination offers a
consoling permanence and indestructibility. The poet must
therefore write against the grain of experience, must, in
Murry's words, "make the creation of the poem itself a defence against the onset of the doubts and miseries and feverous
speculations." But the defense has proved both ineffective and
unwise, and as he concludes his address to the Native Muse
Keats quietly abandons it:

> Long have I said, how happy he who shrives
> To thee! But then I thought on poets gone,
> And could not pray:—nor can I now—so on
> I move to the end in lowliness of heart.—
>
> (IV, 26–29)

This is followed without transition by the sorrowful lament
of the Indian maid which, in spite of its sentimentality, picks
up directly from the dark tone, and even the content—she
longs for her "native land"—of the prologue. Keats has lost
faith in his old view of art as therapy, as compensation or consolation for the human condition. The poet can no longer
turn away from his own immediate awareness toward the
healing brightness of the imagination. He will have to deal
with his experience, with its darker as well as its lighter
shades, with its griefs as well as joys.

The song "O Sorrow" that the Indian maid sings is closely related to this. First she repeats Endymion's assertion (from Book I) of the dependence even of external nature on human love:

> "There is no lightning, no authentic dew
> But in the eye of love: there's not a sound,
> Melodious howsoever, can confound
> The heavens and earth in one to such a death
> As doth the voice of love: there's not a breath
> Will mingle kindly with the meadow air,
> Till it has panted round, and stolen a share
> Of passion from the heart!—"
>
> (IV, 78–85)

Yet this restatement, with its suggestion of an apocalyptic confounding of heaven and earth and its reverse Prometheanism (the stealing of fire *from* humanity), has a threatening element quite absent from Endymion's fanciful speech. This emerges clearly in her song, which suggests that the beauty of external nature is dependent not only on love but on sorrow as well:

> "O Sorrow,
> Why dost borrow
> The natural hue of health, from vermeil lips?—
> To give maiden blushes
> To the white rose bushes?
> Or is't thy dewy hand the daisy tips?
>
> "O Sorrow
> Why dost borrow
> The lustrous passion from a falcon-eye?—
> To give the glow-worm light?
> Or, on a moonless night,
> To tinge, on syren shores, the salt sea-spry?"
>
> (IV, 146–57)

This has usually been interpreted as a form of compensation: sorrow removes the beauties of its victims but resurrects them in the beauty of nature; that is, they are "in their sublime, creative of essential Beauty." But this reading ignores the actual wording of the song, in which the victimization is definite but the positive compensation only hypothetical, a series of question marks. Even if the metamorphosis does take place, it is of ambiguous value: nature feeds upon the sufferings of humanity—or perhaps, if we take it to refer to subjective perception, our sense of the beauty of nature depends on (or at least is heightened by) the poignant contrast with our own miseries.

In any case, the resolution of the song betrays no sense of compensation or joy in the feelings of the Indian maid:

> "To Sorrow,
> I bade good-morrow,
> And thought to leave her far away behind;
> But cheerly, cheerly,
> She loves me dearly;
> She is so constant to me, and so kind:
> I would deceive her
> And so leave her,
> But ah! she is so constant, and so kind."
>
> (IV, 173–81)

As Endymion had said in the first book, "pleasure is oft a visitant; but pain / Clings cruelly to us" (906–7). Love may be fickle, but sorrow alas is virtuous, and faithful to those she embraces. This destructive attachment is presented as the travesty of an ideal love relationship, just as Circe's bower is a parody of the true love nest. The Indian maid tells how she tried to drown her melancholy in ecstatic self-annihilation by joining the Bacchic procession, "in search of pleasure throughout every clime" (IV, 275)—a loose parallel to En-

dymion's own "strange journeyings" in search of "enthralments far / More self-destroying." But at last she gives up
and (with echoes of Cleopatra taking up the asp) accepts the
adversity to which she feels destined:

> "Come then, Sorrow!
> Sweetest Sorrow!
> Like an own babe I nurse thee on my breast:
> I thought to leave thee
> And deceive thee,
> But now of all the world I love thee best."
>
> (IV, 279–84)

What the Indian maid says here in a somewhat ludicrous
manner is given much more power and meaning later by
Endymion, when he too renounces his quest and accepts the
human fate that the new-found maiden seems to offer him:

> "Alas!" said he, "were I but always borne
> Through dangerous winds, had but my footsteps worn
> A path in hell, for ever would I bless
> Horrors which nourish an uneasiness
> For my own sullen conquering: to him
> Who lives beyond earth's boundary, grief is dim,
> Sorrow is but a shadow: now I see
> The grass; I feel the solid ground."
>
> (IV, 615–22)

This is a different road to fulfillment than the one Endymion
had described in his speech on happiness, different from
Endymion's whole excursion "beyond earth's boundary."
Endymion recognizes the reality of suffering but does not
capitulate to it. He expresses one of the fundamental ideas of
tragedy: the "soul-making" that takes place in the confrontation with pain and adversity. Endymion praises not the
"blending pleasureable" that will lead to self-annihilation but

the disorienting "uneasiness" that may call into play the resources of the self.[51]

The "horrors" to which Endymion refers are those we witnessed a few lines earlier in one of the most successful passages of the poem, the description of the Cave of Quietude. Endymion, torn between Cynthia and the Indian maid, has been initiated for the first time into the hell of radical self-division. ("I have a triple soul," "I feel my heart is cut for them in twain," "My tortur'd brain begins to craze," 95, 97, 116). He is tormented by his own inconsistency, and sees it as the symptom of a deeper absence of selfhood or identity. ("What is this soul then? Whence / Came it? It does not seem my own, and I / Have no self-passion or identity," 475–77). Endymion, flying high above the earth with the Indian maid, is torn by "a grievous feud" which leads him into a kind of solipsistic withdrawal (symbolized by the Indian maid's gradual disappearance while Endymion, seizing desperately at her hand, kisses his own).

At this point Endymion undergoes an extraordinary experience. Keats adapts the Spenserian device of spatializing a psychological state into a visual picture-myth, to give us the last and most remarkable of the bowers in *Endymion*. The Cave of Quietude provides some of the traditional rewards of the bower, sleep and renewal, but this sleep does not, as in Book I, provide visionary access

51. The same tragic attitude begins to appear in Keats' letters at this time. On 22 November, halfway through the fourth book, he writes to Bailey: "I scarcely remember counting upon any Happiness —I look not for it if it be not in the present hour. . . . The first thing that strikes me on hearing a Misfortune having befalled another is this. 'Well it cannot be helped.—he will have the pleasure of trying the resources of his spirit' " (1:186). The same day he writes to Reynolds in a similar though more confident vein: "Why dont you, as I do, look unconcerned at what may be called more particularly Heart-vexations? They never surprize me—lord! a man should have the fine point of his soul taken off to become fit for this world" (1:188).

To golden palaces, strange minstrelsy,
Fountains grotesque, new trees, bespangled caves,
Echoing grottos, full of tumbling waves
And moonlight.

(I, 457–60)

Instead the Cave offers "a dreamless sleep," for its goal is not
vision but survival, not transcendence but a regeneration of
the "whole" of the distinctively human, suffering being:

O wondrous soul!
Pregnant with such a den to save the whole
In thine own depth. Hail, gentle Carian!
For, never since thy griefs and woes began,
Hast thou felt so content: a grievous feud
Hath led thee to this Cave of Quietude.

(IV, 543–48)

The emphasis on "griefs and woes" also makes this very much
of an anti-bower, though it is equally the bower that provides
contentment beyond these woes. As Bernard Blackstone has
valuably emphasized, there are two distinct stages in Keats'
description.[52] The first is the stage of anguish and suffering
which Keats sees as a common and almost universal part of
human experience:

There lies a den,
Beyond the seeming confines of the space
Made for the soul to wander in and trace
Its own existence, of remotest glooms.

(IV, 512–15)

Keats begins with a palinode, a turn upon himself, for "the
seeming confines" were those of a more hopeful but naive

52. *The Consecrated Urn,* pp. 183–84. But Keats does not, as
Blackstone implies, consistently call one stage the "den" and the
second the Cave, nor do they seem separated spatially, with the Cave
at the center.

self, which had sought like Endymion to trace its own existence only in the brighter regions of experience.

> Dark regions are around it, where the tombs
> Of buried griefs the spirit sees, but scarce
> One hour doth linger weeping, for the pierce
> Of new-born woe it feels more inly smart:
> And in these regions many a venom'd dart
> At random flies; they are the proper home
> Of every ill: the man is yet to come
> Who hath not journeyed in this native hell.
>
> (IV, 516–23)

This is a different journey from Endymion's quest for "love's elysium," and it makes the Indian maid's evocation of Sorrow seem like feeble sport. But there is a second stage, when the soul somehow passes through and beyond anguish:

> But few have ever felt how calm and well
> Sleep may be had in that deep den of all.
> There anguish does not sting; nor pleasure pall:
> Woe-hurricanes beat ever at the gate,
> Yet all is still within and desolate.
> Beset with painful gusts, within ye hear
> No sound so loud as when on curtain'd bier
> The death-watch tick is stifled. Enter none
> Who strive therefore: on the sudden it is won.
> Just when the sufferer begins to burn,
> Then it is free to him; and from an urn,
> Still fed by melting ice, he takes a draught—
> Young Semele such richness never quaft
> In her maternal longing! Happy gloom!
> Dark Paradise! where pale becomes the bloom
> Of health by due; where silence dreariest
> Is most articulate; where hopes infest;
> Where those eyes are the brightest far that keep
> Their lids shut longest in a dreamless sleep.
>
> (IV, 524–42)

Like the bowers in early Keats, the Cave provides security and rest, but it is a process rather than a place, an internal debate, a dialectical bower-in-the-making. Keats' early bowers offer a simple refuge from the pains of the world, usually achieved by flight and escape. But this bower is reached only by passing through the world. It is a description of the mind *in extremis,* in dialogue with the world, finally discovering its own inner resources. This cannot be willed or sought, but comes as a kind of involuntary grace when least expected: "Enter none / Who strive therefore: on the sudden it is won." It is a cooling draught that can come only "when the sufferer begins to burn." Yet the salvation this bower offers is an ambiguous and temporary one, an affectlessness that is replete with associations of death, but also a renewal which aims to restore us to the world. This is the burden of the contradictory terms that Keats uses to describe it. Keats often uses oxymorons, like synaesthesia, to indicate a high intensity of being, when we have passed beyond simple judgments and the clear intelligence of the individual senses. Here the oxymorons represent an intensity of nonbeing, a deathlike oblivion that foreshadows such poems as the sonnet to sleep, rather than merely "a stance beyond the reach of primary human emotions," as Harold Bloom calls it.[53] Yet it is a death that provides regeneration, a part that renews the whole. The best analogue is not the "peace which passeth understanding" that some critics with mystical inclinations have invoked, but rather the purgatorial passage through death that Keats attributes to Apollo in *Hyperion* and the poet in *The Fall of Hyperion.*

53. *The Visionary Company,* p. 395. But Professor Bloom's attempt to paraphrase the Cave in aesthetic rather than mystical or psychological terms is provocative: "A poet needs a stance beyond the reach of primary human emotions before he can attain an art relevant to them. Endymion comes out of the Cave sufficiently disinterested to disqualify him for more questing." Hence the renunciation that follows.

This experience returns Endymion with a shock to earth
("His first touch of the earth went nigh to kill," IV, 614) and
and leads him to praise "horrors which nourish an uneasiness
/ For my own sullen conquering." It also leads to his choice
of the Indian maid and renunciation of the visionary quest.
This is an astonishing reversal, though we should not be completely unprepared for it. Its archetype, though with a different emphasis, is that extraordinary moment of nakedness and
disintoxication in "Sleep and Poetry," when the chariot of
the imagination disappears, leaving a void, and a new awareness, more sharply felt than the preceding vision:

> The visions are all fled—the car is fled
> Into the light of heaven, and in their stead
> A sense of real things comes doubly strong,
> And, like a muddy stream, would bear along
> My soul to nothingness.
>
> (155–59)

It is a moment that has had its echo in the proem to *Endymion,* in which we are bound to the earth, and in each
"journey homeward to habitual self" on Endymion's part,
each return of self-consciousness and "a sense of real things"
at the end of a visionary cycle. But now for the first time
Endymion renounces his quest, embraces the earth in place
of "cloudy phantasms . . . air of visions, and the monstrous
swell / Of visionary seas" (the loci of his travels), and accepts
self-consciousness as the "proper glory" of his soul:

> I have clung
> To nothing, lov'd a nothing, nothing seen
> Or felt but a great dream! O I have been
> Presumptuous against love, against the sky,
> Against all elements, against the tie
> Of mortals each to each, against the blooms

Of flowers, rush of rivers, and the tombs
Of heroes gone! Against his proper glory
Has my own soul conspired: so my story
Will I to children utter and repent.
There never liv'd a mortal man who bent
His appetite beyond his natural sphere,
But starv'd and died. My sweetest Indian, here,
Here will I kneel, for thou redeemed hast
My life from too thin breathing: gone and past
Are cloudy phantasms. Caverns lone, farewell!
And air of visions, and the monstrous swell
Of visionary seas! No, never more
Shall airy voices cheat me to the shore
Of tangled wonder, breathless and aghast.
                                    (IV, 636–55)

This is a decisive turn not only in the poem but in Keats'
whole career, the moment when the intoxication of vision
wears off and the dream of transcendence gives way to a
chastened acceptance of human limitation and earthly reality.
In a like manner, Wordsworth, in the "Elegiac Stanzas" on
Peele Castle, bids farewell to "the heart that lives alone, /
Housed in a dream, at distance from the Kind!" Wordsworth,
with his new sense of tragedy, sees fit to deny the truth of
imagination, but he preserves a full sense of its illusory beauty.
It is

The light that never was, on sea or land,
The consecration, and the Poet's dream.

Endymion, however, goes much further. He has "clung / To
nothing, lov'd a nothing, nothing seen / Or felt but a great
dream." I cannot agree therefore with those who feel that
Keats should have ended the poem here, without the mechanical contrivances that serve for a conclusion. Like so many of
his fellow Romantics in their best and most characteristic
work, the later Keats will set up an urgent dialectic between

the visionary possibility and the limiting actuality; he will continually reenact every stage of the quest cycle, as if only by going outside of itself could the self ultimately find itself, as if only by dreaming more dreams can the self rediscover and value the waking world. But Endymion dismisses the quest, dismisses the entire poem, loses himself in what Keats later calls "fancies vain and crude" (IV, 722).

Keats is groping for a perspective beyond vision, one that includes vision yet is aware of its limitations. He falls back instead to a position that is prior to vision, wary of it from without. Endymion echoes the Peona of the first book when he tells the Indian maid that she has redeemed his life "from too thin breathing." This is the same phrase that Peona had used (I, 751) in her attack on "visions, dreams, / And fitful whims of sleep." The Indian maid, though she is a sexual being and represents the new possibility of *human* love for Endymion, in many ways recalls Peona, for whom she is partly a surrogate. Endymion asks her to be his "nurse" (IV, 117) and she invokes the healing power of nature to counter his despair:

> "Are not these green nooks
> Empty of all misfortune? Do the brooks
> Utter a gorgon voice? Does yonder thrush,
> Schooling its half-fledg'd little ones to brush
> About the dewy forest, whisper tales?—
> Speak not of grief. . . ."
>
> (IV, 127–32)

Significantly, when Endymion kneels before the maid and repents his quest, he describes it as an offense against nature, "against the blooms / Of flowers, rush of rivers." He sees his choice of the maid as a return to "his natural sphere" and places himself once more under the protection of Pan (IV, 633–36). He offers her a purely natural existence. "No more of dreaming," he says, and then goes on to outline an elaborate dream of a life within nature, in a nature remarkably simple and pristine, stripped of myth and mystery.

> Honey from out the gnarled hive I'll bring,
> And apples, wan with sweetness, gather thee.
> (IV, 682–83)

Thus his love for the Indian maid, while in some ways a great advance over the quest for Cynthia and "an immortality of passion," is also a reversion to the nature of the first book, from which Endymion separated himself to embark on his quest.[54] Similarly, the critique of vision, just like the exposure of the bower in Glaucus' account of Circe, is made less interesting by a note of conventional moralizing. Thus, just as Glaucus sometimes borders on a complete revulsion from the

54. Harold Bloom finely catches the element of reversion in Endymion's choice but justifies it in Blakean terms: "He has passed from innocence to experience, touched the hell within experience, and is ready for a more organized innocence that *may* precede the vision of art" (p. 395, my italics).

Northrop Frye, far more dubiously, reads the structure of the whole poem in terms of these Blakean stages. He sees Latmos as a dreamlike "unborn" world of illusory innocence, like Thel's. Endymion, in the descent of the second and third books, is said to strike "roots into experience," while also falling, however, into a solipsistic state of "individual and subjective consciousness." Frye then sees the fourth book as Endymion's emergence into a higher innocence, "the world of the awakened imagination, where we pass beyond the elemental spirits to become united with the gods." But Frye's scrappy account of this last book, much inferior to his first-rate commentary on Glaucus and Book III, makes this part of his reading least convincing. (He merely compounds the obscurity when he explains that "this last stage of Endymion's pilgrimage is illustrated by the divine figures with which *Hyperion* and the great odes are so largely concerned." *A Study of English Romanticism*, p. 148.) It is Frye's general view of Romanticism that leads him to impose upon *Endymion* a final movement from "pure subjective consciousness" to "the awakened imagination" (whatever that means). Unlike Bloom he seeks to justify Endymion's apotheosis, but to do so he must ignore Keats' own qualms and misgivings, which are expressed most forcefully in the renunciation speech.

body and from sexuality, a position we would be unwise to attribute to Keats, so Endymion in his recoil from his visionary goal stresses the theme of the overreacher: "There never liv'd a mortal man who bent / His appetite beyond his natural sphere / But starv'd and died." These are but momentary stopping places for Keats, as yet unable to work out the new position toward which he is tending.

It seems clear then that Keats could not have ended the poem on Endymion's renunciation, for his imagination is caught between contradictory impulses. The most genuine note in the last three hundred lines of the poem is the passage in which Keats avows his own divided consciousness and admits his departure from the original myth and the poem's own plan. He apologizes to Endymion for his long delay in seeing him "enskyed":

> Yes, moonlight Emperor! felicity
> Has been thy meed for many thousand years;
> Yet often have I, on the brink of tears,
> Mourn'd as if yet thou wert a forester;—
> Forgetting the old tale.

> (IV, 776–80)

Keats sees that he has turned the joyous tale of an apotheosis into one seasoned with sorrow, frustration, and uncertainty. But the foreordained end does take place and Keats wrenches the story back to its original course. In line with the tone of the fourth book, Endymion wins his immortality in a notably modest and subdued way (especially as compared with the delirious climax of Book III), as if Keats were deliberately making none but the smallest claims for his hero's achievement. By a trick of the plot Endymion's divided loyalties are reconciled. Cynthia and the Indian maid turn out to be one and the same: spirit and nature, vision and actuality are tentatively and all too easily united. The quest for transcendence, having departed from nature, makes full circle

and embraces nature again. Endymion returns to his home-
land and to the natural scenes of his childhood:

> The spirit culls
> Unfaded amaranth, when wild it strays
> Through the old garden-ground of boyish days.
> A little onward ran the very stream
> By which he took his first soft poppy dream;
> And on the very bark 'gainst which he leant
> A crescent he had carv'd, and round it spent
> His skill in little stars. The teeming tree
> Had swollen and green'd the pious charactery,
> But not ta'en out.
>
> (IV, 782–91)

From these lines we get a small but suggestive hint at the
reconciliation toward which Keats is reaching out. We can
see the celestial carving on the tree as the poetic consciousness
itself, which, as in *Endymion,* imposes its visionary ideal, the
moon-ideal, onto the bark of nature. The tree neither dies nor
obliterates the boyish sketch, but somehow comes to terms
with it, transforming it through its own organic and temporal
growth, and at the same time being transformed by it.

The last part of the poem therefore neither capitulates to
nature nor leaves nature behind in the achievement of transcendence. Peona reenters the poem and offers Endymion
what amounts to a complete return to the world of the first
book. He refuses, turns hermit, and begins to prepare for
death. Finally Cynthia reveals herself and Endymion is
"spiritualiz'd" by an "unlook'd for change" (IV, 992–93).
Yet he and Cynthia will still "range / These forests," not far
from Peona and "the old garden-ground of boyish days." The
reconciliation will hardly be a lasting one. Within days after
completing *Endymion* Keats will write "In drear-nighted
December," the first of a long series of poems in which nature
and consciousness are painfully and irrevocably separated.

4

Crisis and Change

ENDYMION challenges criticism partly because it is less a unified poem than a poem-in-process: we can see Keats develop-
ing and changing amid the labors of composition. But if
Endymion has ultimately confused or frustrated its critics,
the poems written during the eight or nine months between
the completion of the first draft of *Endymion* in December
1817 and the commencement of *Hyperion* in September 1818
have had a sadder fate: they have hardly succeeded in en-
gaging criticism at all. Most chronological accounts turn at
this point from the poems to the incomparably rich letters,
with some justice, for after November 1817 a major portion
of Keats' creative energy does shift into prose. Many of the
poems of this period are occasional or improvised, and Keats
seems to have shared the subsequent estimate of them. The
one longer poem, *Isabella,* Keats rapidly came to dislike, and
he seems to have included it in the 1820 volume only under
pressure from his friends and publisher.[1] Only two of the
shorter poems, "Robin Hood" and "Lines on the Mermaid

1. *Letters,* 2:174.

Tavern," were granted admission to that volume, the last to appear during Keats' lifetime.

To a student of Keats' development the poems of this period have great interest in spite of their weaknesses. They tell us what we could not so readily understand from the letters alone—that Keats was undergoing a major crisis, of which the weakness of the poems and the shift to prose are both symptoms. The poems themselves, even some of the most trivial, grapple with the crisis: the same issues recur from poem to poem like painful but unpurgeable obsessions, repeatedly attacked but never resolved. Yet the crisis leads to a transformation that makes Keats' earlier development seem insignificant. The difference between the first and fourth books of *Endymion* is small compared with what separates the poet of *Endymion* from the poet of *Hyperion*. To understand the crisis and the metamorphosis we must be willing to pay close attention to poems that are far from achieved works of art.[2]

Elements of crisis had already appeared in the fourth book of *Endymion* and had engendered contradictions large enough to explode that book into virtual incoherence. The poems of the months that follow read like painful footnotes to that book, repeated attempts to deal with its discoveries more honestly than the ending had done. "In drear-nighted December," the first of these poems, takes up unflinchingly the tragic awareness that had intruded into the fourth book. The winter of 1817–18 must have been fierce for Keats: in

2. As with Keats' earliest work it is almost impossible to study these poems properly in Garrod's editions, which rigidly preserve not only the three volumes of Keats' lifetime but also the accidents of various posthumous editions. A strictly chronological ordering, such as Clarence D. Thorpe's complete (but by now somewhat dated) Odyssey Press edition, *Complete Poems and Selected Letters* (New York, 1935), is virtually indispensable.

this lyric, winter signifies all the pain and adversity of experience. Such a symbolic association is hardly original, but for Keats, who had always been attracted to the lush and luxurious in nature, whose primary natural symbol had been the bower, this new consciousness of winter indicates a change of emphasis. Keats did not cease to be attracted to summer and the delights of nature. On the contrary, amid the bare branches and frozen landscape of "In drear-nighted December," the "green felicity" of trees in bloom and the brightness of "Apollo's summer look" seemed all the more desirable for their absence.

In February, in a sonnet to Spenser, Keats is still "an inhabitant of wintry earth," and therefore cannot hope to receive inspiration from the poet of romance:

> But Elfin Poet 'tis impossible
>   For an inhabitant of wintry earth
> To rise like Phoebus with a golden quell
>   Fire-wing'd and make a morning in his mirth.
> It is impossible to escape from toil
>   O' the sudden and receive thy spiriting:
> The flower must drink the nature of the soil
>   Before it can put forth its blossoming.
>
>   (5–12)

He concludes by asking Spenser to "Be with me in the summer days," in the hope that he will then be able to write again, and write more in the spirit of the Elfin Poet. This sonnet raises too many issues to be dealt with at once. I shall return to the distance between Keats and his "toil" on the one hand, and the "spiriting" of Spenser, of Hunt (who proposed the sonnet), and of fire-winged Phoebus with his golden quill. At this point it is important to note how Keats resolves the poem and bridges the distance with an organic metaphor. Just as winter will be followed by spring and summer, just as the flower is nourished by the soil, so too the winter of human adversity will be followed by a redemptive summer. Keats expresses a similar hope in the octave of the lovely blank-verse sonnet "What the Thrush Said," written two weeks afterward:

> O Thou whose face hath felt the Winter's wind,
>   Whose eye has seen the snow-clouds hung in mist,
>   And the black elm tops 'mong the freezing stars,
>   To thee the spring will be a harvest-time.
> O Thou, whose only book has been the light
>   Of supreme darkness which thou feddest on
>   Night after night when Phoebus was away,
>   To thee the Spring shall be a triple morn.

The same hopeful identification of human life with the natural cycle occurs in two other sonnets of the period, "The Human Seasons," which I discussed in the opening chapter, and the sonnet to Homer:

> Aye, on the shores of darkness there is light,
>   And precipices show untrodden green;
> There is a budding morrow in midnight;
>   There is a triple sight in blindness keen.
>   (9–12)

The exact date of these lines is not known, but the Shake-spearean form of the sonnet and the direct echoes of the thrush poem enable us to place it in this period with some certainty. Both sonnets, with their evocations of an almost apocalyptic light and darkness, indicate that the symbolic meaning of winter grew more radical as the winter progressed. Winter represents not only the absence of the "passed joy" of summer, but also a winter of the spirit, which is making poetry impossible for Keats. The sonnet to Homer is explicitly about poetic creation, and the echoes indicate that this too is one of the meanings of the "book" and the absence of Phoebus in "What the Thrush Said." Not only the sun has departed, but the spirit of poetry as well. The redemptive tone of both sonnets is strictly conditional; they express but an uncertain hope that the natural cycle is relevant to the poet's predicament, that he is capable of renewal just as midnight contains the seeds of daylight. But the example of Homer, though encouraging, is as distant from Keats as the example of Spenser. For blind Homer the veil of earth, heaven, and hell had been rent. But Keats, though blind as well ("in giant ignorance"), still

> sits ashore and longs perchance
> To visit dolphin-coral in deep seas.
> (3–4)

"Perchance." There is a contradiction in both this sonnet and the message of the thrush. On one hand Keats longs for an apocalyptic light out of darkness, sight out of blindness, an uncurtaining of heaven, or a visit like Endymion's to the depths of the sea. These months are full of appeals to the great poets, to Milton and Shakespeare in January, to Spenser in February, now to Homer, in which Keats must combat a longing for a miraculous transformation, for he knows that "it is impossible to escape from toil / O' the sudden." Only in the sonnet to Homer does he yield to this apocalyptic longing. On the other hand, in the same sonnet he yearns for a strictly natural renewal, for the "budding morrow in midnight," as in the sonnet to Spenser, where he had hopefully compared himself to the flower that "must drink the nature of the soil / Before it can put forth its blossoming." If man too can be assured of renewal, then Keats need only follow the advice of the thrush—"O fret not after knowledge"—or, as he himself paraphrases it (in the same letter that includes "What the Thrush Said"): "Let us open our leaves and be passive and receptive—budding patiently under the eye of Apollo" (1:232).

Both of these hopes, as Keats himself (with supreme if self-contradictory honesty) recognizes, are illusory. In *Endymion* Keats had depicted a quest to be "enskyed" and lifted into "endless heaven." Now his faith in such transfiguration has disappeared:

> 'tis impossible
> For an inhabitant of wintry earth
> To rise like Phoebus with a golden quell
> Fire-wing'd and make a morning in his mirth.

This is the golden Phoebus of the early poems of Keats, to whom the poet now bids farewell; it is not the later Apollo of the third book of *Hyperion,* who is very differently transfigured, who is convulsed by "knowledge enormous" and dies into life. The sonnet, despite its emphasis on "toil," does preserve an ambiguous faith in *natural* regeneration.[3] But this faith is undercut in "The Human Seasons" where man's "Winter . . . of pale misfeature" implicitly breaks the cycle and reminds Keats of his "mortal nature." It was the latter poem that proved more prophetic. Hindsight enables us to look forward to that hoped-for summer of 1818 to see Keats not receiving the "spiriting" of Spenser but crying out before the "cold Beauty" of the North that "pain is never done":

> The short-liv'd, paly Summer is but won
> From Winter's ague, for one hour's gleam;
> Though sapphire-warm, their stars do never beam:
> All is cold Beauty; pain is never done.
> ("On Visiting the Tomb of Burns," 5–8)

3. Ambiguous because the crucial lines, "The flower must drink the nature of the soil / Before it can put forth its blossoming," describes a process which, for the flower, would be inexorable and involuntary, but which for Keats is also a deliberate and active rooting of his flight-worn poetic consciousness in the soil of reality. Keats' impulses pull both ways in the poem.

It did not require the summer in Scotland for Keats to be alerted to the fallacy of both the apocalyptic and the purely natural solutions. In two crucial poems written in January 1818, at the very beginning of this period, Keats had already charted a third course of self-transformation. In the "Lines on Seeing a Lock of Milton's Hair," written at Leigh Hunt's house on January 21, Keats turns what seems at first to have been an awkward moment into an act of self-consecration. In the stiff and undistinguished first half, Keats makes the conventional act of homage and requests the blessing of the great poet on a young novice. What is notable about these lines is that Keats, who had so long associated poetic creation with sleep and passivity, now imagines a poet who is a model of intense activity and energy:

> Thy spirit never slumbers,
>   But rolls about our ears,
> For ever, and for ever!
> O what a mad endeavour
>   Worketh he,
> Who to thy sacred and ennobled hearse
> Would offer a burnt sacrifice of verse
>   And melody.

(3–10)

The very conventionality of the language helps convey Keats' sense of intimidation at his own new project, symbolized by his gesture to Milton. His feeling of inadequacy in Milton's presence brings to mind his more radical uncertainty after seeing the Elgin Marbles, ten months earlier:

> My spirit is too weak—mortality
>   Weighs heavily on me like unwilling sleep,
>   And each imagin'd pinnacle and steep
> Of godlike hardship tells me I must die
> Like a sick Eagle looking at the sky.

(1–5)

On both occasions Keats is excited both by a model of achieved greatness, by the unexpectedly palpable incursion it makes into his life. But here, more explicitly than in the earlier poem, he turns the moment into one of high aspiration, and writes a manifesto for a new and different poetic career:

> When every childish fashion
>   Has vanish'd from my rhyme,
> Will I, grey-gone in passion,
>   Leave to an after-time
>   Hymning and harmony
> Of thee, and of thy works, and of thy life;
> But vain is now the burning and the strife,
> Pangs are in vain, until I grow high-rife
>   With old Philosophy,
> And mad with glimpses of futurity!
>
> For many years my offerings must be hush'd;
>   When I do speak, I'll think upon this hour,
> Because I feel my forehead hot and flush'd
>   Even at the simplest vassal of thy power,—
>   A lock of thy bright hair,—
>   Sudden it came,
> And I was startled, when I caught thy name
>   Coupled so unaware;
> Yet, at the moment, temperate was my blood.
> I thought I had beheld it from the flood.
>   (23–42)

The farewell to early Keats could not be more explicit. The poet is startled as if by an apparition, but he reacts against his own excitement. The message is the same as the one which he was shortly to address to Spenser:

> It is impossible to escape from toil
> O' the sudden and receive thy spiriting.

There will be no apocalyptic transformation. It was only the early Keats who could put his trust in that kind of "spiriting." Keats now sees a path of "toil," a long period of growth toward wisdom and intellectual maturity, a labor of "knowledge enormous." In April he was to put the same thought to his publisher in prose: "I know nothing I have read nothing and I mean to follow Solomon's directions of 'get Wisdom—get understanding'—I find cavalier days are gone by. I find that I can have no enjoyment in the World but continual drinking of Knowledge . . . the road lies through application, study and thought. I will pursue it and to that end purpose retiring for some years. I have been hovering for some time between an exquisite sense of the luxurious and a love for Philosophy—were I calculated for the former I should be glad—but as I am not I shall turn all my soul to the latter" (1:271). The poet exchanges the luxury of Spenser for the intellectual grandeur of Milton. He can neither be satisfied to open his leaves and be passive and receptive nor expect that Jove will rend the veil of heaven to end his "giant ignorance." The realization of his powers must be a self-realization.

The day after his address to Milton Keats wrote an even more important poem. He sits down to read *King Lear,* perhaps as a first step toward that self-realization through knowledge to which he had just pledged himself, and commemorates the moment in verse. This gives the reading of the play the significance of a ritual act ("the thing appeared to demand the prologue of a Sonnet, I wrote it & began to read," 1:214). Here Keats makes the renunciation of his earlier poetic mode explicit and gives a new complexity and weight to the task of self-creation.

> O golden-tongued Romance with serene lute!
> Fair plumed Syren! Queen of far away!
>   Leave melodizing on this wintry day,
> Shut up thine olden pages, and be mute:
> Adieu! for once again the fierce dispute

> Betwixt damnation and impassion'd clay
>   Must I burn through; once more humbly assay
> The bitter-sweet of this Shakespearian fruit.
> Chief Poet! and ye clouds of Albion,
>   Begetters of our deep eternal theme,
> When through the old oak forest I am gone,
>   Let me not wander in a barren dream,
> But when I am consumed in the fire,
> Give me new Phoenix wings to fly at my desire.[4]

For the early Keats there had been no more honorific word or attractive art than romance. Even two months later he was to insist, over his publishers' objection, on giving *Endymion* the subtitle "A Poetic Romance," with the assertion that "a ramance is a fine thing notwithstanding the circulating Libraries" (1:253). But here he puts aside romance—putting aside not only *Endymion* but his erstwhile romantic masters, such as Spenser—for the very different poetry and experience that *Lear* represents.

What is it about romance that Keats now rejects? Its serenity? Its ornamental beauty? Its melody? It is not that these qualities no longer attract him but that on a "wintry day," in a certain kind of world, they seem at best but a part of the truth. Romance is the kind of art that he had so beautifully praised in the proem to *Endymion,* which, in a world of despondence and dearth,

> still will keep
> A bower quiet for us, and a sleep
> Full of sweet dreams, and health, and quiet breathing.

Its greatest attraction had always been its distance from actuality: "Queen of far away."[5] In his "Epistle to Reynolds" in

4. Like Professor Bate (*John Keats*, p. 287 n.), I have not followed Garrod's quaint, distracting over-punctuation. See also Bush, ed., *John Keats: Selected Poems*, pp. 132–33.

5. For Keats the greatest art, like that of *Lear*, has the power to transform empirical reality by way of "intensity" or a "momentous

March, Keats, after describing a vision of "eternal fierce destruction," would turn away and hope to "take refuge" from "detested moods in new Romance" (111–12). Romance had always been a refuge from the harshness of reality and the mind's despair. But now the poetry of dream seems barren as Keats prepares to face in *Lear,* then himself to write, another kind of poetry, tragic and purgatorial, a poetry of actuality, that can deal with the bitter as well as the sweet, that brings into play knowledge as well as sensation, that requires of both its creator and reader an active transformation of the self ("to fly at my desire") rather than passive and self-annihilating receptivity. In a letter to his brother Keats instances the *Lear* sonnet as evidence of a change in his temperament: "I think a little change has taken place in my intellect lately—I cannot bear to be uninterested or unemployed, I, who for so long a time, have been addicted to passiveness—Nothing is finer for the purposes of great productions, than a very gradual ripening of the intellectual powers" (1:214).[6] The change from passivity to activity is parallel to the change from romance to tragedy. In this new attitude toward both intellectual knowledge and the active knowledge of self, Keats is setting for himself the goal of personal openness and an ex-

---

depth of speculation" (see pp. 62–63, above). Romance, on the other hand, when it does not merely evade reality, can at best supply it with an interesting "colouring," as Keats had indicated a few weeks earlier in explaining his preference for the realistic Smollett over Scott: "Scott endeavours to th[r]ow so interesting and ramantic a colouring into common and low Characters as to give them a touch of the Sublime—Smollet on the contrary pulls down and levels what other Men would continue Romance" (1:200).

6. It is worth noting that even the shift from sensation to knowledge Keats can describe only in the language of nature or sensation itself. Thus he consecrates himself to a "continual drinking of Knowledge" and "a very gradual ripening of the intellectual powers," which indicates that his antinomies are far from dualistic and his sensibility never becomes dissociated. Keats surely rivals the Metaphysicals in the power, which Eliot praised, to unite thinking with feeling.

panding consciousness which he will find very painful to achieve.

What is the nature of this new goal, and of the new poetry that *Lear* represents? Long afterwards Keats was to compare the Italian poet Boiardo with Shakespeare:

> He had a Castle in the Appenine. He was a noble Poet of Romance; not a miserable and mighty Poet of the human Heart. The middle age of Shakspeare was all c[l]ouded over; his days were not more happy than Hamlet's who is perhaps more like Shakspeare himself in his common every day Life than any other of his Characters. (2:115–16)

In a remarkable letter to Reynolds on May 3 Keats was to compare Milton unfavorably to Wordsworth on the score of "Miltons apparently less anxiety for Humanity." Wordsworth, on the other hand, seemingly "martyrs himself to the human heart, the main region of his song." To explain himself Keats adds, a few lines later, "you will know exactly my meaning when I say, that now I shall relish Hamlet more than I ever have done" (1:278–79). Against romance, and against Miltonic epic, is a tragic poetry whose human concern is grounded in the consciousness of self. The references to Hamlet, the most self-conscious character in English literature, make Keats' meaning especially clear. As Professor Bate says, "Keats saw, in effect, that he was and could only be a modern poet: that he could hardly escape a poetry that was turned more to the inner life."[7]

We can now come closer to understanding the central lines of the *Lear* sonnet:

> once again the fierce dispute
> Betwixt damnation[8] and impassion'd clay
> Must I burn through.

---

7. *John Keats,* p. 322. This is the central point of Professor Bate's fine chapter on this period called "The Emergence of a Modern Poet."

8. Keats originally wrote "Betwixt Hell torment." *Letters,* 1:215.

What Keats describes is a dialectic between suffering and consciousness,[9] between a world of hellish torment such as the world of *Lear* and a self-consciousness as acute as that of the suffering Lear himself, or Shakespeare, or the man who "can read and perhaps understand Shakspeare to his depths" (1:239). Keats is under no illusion of ease. This "fierce dispute" will be greater than the "undescribable feud" that Keats felt in contemplating the Elgin Marbles or the "grievous feud" that led Endymion to the Cave of Quietude. But he welcomes it, and in doing so he leads us to recall Endymion's own renunciation of romance in Book IV, when he had blessed "Horrors which nourish an uneasiness / For my own sullen conquering" (618–19). But Keats anticipates more than "an uneasiness," nor is he confident that he can readily conquer. He expects a purgatorial death ("when I am consumed in the fire")—perhaps like the martyrdom he metaphorically attributes to Wordsworth—out of which he can only *hope* for a Phoenix-like rebirth.[10]

Keats had anticipated the difficulty of his new commitment even before the fourth book of *Endymion,* in all of those moments of unprotected nakedness when Endymion must make "the journey homeward to habitual self." But perhaps he was not aware of the extent of his inner recalcitrance, in-

9. Cf. Trilling, *The Opposing Self,* p. 47: "between . . . the knowledge of evil and the knowledge of self."

10. Shakespeare himself comes to this theme of rebirth by moving in precisely the opposite direction: from the great tragedies to the final romances. Each of the last plays recapitulates this progress, which is already anticipated by several of the last tragedies, especially *Antony and Cleopatra*: each of the romances begins with a tragedy in miniature, followed by motifs of redemption and resurrection.

Keats is undoubtedly unfair to romance when he reduces it to fancy and faery and uses it to represent his own escapist impulses. Still, that he does so is important, and should give pause to those recent critics who have been trying to root Romanticism in the myths and archetypes of romance.

deed revulsion, which had been fully foreshadowed in "In drear-nighted December," the first of a whole series of poems on the pains of consciousness. These poems constitute a sustained and troubled meditation on the nature of the mind and its relation to reality. That first poem describes a harsh wintry world which batters both man and nature, but the poem is built upon the distinction between them. Nature, Keats feels, cannot be said to suffer, because it is neither aware of loss nor anxious about renewal; man, however, is conscious of both, of the past and the future, and this consciousness makes his present hellish but meaningful. The distinction recalls the memorable *pensée* of Pascal:

> Man is but a reed, the most feeble thing in nature; but he is a thinking reed. The entire universe need not arm itself to crush him. A vapour, a drop of water suffices to kill him. But, if the universe were to crush him, man would still be more noble than that which killed him, because he knows that he dies and the advantage which the universe has over him; the universe knows nothing of this.
>
> All our dignity consists, then, in thought. . . .[11]

But Keats' emphasis is the reverse of Pascal's. For Pascal this consciousness, while it is man's agony, is also the essence of his glory. But Keats here—unlike the *Lear* sonnet, with its ennobling tragic commitment—stresses the agony alone. He envies the static unconsciousness of the "happy, happy tree," which does not know that it has lost its leaves, and the "sweet forgetting" of the "happy, happy Brook" which cannot recall the summer, when it was free of ice. He longs for insentience, for "the feel of not to feel it."

In the context of this longing the new resolution which Keats announces in the lines to Milton and the *Lear* sonnet leads to a deep inner crisis. Little more than a week after those poems were written, a light-hearted epistolary verse tribute

11. *Pascal's Pensées,* trans. W. F. Trotter (New York, 1958), p. 97.

to "the glory and grace of Apollo" suddenly turns into the anxious cry of an alarmed and divided consciousness:

> God of the Meridian,
>   And of the East and West,
> To thee my soul is flown,
>   And my body is earthward press'd.
> It is an awful mission,
> A terrible division;
> And leaves a gulph austere
> To be filled with worldly fear.
> Aye, when the soul is fled
> To high above our head
> Affrighted do we gaze
> After its airy maze,
> As doth a mother wild,
> When her young infant child
> Is in an eagle's claws—
> And is not this the cause
> Of madness?—God of Song,
> Thou bearest me along
> Through sights I scarce can bear:
> O let me, let me share
> With the hot lyre and thee,
> The staid Philosophy.
> Temper my lonely hours,
> And let me see thy bowers
> More unalarm'd!

Now that the imagination has undertaken to burn through experiences like that of *King Lear,* the bowers of poetry, which once promised "a sleep / Full of sweet dreams, and health, and quiet breathing," become perilous and threatening. The image of the eagle recalls the sonnet on the Elgin Marbles. "Why should we be owls, when we can be Eagles?" Keats was to ask Reynolds three days later, comparing Wordsworth and Hunt unfavorably to the Elizabethans (1:224).

But I think Keats' anxiety is more radical than simply "the fear of failing through sheer incapacity," as Bate suggests.[12] As in the Elgin Marbles sonnet, where he had turned his sense of incapacity into a deeper meditation on time and mortality, Keats makes his case as a poet a more intense version of his situation as a man. In Book IV of *Endymion* Keats had contrived for his hero a similar experience of "terrible division." But for Keats, unlike Endymion, there can be neither a simple choice nor a mechanical reconciliation of opposites. His "body is earthward press'd" not simply out of inability but from mortality as well. As a man he is bound to the earth, but he is not yet willing, as a poet, to "drink the nature of the soil." He glories in his capacity for mental and imaginative flight but is tormented by the chasm that it opens up, the human awareness that it brings home. He longs for knowledge here ("the staid Philosophy") to "ease the Burden of the Mystery," to cool the fever that has become part of the creative process ("the hot lyre"). This reminds us of the fire images of the *Lear* sonnet and the "forehead hot and flush'd" of the lines to Milton, but Keats will later explain that this is the lot not only of poets but of all men of "high Sensations": "An extensive knowledge is needful to thinking people—it takes away the heat and fever; and helps, by widening speculation, to ease the Burden of the Mystery" (1:277).

Yet the "terrible division" in this poem, between the roaming spirit, hostage to Apollo, and the earth-bound self, indicates that such reconciling knowledge is not yet available, that Keats feels a growing gulf between his venturesome mind and his chances of personal stability and happiness ("And is this not the cause / Of madness?") It is typical of this period of stress and shifting allegiances that at the same time that Keats puts new faith in mind and self-consciousness

12. *John Keats,* p. 292.

he also recoils most intensely from them, in fierce dialogue with himself, in fearful response to his own new commitment. He gave expression to this renewed animosity a few days later, in a very bad poem over which no critic, I believe, has previously seen fit to linger. The sonnet "To the Nile" was written in fifteen minutes, in competition with Shelley and Hunt.[13] (Hunt, who suggested the topic, worked on into the night and wrote one of his best poems.) Weak as it is, however, Keats' sonnet, which is about the relation of the mind to reality, tells us much about the crisis he is undergoing:

> Son of the old moon-mountains African!
>   Stream of the Pyramid and Crocodile!
>   We call thee fruitful, and, that very while,
> A desert fills our seeing's inward span;
> Nurse of swart nations since the world began,
>   Art thou so fruitful? or dost thou beguile
>   Such men to honour thee, who, worn with toil,
> Rest them a space 'twixt Cairo and Decan?
> O may dark fancies err! they surely do;
>   'Tis ignorance that makes a barren waste
> Of all beyond itself. Thou dost bedew
>   Green rushes like our rivers, and dost taste
> The pleasant sun-rise. Green isles hast thou too,
>   And to the sea as happily dost haste.

Not many poems could recover, even to this limited extent, from two such opening lines. Yet within the context of the whole poem even they have a purpose. Keats begins by placing the Nile in a pseudomythological setting, in order to question the myth. Keats will set out to demythologize the Nile, to get at its reality. One of the movements of the poem—the poem is remarkable for nothing so much as its movement—

13. Even an article devoted to "Keats and Egypt" gives it no more than passing mention. Helen Darbishire, "Keats and Egypt," *Review of English Studies* 3 (1927): 1–11.

is from the exotic to the familiar. But the familiar turns out to be different from the real—Keats retreats to the familiar in recoil from questions that are *too* real—and he ends by straining to confirm the myth.

What Keats questions is the myth of the Nile's fruitfulness. This is characteristic of his 1818 mood, of the new tragic awareness that draws him to the darker side of both nature and human life. Against the river he raises the image of the desert, and they symbolize the doubleness of nature and of experience. The human counterparts of the desert are the men "who, worn with toil, / Rest them a space 'twixt Cairo and Decan." Is the river, he asks, but a small oasis in a vast desert that is this world of toil? And further, is not this oasis, that is, our belief in nature's ultimate goodness, a mirage, the illusory though necessary creation of our own toilworn minds? At this point Keats recoils from the adventurousness of his own imagination. He labels his questions "dark fancies" and denounces his own "ignorance." But he must convince himself as much as convince us. The ejaculation "O may dark fancies err!" is a hope turning fluidly into an assertion. Dark fancies *may* err, he says at first, which by the addition of the exclamation mark turns into a fervent wish (May they only err in this case!) and a feeling of confidence (They may indeed!), and then concludes in the certitude of "they surely do." Keats then generalizes his new discovery: " 'Tis ignorance that makes a barren waste / Of all beyond itself." What Keats seems to mean is not so much ignorance as subjectivism or solipsism. Just as he had previously suggested that the fruitfulness of the Nile could be imaginary, Keats turns and denounces the barrenness of the desert in the same way. He objects not so much to the "barren waste" as to the mind that dwells upon—even, he says, creates—the image of the barren waste. He turns harshly upon his own tragic perceptions, on the consciousness that would spoil our happiness by exploring the dark side of things. In this respect he goes even further than in "In drear-nighted December." In that poem he had isolated human consciousness as a source of suffering, but had at least granted that, though unpleasant, it remained a consciousness of something *real*. Here the idea that there is evil or adversity in the world is no more than a subjective fantasy.

Wordsworth had written "Tintern Abbey" "knowing that Nature never did betray / The heart that loved her," which indicates that, despite his faith, the idea of betrayal was very much on his mind. Keats, after living so long with a nature that seemed benign and with an imagination content with images of delight, feels genuinely betrayed, both by nature (which, like Wordsworth, he cannot admit) and by his imagination (which therefore must take all the blame). Even in the *Lear* sonnet in which he had anticipated the capacity of the imagination to cause him pain, he could still hope to be purged and reborn in the end. Even this is now denied to him. The last three and a half lines of the sonnet therefore make, depending on how we interpret them, either a full or a partial retreat. With a good deal of strain and wishfulness they seek to restore the safe and peaceful nature of the early Keats. The Nile is fruitful after all, and as untroubled as "*our* rivers," which, in spite of our speculative flight to Egypt, we knew were there all along, a safe haven for our erring fancies. Yet these lines may not be so radically willful and dishonest. Until now—and this is certainly one of the reasons for the poem's failure—Keats had burdened his subject with a staggering freight of symbolism; now he tries to resolve his metaphysical dilemma by seeking out the actual landscape lost beneath symbolic significances, the real river, with its rushes and islets, moving toward the sea. Keats, in other words, *demonstrates* the violence that the imagination has done to its material, to the phenomenal world.

Even in doing so Keats cannot resist a final symbolic thrust.

Until now the fundamental weakness (indeed impossibility) of the poem's metaphysics has been its absolutism, expressed in the rigidity of the symbolic alternatives. Either our vision of the desert and of the men "worn with toil" belies the claims of the river, or our belief in the fruitful river turns the desert into a "dark fancy." Nature is either absolutely evil, making good an illusion, or absolutely good, demeaned only by our own fantasies. Keats has yet to suffer what E. M. Forster in *The Longest Journey* calls "the Primal Curse, which is not the knowledge of good and evil, but the knowledge of good-and-evil." He seems as yet unable to imagine the river and the desert existing side by side. But in the last lines there is a hint of a more balanced recognition, for the river, besides becoming an actual river meandering toward the sea, also comes to represent ordinary human experience, with its combination of pleasure and transience, life and mortality ("... dost taste / The pleasant sun-rise. . . . / And to the sea as happily dost haste"). On the whole Keats brings his exotic symbolism into the ken of the familiar, where it can no longer threaten him, but he does so only by suppressing his own speculative misgivings, and constricting his imagination. Devotion to an expanding consciousness and the turn to a tragic perspective seem forgotten.

Not long afterward, in one of the central crisis poems of the period, Keats provided both a thorough gloss on the Nile sonnet and a striking repetition of its movement. This takes place in the verse epistle which Keats sent from Devon to his ailing friend Reynolds on March 25. The well-known general argument comes first:

> O that our dreamings all of sleep or wake
> Would all their colours from the Sunset take:
> From something of material sublime,
> Rather than shadow our own Soul's daytime
> In the dark void of Night. For in the world

We jostle—but my flag is not unfurl'd
On the Admiral staff—and to philosophize
I dare not yet!—Oh never will the prize,
High reason, and the lore of good and ill
Be my award. Things cannot to the will
Be settled, but they tease us out of thought.
Or is it that Imagination brought
Beyond its proper bound, yet still confined,—
Lost in a sort of Purgatory blind,
Cannot refer to any standard law
Of either earth or heaven?—It is a flaw
In happiness to see beyond our bourn—
It forces us in Summer skies to mourn:
It spoils the singing of the Nightingale.

(67–85)

The unevenness of this verse is not entirely due to the un-worked spontaneity of the epistolary form. Keats is genuinely confused by his speculations ("to philosophize / I dare not yet!"). His own imagination is "lost in a sort of Purgatory blind." In the first half of the epistle, Keats had rambled through a chain of half-serious thoughts and fantasies, mostly of a demonic cast, with the assertion that "few are there who escape these visitings" (13). Keats is reflecting once more, as in the Nile sonnet, on the tendency of the mind, or at least *his* mind, to harbor "dark fancies." This is what he means by "Imagination" here: human consciousness in general, not just the creative faculty. Keats leaves no doubt about what he considers the "proper bound" of that consciousness: it is the "material sublime" evoked also in the last lines of the Nile sonnet: sunset and summer skies, and the singing of the nightingale—the happy colors of nature, that is, untroubled by the darker hues of self-consciousness. Keats returns to the aesthetic of *Endymion,* of "dreamings" that are wholly separate from, and console us for, the jostling world of actuality. Keats had included one such dream earlier in the poem, an evocation of

> ... Titian colours touch'd into real life.—
> The sacrifice goes on; the pontiff knife
> Gleams in the sun, the milk-white heifer lows,
> The pipes go shrilly, the libation flows:
> A white sail shews above the green-head cliff
> Moves round the point, and throws her anchor stiff.
> The Mariners join hymn with those on land.
>
> (19–25)

This is the world of the first book of *Endymion,* the preconscious ritual harmony of the golden age. But large as Keats' nostalgia may be, his sense of separation is decisive. The very longing for "something of *material* sublime" indicates that he is not wholly satisfied with dream as *against* reality: he looks for a locus of unity between dream and reality in the objective world. His own imagination has not been content to provide him with happy dreams and natural images. It has gone "beyond its proper bound" and spoiled his happiness, just as Keats, in a letter the previous day to Rice, had said that it must:

> What a happy thing it would be if we could settle our thoughts, make up our minds on any matter in five Minutes and remain content—that is to build a sort of mental Cottage of feelings quiet and pleasant—to have a sort of Philosophical Back Garden, and cheerful holiday-keeping front one—but Alas! this can never be: for as the material Cottager knows there are such places as france and Italy and the Andes and the Burning Mountains—so the spiritual Cottager has knowledge of the terra semi incognita of things unearthly; and cannot for his Life, keep in the check rein. (1:254–55)

This passage indicates to what extent the image of the bower still holds Keats, while also revealing how far he has left it behind. The impulse is there, but a larger recognition counterbalances it. "What a happy thing . . . but Alas! this can never be"—such is the dialectic of this longing. In this case the "Back Garden" is an intellectual one, and against it Keats asserts the openness (*not* self-annihilation) that is the essence of Negative Capability, "to let the mind be a thoroughfare for all thoughts. Not a select party" (2:213). Yet a day later he has to denounce this consciousness. To Reynolds he would call this "terra semi incognita of things unearthly" a "Purgatory blind" in which one "cannot refer to any standard law / Of either earth or heaven." This day-to-day contradiction is characteristic of Keats' mind during these months. In the poem Keats, like Endymion in Book IV, feels that he has overreached himself, and he echoes Endymion's speech of repentance ("There never liv'd a mortal man, who bent / His appetite beyond his natural sphere, / But starv'd and died," IV, 646–48).

But Keats' notion of imagination had changed since *Endymion*. It is no longer essentially a visionary flight "to burst our mortal bars" but rather—though Keats still uses the old transcendental notation of "things unearthly" or "ethereal"— to "burn through" the "fierce dispute / Betwixt damnation and impassion'd clay." This is the key to the "Purgatory blind," for it was in the *Lear* sonnet that Keats for the first time described imagination as a purgatorial process. In the sonnet, in spite of the pain that he expected to undergo, Keats could still hope in the end to rise Phoenix-like from the consuming fire. But the thwarting of this hope has turned the tragic catharsis of *Lear* into a "Purgatory blind" and turned Keats against his own acceptance of both suffering and consciousness. The unchecked course of his imagination, its confrontation with pain and adversity, has raised questions that Keats had not fully anticipated. He finds himself a little like Arnold, without a "standard law" to which he can refer,

> Wandering between two worlds, one dead,
> The other powerless to be born.[14]

He despairs of ever attaining to "high reason, and the lore of good and ill," and as the vision that follows will show, he is troubled by the discovery of evil and cruelty in nature. But in spite of this language Keats' preoccupation here is not, like Arnold's, primarily ethical. His concern is prior: to understand and accept that autonomy of the spirit which his commitment to poetry has always implied, and which is one of the roots of all the subsequent ethical dilemmas of the nineteenth century. In a very great moment in the "Ode to Psyche," Keats would turn away from that world of "antique vows" and ritual harmony of which he so fondly dreams early in this epistle, to arrogate for the poet the roles of prophet and priest both, to assert that

> I see, and sing, by my own eyes inspir'd.
> (43)

This sort of assertion, for Arnold's and Nietzsche's generation, will already have become part of cultural history. Their forebears will have liberated and orphaned the self, and they will build upon new foundations. But Keats is still struggling toward that primary scission. Here in the epistle, though as man and poet he is hopelessly cut off from his older limited "natural sphere," he looks back upon it nostalgically. His only concession to a larger vision and a more burdensome imaginative enterprise is a single phrase, "but still confin'd." The imagination, he says, ought to go back to "its proper bound" or *go further,* to rest happily on earth, preserving a sense of nature's benignity, or storm heaven for a new "standard law"; it ought to be content with the material sublime of sunset and summer skies or go forward the whole

14. Matthew Arnold, "Stanzas from the Grande Chartreuse," 85–86.

way of the *Lear* sonnet and (as time would show) the odes.

In the light of this argument, the passage that follows is uniquely interesting, for it exhibits both the larger vision that Keats cannot repress, and yet also the full force, already adumbrated in the Nile sonnet, of his attempt during this period to repress it, of his recoil from his own most adventurous thoughts. The passage lays bare the painful division of a soul in perplexity:[15]

> Dear Reynolds, I have a mysterious tale
> And cannot speak it. The first page I read
> Upon a Lampit Rock of green sea weed
> Among the breakers—'Twas a quiet Eve;
> The rocks were silent—the wide sea did weave
> An untumultuous fringe of silver foam
> Along the flat brown sand.
>
> (86–92)

The scene is carefully set. It is, significantly, a landscape that could be from "Sleep and Poetry" or the first book of *Endymion*,[16] the serene and untroubled landscape that Keats had marshaled at the close of the Nile sonnet to exorcise his "dark fancies."

> I was at home,
> And should have been most happy—but I saw
> Too far into the sea; where every maw

15. I don't wish to overemphasize the element of crisis in the poem, but even a critic as little given to exaggeration as Douglas Bush describes it as "tormented." *John Keats: His Life and Writings* (New York, 1966), p. 140.

16. The setting is not only in the spirit of early Keats but recalls several actual descriptions of the sea, such as this one in "Sleep and Poetry":

> as when ocean
> Heaves calmly its broad swelling smoothness o'er
> Its rocky marge, and balances once more
> The patient weeds; that now unshent by foam
> Feel all about their undulating home.
>
> (376–80)

The greater on the less feeds evermore:—
But I saw too distinct into the core
Of an eternal fierce destruction,
And so from Happiness I far was gone.
Still am I sick of it: and though to-day
I've gathered young spring-leaves, and flowers gay
Of Periwinkle and wild strawberry,
Still do I that most fierce destruction see,
The Shark at savage prey—the hawk at pounce,
The gentle Robin, like a pard or ounce,
Ravening a worm—Away ye horrid moods,
Moods of one's mind! You know I hate them well,
You know I'd sooner be a clapping bell,
To some Kamschatkan missionary church,
Than with these horrid moods be left in lurch.

(93–109)

A recent critic, Walter Evert, has written a thorough commentary on this poem in which he argues that the lines on the "eternal fierce destruction" have almost always been quoted out of context and therefore "universally misunderstood." He rightly says that "they actually serve as an exemplum of the argument on imagination just presented." Keats, far from announcing his discovery of the destructive element in nature, is instead berating himself for seeing *"too far* into the sea . . . *too distinct* into the core / Of an eternal fierce destruction." Far from being realities, these are "horrid moods, / Moods of one's mind!" They have made Keats sick, though he "was at home, / And should have been most happy." "It is not the world that is at fault," Evert says, "but the mind that interprets the world."[17]

This reading, though it restores to us the literal sense of the passage, is actually as misleading as the lazy view it replaces,

17. Walter H. Evert, *Aesthetic and Myth in the Poetry of Keats* (Princeton, 1965), pp. 209–11. These are easily the best pages in an otherwise unexciting book.

for neither catches the full dialectic of the passage. In a sense the central lines on what is generally called the "struggle for existence," Tennyson's nature "red in tooth and claw," deserve to be torn out of context. "The shark at savage prey— the hawk at pounce" and "the gentle Robin . . . Ravening a worm" are realized with much greater vividness than the periwinkle and wild strawberry, symbols of the old serene and bowery Nature. Keats' own poetical power betrays his argument, which, even more explicitly than in the Nile sonnet, is an attempt to convince himself as much as his reader. As in the sonnet, Keats is attempting to suppress his new and insistent tragic perceptions by attributing them to a diseased excess of consciousness. By doing so he seeks to discredit at once the knowledge of evil and the knowledge of self, both parts of his profound new awareness in the *Lear* sonnet. He concludes the epistle aptly with a promise to "take refuge" from these "detested moods in new Romance." His turn upon himself, upon the resolution he had taken in January before sitting down to read *King Lear,* is now symbolically complete.

Deeply as Keats may at moments have tried to recoil from them, he could not undo the remarkable changes that were taking place in his temperament and mental life since the fourth book of *Endymion.* Let us review these changes briefly. His concern with the problem of evil now becomes a continuing one. A day after he writes his sonnet and sets about to read *King Lear,* his mind returns to some words he had heard from Bailey months earlier: *"Why should Woman suffer?"* This is a question which he feels a poet of romance would be unable to deal with: "These things are, and he who feels how incompetent the most skyey knight errantry is to heal this bruised fairness is like a sensitive leaf on the hot hand of thought" (1:209). Five months later, writing to Bailey again, he is still brooding about the problem. It seems to make his earlier naive commitment to poetry all the more inappropriate, indeed, monstrously insensitive. He tells Bailey, who had written a generous review of *Endymion* for an Oxford paper, that "you are too simple for the World": "Were it my choice I would reject a petrarchal coronation—on account of my dying day, and because women have Cancers." His conviction has been strengthened by the events of the spring. "I have two Brothers one is driven by the 'burden of Society' to America the other, with an exquisite love of Life, is in a lingering state . . . I have a Sister too and may not follow them, either to America or to the Grave—Life must be undergone" (1:292–93).

As the last four words indicate, Keats is concerned not with the abstract question of evil, but with the problems of survival and self-affirmation in a world in which suffering exists and evil is a reality. A year later he was to give a memorable account of this process, under the head of "soul-making" (2:101–3), and in a May 3 letter to Reynolds he makes a remarkable preliminary sketch of it. He compares human life to a "large Mansion of Many Apartments," the first of which is "the infant or thoughtless Chamber, in which we remain as long as we do not think." The second chamber, the Chamber of Maiden Thought, toward which we "are at length imperceptibly impelled by the awakening of the thinking principle—within us," has two stages. At first (in what seems very much like Keats' account of his own earlier poetry and sensibility),

> we become intoxicated with the light and the atmosphere, we see nothing but pleasant wonders, and think of delaying there for ever in delight: However among the effects this breathing is father of is that tremendous one of sharpening one's vision into the heart and nature of Man—of convincing one's nerves that the World is full of Misery and Heartbreak, Pain, Sickness and oppression—whereby This Chamber of Maiden Thought becomes gradually darken'd. . . .

But this discovery of evil is not an end in itself. For the poet especially, it is just the beginning. Now, Keats indicates, he has found his true subject, one which will try the resources of his spirit. The subject is not negativity but the struggle of the self with negativity:

> . . . and at the same time on all sides of it many doors are set open—but all dark—all leading to dark passages—We see not the ballance of good and evil. We are in a Mist—*We* are now in that state—We feel the "burden of the Mystery," To this point was Wordsworth come, as far as I can conceive when he wrote 'Tintern Abbey' and it seems to me that his Genius is explorative of those dark Passages. Now if we live, and go on thinking, we too shall explore them. (1:280–81)

Keats is not in less of a mist than when he had written the March verse epistle, but he then had despaired ever of acquiring "the lore of good and ill," had shrunk from his perplexities into a makeshift natural bower and a "select party" of happy thoughts. Now he resolves to face these dark passages, to go on thinking and thus to explore them. This resolution implies a new tutelage to Wordsworth, a new acceptance of the unsparing examination of the self that Wordsworth had shown to be the inescapable burden of the modern poet. Milton will not pass muster here. "He did not think into the human heart, as Wordsworth has done" (1:282). Only three months earlier he had seen fit to denounce this self-consciousness as egotism: "for the sake of a few fine imaginative or domestic passages, are we to be bullied into a certain Philosophy engendered in the whims of an Egotist—Every man has his speculations, but every man does not brood and peacock over them till he makes a false coinage and deceives himself. . . . I will have no more of Wordsworth or Hunt in particular" (1:223–24). In the verse epistle he had, by implication, renewed the attack by dismissing his own sombre thoughts as "horrid moods, / Moods of one's Mind." Wordsworth himself had grouped a number of his poems under the collective title of "Moods of my own mind," a label Keats found damaging and revealing. The new sympathy for Wordsworth is thus a decisive clue to the kind of poet that Keats will become.

Another interesting though minor development in early 1818 is the appearance of a certain social consciousness in Keats' work, related, I think, to his general turn toward actuality and to the heightening of that skeptical strain that had always been a part of his temperament. Keats is generally regarded as the least political of all the Romantic poets, and in a narrow sense this is true. One does not deny his sincere attachment to liberty, but his early liberal politics, though they led to much abuse from the reviewers (because of the association with Hunt), amount to little more than an admiration of certain heroic figures and a genuine abhorrence of tyrants. His reaction to the city, for example, is so simple as to be almost a caricature of the Wordsworthian desire just to be somewhere else, to get out of it. There is little during this period to prepare us for that concrete interest in "the present state of society" (1:320), in how men live and how their lives are affected by communal conditions, that appears strikingly in the letters of the Scottish tour. But it is hardly necessary for Miss Ward to conjecture that the famous stanzas 14–16 of *Isabella,* which Shaw proclaimed to be an anticipation of "the immense indictment of the profiteers and exploiters with which Marx has shaken capitalistic civilization to its foundations,"[18] may therefore have been added to the poem after Keats' return from Scotland.[19] Keats had already written a more jocular version of the same critique at the beginning of February, before having begun *Isabella,* in the

18. George Bernard Shaw, "Keats," in *The John Keats Memorial Volume,* ed. G. C. Williamson (London, 1921), p. 175.

19. Ward, *John Keats: Making of a Poet,* p. 189.

fine lines on "Robin Hood." This poem, which Keats included in the 1820 volume, is usually remembered for its salutatory last stanza, as a toast to the age of romance:

> Honour to the old bow-string!
> Honour to the bugle-horn!
> . . . .
> Honour to bold Robin Hood,
> Sleeping in the underwood!
> Honour to maid Marian,
> And to all the Sherwood-clan!
> (50–51, 57–60)

Actually the toasting vein of the last stanza is tinged with irony; the poem is no exercise in nostalgia. It is the work of a poet who a few days earlier had put aside romance; if anything it is too harsh in its realism. The poem is a reply to two sonnets on Robin Hood that Reynolds had sent to Keats. In one of them Reynolds asks: "The trees in Sherwood forest . . . are they deserted all?" No, Reynolds himself answers,

> Go there, with Summer, and with evening,—go
>   In the soft shadows like some wandering man,—
> And thou shalt far amid the forest know
> The archer men in green, with belt and bow,
>   Feasting on pheasant, river-fowl, and swan,
>   With Robin at their head, and Marian.[20]

Keats begins his poem with a direct rebuttal:

> No! those days are gone away,
> And their hours are old and gray,
> And their minutes buried all
> Under the down-trodden pall
> Of the leaves of many years:
> (1–5)

20. John Hamilton [Reynolds], *The Garden of Florence and Other Poems* (London, 1821), pp. 124–25.

Robin Hood has been destroyed not simply by inevitable historical change, whose brutality Keats again expresses in terms of winter, but also by the state of society:

> Many times have winter's shears,
> Frozen North, and chilling East,
> Sounded tempests to the feast
> Of the forest's whispering fleeces,
> Since men knew nor rent nor leases.
>
> (6–10)

It is this state of society that is hostile to romance, hostile to beauty, hostile to the principle of distinterestedness or benevolence that Robin Hood represents:

> All are gone away and past!
> And if Robin should be cast
> Sudden from his turfed grave,
> And if Marian should have
> Once again her forest days,
> She would weep, and he would craze:
> He would swear, for all his oaks,
> Fall'n beneath the dockyard strokes,
> Have rotted on the briny seas;
> She would weep that her wild bees
> Sang not to her—strange! that honey
> Can't be got without hard money!
>
> (37–48)

The gesture of protest that Keats makes, skeptical here, impassioned in *Isabella,* is interesting but all too easy. It is an invocation of actuality but is not supported by the *knowledge* of actuality that could make it more than a gesture. One of the purposes of the fateful walking tour to the Lake District and Scotland that Keats and Charles Brown undertook in June was to rectify that "inexperience of life, and simplicity of knowledge" that brought Keats to dislike *Isabella.* "I should not have consented to myself these four Months tramping in the highlands," Keats wrote from Scotland, "but that I thought it would give me more experience, rub off more Prejudice, use [me] to more hardship, identify finer scenes load me with grander Mountains, and strengthen more my reach in Poetry, than would stopping at home among Books even though I should reach Homer" (1:342). But this letter, with its renewal of what Keats had said in November about "Heart-vexations,"[21] tells us only part of the story of the Scottish tour. It was written in late July, when unanticipated hardship had become a pressing reality. Still, the Scottish tour was never intended as a holiday for Keats. He always saw it as a step in his intellectual life, in his progress as a poet and as a man, even more important to him than mastery of Homer.[22] To understand Keats' development we must deal with the complex and in the end contradictory motives of this fateful journey.

On the one hand the Scottish tour is a step in that turn toward actuality which is so important to the Keats of 1818, the Keats in full reaction from the excessively mental traveling of *Endymion*. One cannot read Keats' letters from the North, especially the earlier ones, without noting his persistent attempt to submerge himself in reality, to be as intelligently descriptive as possible, and always to test his unavoidable preconceptions against lived experience. "I cannot make my journal as distinct and actual as I could wish," he writes regretfully to Tom, "from having been engaged in writing to George" (1:305). The account he wishes to give requires a creative engagement and would not bear mechan-

21. "A man should have the fine point of his soul taken off to become fit for this world" (1:188), an early expression of the notion of soul-making.

22. "I purpose," he said of the trip in April, ". . . to make a sort of Prologue to the Life I intend to pursue—that is to write, to study and to see all Europe at the lowest expence" (1:264).

ical repetition. The actuality that Keats seeks has two very different faces, one social and human, the other purely natural, and they were not easily to be reconciled. Twenty years later, mingling apology with buoyant self-assurance, Brown himself avowed the contradiction, and supplied his own emphasis:

> We were not bound on a journey of discovery into "the busy haunts of men." Not that cities, their rise, progress, and increasing prosperity, or the reverse, or their prevailing interests and politics, were objects of indifference; but attention to them, and a love of the beauty and sublimity of nature are so widely distinct in character as not to be harmonized together.

They had slighted the temporal world, to gain access to an eternal and unchanging one: "A score of years will scarcely alter the appearance of a woodland scene; and a thousand years cannot affect the imperishable and unchangeable grandeur of mountain, rock, and torrent."[23]

Keats was at moments less content with that "imperishable and unchangeable grandeur." His letters are full of comments on men and manners. He is quick to compare his discoveries with life as he knows it; he is delighted to confirm in his mind the *otherness* of other people. After giving a vivid rendition of a wild Highland fling and comparing it amusingly with English dances he adds: "I was extremely gratified to think, that if I had pleasures they knew nothing of they had also some into which I could not possibly enter." But this awareness of others leads to an upsurge of humanitarian feelings, about "the glory of making by any means a country happier," and then to qualms about the whole trip: "This is what I like better than scenery. I fear our continued moving from place to place, will prevent our becoming learned in

23. Charles Brown, *Walks in the North* (1840), reprinted by Rollins in Keats' *Letters,* 1:422.

village affairs; we are mere creatures of Rivers, Lakes, & mountains" (1:307–8). Keats had had similar misgivings in March amid the natural beauty (but "dwindled" humanity) of Devonshire: "Scenery is fine—but human nature is finer— The Sward is richer for the tread of a real, nervous, english foot—the eagles nest is finer for the Mountaineer has look'd into it" (1:242)—a stupendous rebuke to mere "nature poetry."

In spite of these misgivings, Keats had indeed gone north primarily for the "scenery," fully conscious that the "grandeur of mountain, rock and torrent" was not easily to be harmonized with the life of the cities. As he told Haydon in April, "I will clamber through the Clouds and exist. I will get such an accumulation of stupendous recollections that as I walk through the suburbs of London I may not see them" (1:264). A day later he told Reynolds, with his wonderful combination of enthusiasm and self-irony, that he would "go to gorge wonders" (1:268). Keats is to embark not so much on a quest for actuality as an excursion to the sublime, not on the wings of imagination but in nature itself. Keats seeks the sublime objectified—the "material sublime"—to obliterate an actuality ("the suburbs of London") that he finds alien to the spirit of poetry, and to his own spirit.

The motif of escape is an important one in many of the poems and letters of the trip. Keats and Brown react harshly to every evidence of London influence. In the lines "On Visiting Staffa," Lycidas, the spirit of the place, departs forever because of the fashionable tourists, because "the stupid eye of mortal / Hath pass'd beyond the rocky portal" (45–46). Keats' first journal-letter to Tom, which is partly a manifesto for the whole trip, presses this dichotomy:

> There are many disfigurements to this Lake—not in the way of land or water. No; the two views we have had of it are of the most noble tenderness—they can never fade away

—they make one forget the divisions of life; age, youth, poverty and riches; and refine one's sensual vision into a sort of
north star which can never cease to be open-lidded and stedfast over the wonders of the great Power. The disfigurement
I mean is the miasma of London. . . . The border inhabitants
are quite out of keeping with the romance about them,
from a continual intercourse with London rank and fashion.
(1:299)

Anticipations of the "Bright star" sonnet here are mingled
with echoes of the opening lines of *Endymion;* Keats is returning to the doctrine of those lines, the doctrine of romance.
He finds in Windermere not only an antidote to London but
a refuge from the contingencies of reality. It projects him with
"sweet forgetting" into a world of timelessness, indivisibility,
and permanence. Earlier in the same letter Keats writes:
"June 26—I merely put *pro forma,* for there is no such
thing as time and space, which by the way came forcibly on
me on seeing for the first hour the Lake and Mountains of
Winander" (1:298). People, even Wordsworth, the presiding
spirit, may betray romance,[24] but the lakes and the mountains
are faithful.

Still, in spite of the recurrent antithesis between nature and
London, the tour is an escape not so much from the world
as from the crisis of self-consciousness in which Keats has
been trapped all year, the "Purgatory blind" of the imagination "brought / Beyond its proper bound." The conflict of

24. One of the main purposes of the visit to the Lake District is to
go to Wordsworth's sources, which are by now in Keats' mind identified with the mainsprings of poetry. But Keats finds that Wordsworth
too is quite out of keeping with the romance about him, not so much
because he is out campaigning for a Tory (Brown, in Rollins, *The
Keats Circle,* 2:61), but because he seems less cut off from London and
the world than Keats had imagined: "Lord Wordsworth, instead of
being in retirement, has himself and his house full in the thick of
fashionable visitors quite convenient to be pointed at all summer long"
(*Letters,* 1:299). This is also new evidence of Wordsworth's egotism.

the March epistle between the imagination and personal happiness was still weighing upon Keats in June, less than two weeks before he was to set out for the North. Keats wrote then to Bailey of his new sister-in-law Georgiana:

> To see an entirely disinterrested Girl quite happy is the most pleasant and extraordinary thing in the world—it depends upon a thousand Circumstances—on my word 'tis extraordinary. Women must want Imagination and they may thank God for it—and so m[a]y we that a delicate being can feel happy without any sense of crime. It puzzles me and I have no sort of Logic to comfort me—I shall think it over. (1:293)

"Disinterrested" here means unselfish, aware of others. What that "sense of crime" would be we know from an earlier letter: the self-conscious guilt feelings of one who is sensitive to a world full of heartbreak and misery, and therefore ashamed of his own happiness. "Health and Spirits can only belong unalloyed to the selfish Man—the Man who thinks much of his fellows can never be in Spirits" (1:175). That Georgiana is neither insensitive nor morbidly unhappy strikes Keats as extraordinary. But creatures who so felicitously "want Imagination" are not likely to write great poetry, or to write poetry at all. Keats himself cannot abandon Imagination, but his imagination refuses to abandon reality. He goes north therefore to seek out a different reality, ready made for poetry, less problematic because it is *inherently imaginative*. No interposition of self is necessary.

One use of the tour, as Keats himself avows about one episode, is as a "means of annulling self" (1:323), of resisting the growing dependence of poetry on the self, that is, on the treacherous contingencies of personal identity and free consciousness. That same first letter to Tom concludes on almost a utopian note:

> I shall learn poetry here and shall henceforth write more than ever, for the abstract endeavor of being able to add a

mite to that mass of beauty which is harvested from these grand materials, by the finest spirits, and put into etherial existence for the relish of one's fellows. I cannot think with Hazlitt that these scenes make man appear little. I never forgot my stature so completely—I live in the eye; and my imagination, surpassed, is at rest. (1:301)

For the "finest spirits" these mountains and lakes are Beauty itself. Poems need only be "harvested" from them. Observation alone is necessary; imagination need hardly be brought into play. Reality for once surpasses and suppresses the mind's demands upon it. Man can forget himself, submerge himself in the grandeur of the external world. Wordsworth country would magically liberate Keats from Wordsworth's complex example. As Middleton Murry points out, Keats is echoing the older poet in this letter:[25]

> Beauty—a living presence of the earth,
> Surpassing the most fair ideal Forms
> Which craft of delicate Spirits hath composed
> From earth's materials—waits upon my steps.

But in the same Prospectus to *The Recluse* Wordsworth writes of "the Mind of Man— / My haunt, and the main region of my song." And later:

> Such grateful haunts foregoing, if I oft
> Must turn elsewhere—to travel near the tribes
> And fellowships of men, and see ill sights
> Of madding passions mutually inflamed;
> Must hear Humanity in fields and groves
> Pipe solitary anguish; or must hang
> Brooding above the fierce confederate storm
> Of sorrow, barricadoed evermore
> Within the walls of cities—may these sounds
> Have their authentic comment.[26]

25. *Keats,* p. 287.
26. Wordsworth, "Prospectus" to *The Recluse,* 42–45, 40–41, 72–81.

Keats has not solved the problem which had haunted him for many months—the relation of the imagination to reality. By going north Keats manages to avoid the problem by focusing on a more narrow and limited reality, powerful enough to suppress the darker tendencies of his mind. But the content and tone of this utopian first letter are not repeated either in prose or verse as the tour progresses. Keats begins to find a regular diet of the sublime at once inaccessible and cloying—he cannot continually "gorge wonders." The actual world, not only with its miseries but with its dogged ordinariness reasserts itself. The native skepticism of Keats' temperament reasserts itself. "Sickly imagination and sick pride" reassert themselves. The tour, so clearly intended as a resolution of Keats' crisis, in the end becomes a radical extension of it.

Signs of this counter-movement are in everything Keats writes after the first letter; they appear even in his most trivial and relaxed moments, such as the delightful doggerel letter he sent to his sister:

> There was a naughty Boy,
>   And a naughty Boy was he,
> He ran away to Scotland
>   The people for to see—
>   There he found
>   That the ground
>   Was as hard,
>   That a yard
>   Was as long,
>   That a song
>   Was as merry,
>   That a cherry
>   Was as red—
>   That lead
>   Was as weighty,

That fourscore
Was as eighty,
That a door
Was as wooden
As in England—
So he stood in
His shoes and he wonder'd,
He wonder'd,
He stood in his
Shoes and he wonder'd.
(92–116)

We can only assume that he *did* wonder, a great deal. At the same time he begins to worry, as we noted earlier, that "our continued moving from place to place, will prevent our becoming learned in village affairs. We are mere creatures of Rivers, Lakes, & mountains." He speculates about the Scottish Kirk. The poverty of the cottage weavers sets him thinking about "the dignity of human society."

What a tremendous difficulty is the improvement of the condition of such people—I cannot conceive how a mind 'with child' of Philantrophy would grasp at possibility—with me it is absolute despair. (1:321)

In dealing with the lakes and mountains Keats gradually allows a note of irony to creep in. In a letter to Reynolds he summarizes his trip "in the manner of the Laputan printing press—that is I put down Mountains, Rivers Lakes, dells, glens, Rocks, and Clouds, With beautiful enchanting, gothic picturesque fine, delightful, enchancting, Grand, sublime— a few Blisters &c" (1:322). And to Bailey:

I have been among wilds and mountains too much to break out much about their Grandeur. I have fed upon Oat cake —not long enough to be very much attached to it—the first

> Mountains I saw, though not so large as some I have since
> seen, weighed very solemnly upon me. The effect is wearing
> away—yet I like them mainely. (1:342)

One might say, paradigmatically, that the concern with oatcakes takes its toll upon the interest in mountains. Of course, we should be wary of making too much of this diminution, which is the fate of any tourist as his travels begin to wear on. But not every tourist has made the kind of investment that Keats has. Not every tourist sets out to repair his psyche and restore his creative power, "to make a sort of Prologue to the Life I intend to pursue."

The real crisis, if we may call it that, comes not over blisters or oatcakes or even from the diminishing sublimity of the lakes and mountains. It comes from what turns out to be the central event of the tour, the visit to the main shrines of the poet Burns. If we are right to have described the tour as a quest toward the sources of poetry, we should not be surprised that the search for a poet should occasion the three most revealing poems that Keats writes in the North. The place of Burns in the Romantic pantheon is an important one, as a poet, surely, but also as a saint and martyr to the cause of poetry. Wordsworth, in a moving stanza in "Resolution and Independence," had linked him with Chatterton and concluded,

> By our own spirits are we deified:
> We Poets in our youth begin in gladness;
> But thereof come in the end despondency and madness.
>
> (47–49)

These lines are very much in Keats' mind in the Highlands. The three poems he writes convey a disappointment and despondency that finally approach the fear of madness. The first stage of Keats' crisis appears in a fine poem written early in the tour, the sonnet "On Visiting the Tomb of Burns." It describes a simple and perhaps momentary incapacity of response, in which Keats, however, finds deeper meaning:

> The Town, the churchyard, and the setting sun,
>> The clouds, the trees, the rounded hills all seem,
>> Though beautiful, cold—strange—as in a dream,
> I dreamed long ago, now new begun.
> The short-liv'd, paly Summer is but won
>> From Winter's ague, for one hour's gleam;
>> Though sapphire-warm, their stars do never beam:
> All is cold Beauty; pain is never done:
> For who has mind to relish, Minos-wise,
>> The real of Beauty, free from that dead hue
>>> Sickly imagination and sick pride
>> Cast wan upon it? Burns! with honour due
>> I oft have honour'd thee. Great shadow, hide
> Thy face; I sin against thy native skies.[27]

"This Sonnet," Keats tells Tom in a letter, "I have written in a strange mood, half asleep. I know not how it is, the Clouds, the sky, the Houses, all seem anti Grecian & anti Charlemagnish" (1:309). It is less than a week since the manifesto of the first letter to Tom but the scene and mood have changed. Keats, far from being transported to the sublime, fails to respond to the country around him. It remains "objectively" beautiful, but seems somehow distant, eerie, almost unreal. This the first quatrain tells us. Gradually, this sensation

27. This is the text as emended by Garrod (1958). The original text, obscure and problematic, is no more than a corrupt transcript by Jeffrey. It may be found in *Letters*, 1:308. The poem's text and meaning have been the subject of much controversy. Views other than my own (besides Murry's, which I discuss below) include those of J. C. Maxwell, "Keats's Sonnet on the Tomb of Burns," *Keats-Shelley Journal* 4 (1955): 77–80, and George Yost, Jr., "A Source and Interpretation of Keats's Minos," *Journal of English and Germanic Philology* 57 (1958): 220–29. Professor Bate's brief comment is excellent, *John Keats*, pp. 351–52.

reverberates in the mind of the poet, whose defenses are down, who writes "in a strange mood, half asleep." The scene now suggests to Keats the pallor of the whole Northern summer, utterly unlike the warm South that so attracts his imagination, offering only a brief and pitiful respite from the harshness of winter.[28]

But the mention of "Winter's ague"—even if we recall the previous symbolic urgency of the seasons—does little to prepare us for what Middleton Murry calls the "strange and unexpected vehemence" of the eighth line.[29] "All is cold Beauty" summarizes and generalizes what has come earlier; but "pain is never done" makes a remarkable leap. Keats had begun with only a failure of response. The town, the churchyard, and the sun merely "seem" cold. But now "all *is* cold Beauty": the deficiency is in the world as well as in himself, and not in this scene alone but in "all" such beauty. Suddenly this failure of beauty provokes Keats to think of its obverse: the universality of pain. In the central lines that follow Keats recoils from this imaginative leap and grudgingly confirms and explains it. His retreat is most evident in the honorific phrase "the real of Beauty," what Keats in the "Epistle to Reynolds" had called the "material sublime," objective beauty uncolored by the darker hues of self-consciousness, or by tragic speculation. In his first letter to Tom he had boasted of finding at last that elusive beauty, with power to "make one forget the divisions of life; age, youth, poverty and riches," to submerge the self into sheer observation: "I live in the eye; and my imagination, surpassed, is at rest."

Now, so soon afterward, in this sonnet, such "real" beauty palls, becomes a dream: "sickly imagination" (the awareness of pain) and "sick pride" (the sense of self) revive, and Keats once more is the Hamlet who had so weighed on his mind

28. Bate, p. 352.
29. Murry, " 'The Feel of *Not* to Feel It,' " in *Keats*, p. 200.

during the spring, whose "native hue of resolution" had been "sicklied o'er with the pale cast of thought" (*Hamlet,* III, i, 84–85). As in the Nile sonnet and the "Epistle to Reynolds" he turns upon himself in anger for spoiling his own happiness, struggling to confine the evil to the self rather than the world, to ascribe it wholly to his own "dark fancies." This is the turn that Middleton Murry describes but misinterprets in his otherwise fine essay on the poem. "Keats very clearly recognizes," he says of these central lines, "that the apparent defect of the object is a deficiency in his own power of response. There is, he says, 'a Real of Beauty,' independent of his momentary capacity of response, though he wonders, and very justly, who among mortal men has power of mind enough to overcome a momentary incapacity such as his. . . . It is the pride of a preconceived imagination, and it is sick, because it fails to make the 'self-destroying' surrender to the thing that is."[30] This is a Murry who, with un-Keatsian inclinations to mysticism, must overemphasize the self-annihilating empathy that is present but not pervasive in Keats' conception of the poet. This is the Murry who, for all his sensitivity to the troubled and darker side of Keats, insists that "the lore of good and ill" in the "Epistle to Reynolds" must surely be "the *love* of good and ill" (Houghton's reading), for "there is a point of vision to be attained whence the chaos and contradiction of the world can be seen as a harmony and loved as a harmony."[31]

For Murry (as for only one side of Keats) there is indeed a "Real" of Beauty that transcends our feelings and perceptions, that requires that we override all contingency and surrender our subjectivity to "the thing that is." Thus, despite his usually scrupulous sense of the text, he misses the crucial

30. Ibid., p. 206.

31. John Middleton Murry, *Keats and Shakespeare: A Study of Keats' Poetic Life from 1816 to 1820* (London, 1925), p. 66.

word "relish," which expresses Keats' qualms and enables these central lines to cut, perhaps confusedly, both ways. Which of us, if he is to remain human, Keats asks, can be as disinterested as Minos, the severe judge of the underworld? Which of us, he adds, could *enjoy* such disinterestedness, could relish beauty objectively, living entirely in the eye, with the troubled mind at rest? Such enjoyment, attractive as it is, is not only difficult but a shade immoral. ("Health and spirits can belong unalloyed only to the Selfish Man—the Man who thinks much of his fellows can never be in Spirits.") But Keats has come to pay homage to Burns' "native skies," and he feels he has offended against them with his misgivings. He apologizes but does not try, as in the Nile sonnet, to restore the facade of an unspoiled, preconscious nature.

The second and in some ways more grave episode of the Burns affair occurs over a week later. This time the shrine is Burns' cottage. The first part of the following letter to Reynolds was written as Keats and Brown (who "have made continual enquiries from the time we saw his tomb at Dumfries") are approaching the house:

> One of the pleasantest means of annulling self is approaching such a shrine as the Cottage of Burns—we need not think of his misery—that is all gone—bad luck to it—I shall look upon it hereafter with unmixed pleasure as I do upon my Stratford on Avon day with Bailey. (1:323)

But there turns out to be a man at the cottage who knew Burns and who participated in—who for Keats symbolizes—his misery. Later in the same letter, but after the visit, Keats writes:

> We went to the Cottage and took some Whiskey—I wrote a sonnet for the mere sake of writing some lines under the roof —they are so bad I cannot transcribe them—The Man at the Cottage was a great Bore with his Anecdotes—I hate the rascal. . . . O the flummery of a birth place! Cant! Cant!

Cant! It is enough to give a spirit the guts-ache—Many a true word they say is spoken in jest—this may be because his gab hindered my sublimity.—The flat dog made me write a flat sonnet—My dear Reynolds—I cannot write about scenery and visitings. . . . One song of Burns's is of more worth to you than all I could think for a whole year in his native country—His misery is a dead weight upon the nimbleness of one's quill—I tried to forget it—to drink Toddy without any Care—to write a merry Sonnet—it wont do—he talked with Bitches—he drank with Blackguards, he was miserable—We can see horribly clear in the works of such a man his whole life, as if we were God's spies. (1:324–25)

The chasm between the two parts of this letter epitomizes the reversal that Keats undergoes during the whole trip. Keats crystallizes the experience, not without self-irony, in the report that "his gab hindered my sublimity." Keats approaches the Burns shrine as he approaches the lakes and mountains, to annul self, to be tranported to the sublime, there effortlessly to harvest great verse. Keats' desire to write a sonnet in the cottage is symbolic, and his failure is no less significant. (He even goes to the length of destroying it, though not before Brown makes a copy.)[32] The actual world, with all its coarse triviality ("his gab"), with its depressing dead weight (Burns' misery), takes its revenge upon him. He has come to the shrines not to learn about the "real" Burns, but to use Burns as high inspiration. He is instead assaulted with a miserable life.

Two more details are clear. One is Keats' sense of *disappointment* with Burns, almost a feeling of personal betrayal. The other is, paradoxically, Keats' growing identification with Burns, which includes a painful foreboding that he may disappoint himself in the same way. Miss Ward, in discussing the sonnet Keats wrote in the cottage, stresses this identification but weakens her argument by an excessively literal read-

32. *Letters*, 1:343.

ing of the poem (claiming that Keats anticipates his own
death within "a thousand days").[33] Actually, Burns' early
death is only one of the ways in which he disappoints Keats.
In the poem, failure to live is intimately connected with
failure in poetry.

> This mortal body of a thousand days
>   Now fills, O Burns, a space in thine own room,
>   Where thou didst dream alone on budded bays,
>   Happy and thoughtless of thy day of doom!
>
> (1–4)

For a moment, Keats was able to put Burns' misery out of his
head: he nostalgically transforms him into a mythicized version of his own younger self, a happy, thoughtless innocent,
dreaming of the laurels of Apollo. Keats' sense of failure is
not so much a foreboding of death as a sense of the impossibility of recapturing one's innocence, of annulling the self and
restoring that paradise that preceded the *consciousness* of
death. This feeling triggers a small crisis; it cheats Keats of
his simple afflatus and makes impossible the sort of poem he
had intended. The sonnet is really about Keats' inability to
get a sonnet written. Like the sonnet at Burns' tomb, it is
about the failure of the poetic imagination.[34]

> My pulse is warm with thine old Barley-bree
>   My head is light with pledging a great soul,
>   My eyes are wandering, and I cannot see,
>   Fancy is dead and drunken at its goal;
>
> (5–8)

Attempting to recapture Burns' joy, his creative afflatus,
Keats, instead reenacts Burns' failure as a man and a poet.

33. *John Keats: Making of a Poet*, pp. 199–201.
34. The seriousness of this failure is clear when we compare the
poem to an early version of the same theme, such as the sonnet "On Receiving a Laurel Crown from Leigh Hunt."

Burns' joy and degradation come together in his beloved Scotch "toddy," and not the least of the ironies of this "shrine" is that Burns' cottage has been turned into a whiskey-shop, presided over by one of his drinking companions. "Poor unfortunate fellow," Keats had written a few days earlier, "his disposition was southern—how sad it is when a luxurious imagination is obliged in self defence to deaden its delicacy in vulgarity, and riot in things attainable that it may not have leisure to go mad after things which are not" (1:319–20). Burns' rioting "in things attainable" refers, I think, to the limitations of Burns' art as well as the "misery" and degradation of his life. Burns' songs, though fine, do not stand high on Keats' scale of imaginative values. Keats is surprised at the beauty of the countryside, and after describing some of the rich views he adds, "as soon as I saw them so nearly I said to myself 'How is it they did not beckon Burns to some grand attempt at Epic' " (1:331). Clearly Keats hopes that the richness of this "material sublime" will beckon him to such an attempt. (*Hyperion* had long been on his mind.) Instead he finds that it can no more transform Keats than it could inspire Burns: "I endeavour'd to drink in the Prospect, that I might spin it out to you as the silkworm makes silk from Mulberry leaves—I cannot recollect it" (1:323).

A similar reenactment of the failure of Burns occurs in the poem. Keats drinks toddy in order to approximate Burns' spirit. Instead he reenacts Burns' misery. "Fancy is dead and drunken at its goal," dead as Burns is, drunk as Burns so often was. So Keats must settle for what he had hoped at all cost to avoid: an approximation not of Burns' spirit but of the actual Burns, the Burns who lived in this cottage:

> Yet can I stamp my foot upon thy floor,
>   Yet can I ope thy window-sash to find
> The meadow thou hast tramped o'er and o'er,—
>   Yet can I think of thee till thought is blind,—

> Yet can I gulp a bumper to thy name,—
> O smile among the shades, for this is fame!
>
> (9–14)

The final episode in the Burns affair, and indeed the final document in the long crisis that Keats has suffered since the previous winter, is a strange and haunted poem quite unlike anything else that Keats wrote.[35] It responds to no particular event, but seems more of a reflection on the whole enterprise of the tour, with its promised joys and unexpected torment. Brown tells us that the "Lines Written in the Highlands after a Visit to Burns's Country" was composed by Keats with more than usual care,[36] yet to the reader it must seem, even more so than the sonnet at Burns' tomb, to have been "written in a strange mood, half asleep."[37] The poem begins, rather artificially, with a description of the quest:

> There is a charm in footing slow across a silent plain,
> Where patriot battle has been fought, when glory
>   had the gain;
> There is a pleasure on the heath where Druids old
>   have been,
> Where mantles grey have rustled by and swept the
>   nettles green;
> There is a joy in every spot made known by times
>   of old,
> New to the feet, although each tale a hundred times
>   be told.

35. "In some of the lines expressing these obscure disturbances of the soul there is a deep smouldering fire, but hardly ever that touch of absolute felicity which is the note of Keats's work when he is quite himself." Colvin, *John Keats: Life . . . and After-Fame*, p. 286.

36. Rollins, *The Keats Circle*, 2:64.

37. The best commentary on the poem is by Caldwell, *John Keats' Fancy*, pp. 38–47. Because of his primary interest in the processes of reverie and association in Keats, he deals particularly with the mood in which the poem seems to have been written.

Keats describes a quest first for the sources of history, then those of prehistory and myth. By seeking out these scenes for ourselves we may have the pleasure of recapturing the past, a past deadened not only by distance but by the inadequacy of historical language. But a deeper and more ambiguous experience awaits the traveler who quests for the sources of poetry:

> There is a deeper joy than all, more solemn in the heart,
> More parching to the tongue than all, of more divine
>   a smart,
> When weary steps forget themselves upon a pleasant turf,
> Upon hot sand, or flinty road, or sea-shore iron scurf,
> Toward the castle or the cot, where long ago was born
> One who was great through mortal days, and died of
>   fame unshorn.
>
> (7–12)

The surest sign that this is a deeper pleasure, Keats indicates confidently, is that it provides a mixture of pain and pleasure, a combination which for Keats signifies an experience of greater intensity, great enough in this case to provide the best pleasure of all, that of self-forgetfulness. Keats seems at last, if only briefly, to have divested himself of "sickly imagination and sick pride," to have forgotten Burns' misery and lost himself in his greatness.

> Light heather-bells may tremble then, but they are
>   far away;
> Wood-lark may sing from sandy fern,—the Sun may
>   hear his lay;
> Runnels may kiss the grass on shelves and shallows
>   clear,
> But their low voices are not heard, though come on
>   travels drear;
> Blood-red the sun may set behind black mountain peaks;
> Blue tides may sluice and drench their time in caves
>   and weedy creeks;

Eagles may seem to sleep wing-wide upon the air;
Ring-doves may fly convuls'd across to some
    high-cedar'd lair;
But the forgotten eye is still fast lidded to the ground,
As Palmer's, that with weariness, mid-desert shrine
    hath found.

(13–22)

The traveler leaves the actual world of nature, with its delicate harmonies, far behind. The wood-lark sings to the sun, the runnels kiss the grass, all to no avail. At this point a remarkable and eerie transformation occurs. Nature, as if responding darkly to the traveler's rejection, turns fierce and demonic. The sun sets "blood-red" behind the black peaks, the tides seem to batter against the prison walls of their channels, the ring-doves fly "convuls'd" through the air. But the traveler is no more conscious of the dark side of what Keats later calls "the sweet and bitter world" than he is of the bright. He is a pilgrim, living entirely in some region of the spirit, aware only of the shrine he seeks, a shrine of the poetic imagination.

Keats' reference here may be to Spenser's Palmer, who steers Guyon safely through the worldly temptations of the Bower of Bliss and finally enables him to destroy the Bower. "There is no such thing as time and space," Keats had written excitedly at the beginning of his first letter from the North. Now, when that destruction of time and space seems a reality, Keats imperceptibly begins to turn upon himself. The poet who had always read Spenser in his diabolic sense, who had always luxuriated in Spenser's bowers, finds himself transformed into the Palmer. The traveler who had hoped to "refine one's sensual vision into a sort of north star which can never cease to be open lidded and stedfast" (1:299) now finds his "forgotten eye . . . fast lidded to the ground."

In the two crucial lines that follow, the poet triumphantly completes his escape from the world and at the same time begins to withdraw his sympathy from that escape:

At such a time the soul's a child, in childhood is the brain;
Forgotten is the worldly heart—alone, it beats in vain.—
                                        (23–24)

The traveler recaptures his lost innocence, but only at the cost
of regressing to the "infant or thoughtless Chamber" of
human life. He repeals the fall into consciousness, yet thereby
loses his hold on reality, in a way that will shortly suggest
madness. The shift is a gradual one. "The soul's a child" is
strengthened, perhaps unconsciously, by a background of
positive Christian associations; but "in childhood is the
brain," though meaning much the same thing, adds a dark
overtone of idiocy. With the evocation of "the worldly heart,"
beating plaintively "in vain" for the poet who has rejected it,
both Keats' perspective and his sympathy shift away from the
quest and toward that of the world. By the next lines the turn
is complete and the analogy of madness has already established itself. The quest becomes a forbidden and dangerous
one:

Aye, if a madman could have leave to pass a healthful day
To tell his forehead's swoon and faint when first began
      decay,
He might make tremble many a one whose spirit had
      gone forth
To find a Bard's low cradle-place about the silent
      North!
Scanty the hour and few the steps beyond the bourn
      of care,
Beyond the sweet and bitter world,—beyond it unaware!
Scanty the hour and few the steps, because a longer
      stay
Would bar return, and make a man forget his mortal way.
                                        (25–32)

In the two earlier Burns poems the attempt to annul self
fails because of the interposition of actuality and self-consciousness. Here the danger is that it will succeed all too well,

that the poet will indeed manage "to burst his mortal bars"
and lose himself beyond the pale of humanity and nature.
The frightening thought recalls the lines to Apollo that Keats
had written in January:

> Aye, when the soul is fled
> To high above our head,
> Affrighted do we gaze
> After its airy maze
>
> . . . .
> And is not this the cause
> Of madness?
>
> (9–12, 16–17)

We need not think that Keats was in genuine danger of losing
his mind that day in the Highlands, but he may for a moment
have felt that "wind from the wing of madness" that once
would pass prophetically over Baudelaire:

> In my moral self as in my physical self I have always had
> the sensation of an abyss, not only an abyss of sleep, but an
> abyss of action, of dreams, of memories, desires, regrets, re-
> morse, beauty, numbers, etc.
>
> I have cultivated my hysteria with pleasure and terror.
> Now, I am always dizzy, and today, January 23, 1862, I felt a
> strange warning. I felt a wind from the wing of madness
> passing over me.
>
> (*Mon coeur mis à nu*)[38]

A great distance, both in personality and of cultural history,
lies between these two poets, but not so great as our modern
critical consensus would indicate. In justifiable reaction to the
sickly and decadent nineteenth-century Keats, we have created a Keats who would yield to few poets in health and

38. Charles Baudelaire, *Flowers of Evil and Other Works (Les
fleurs du mal et oeuvres choisies)*, ed. and trans. Wallace Fowlie (New
York: Bantam Dual-Language Series, 1964), pp. 262, 263. I have
slightly modified Fowlie's translation.

stability. There is much truth, but also a great measure of critical redress, in Lionel Trilling's description of him as "the last image of health at the very moment when the sickness of Europe began to be apparent."[39] That health was won—it was earned—through a fierce inner struggle. He carried within him, if not a true capacity for madness, then certainly the sensation of an abyss. The lines that follow do little more than underline the intensity of that sensation:

> O horrible! to lose the sight of well remember'd
>   face,
> Of Brother's eyes, of Sister's brow—constant to
>   every place;
> Filling the air, as on we move, with portraiture
>   intense;
> More warm than those heroic tints that pain a
>   painter's sense,
> When shapes of old come striding by, and visages
>   of old,
> Locks shining black, hair scanty grey, and passions
>   manifold.
>
>   (33–38)

This is not too clear. Keats seems to be specifying the madness to which he refers as a madness of the imagination, of the shaping spirit lost in its own visionary creations. The visions are simultaneously warm and painful; they at once enable him to capture the past and yet at the same time could involve him, like Faust, with the grotesque and the forbidden. These lines seem to refer back to the beginning of the poem, where Keats had described the quest to the sources of history and myth, materials that will be essential if Keats feels beckoned, as he does, to a grand attempt at epic. Keats is returning to actuality, but without renouncing the ambitions of the imagi-

39. *The Opposing Self*, p. 49.

nation. He is safe after all, but will venture out again. This is
the meaning of the poem's disappointing and not very assured
conclusion:

> No, no that horror cannot be, for at the cable's length
> Man feels the gentle anchor pull and gladdens in its
>   strength:—
> One hour, half-idiot, he stands by mossy waterfall,
> But in the very next he reads his soul's memorial:—
> He reads it on the mountain's height, where chance
>   he may sit down
> Upon rough marble diadem—that hill's eternal crown.
> Yet be his anchor e'er so fast, room is there for a
>   prayer
> That man may never lose his mind on mountains
>   black and bare;
> That he may stray league after league some great
>   birthplace to find
> And keep his vision clear from speck, his inward
>   sight unblind.

(39–48)

This gesture of restraint upon the imagination, involving a
return to the reality of human life, is somewhat parallel to the
one that Wordsworth makes at a terrible moment in "Peele
Castle": "I have submitted to a new control. . . . A deep distress
hath humanised my Soul" (34, 36). But the control to which
Wordsworth submits is terminal and unalterable. For him
"A power is gone, which nothing can restore" (35). The wayward imagination could never again stray at its own sweet
will. It must submit to a new, stoic poetry of tragedy and
suffering, a poetry that Wordsworth's temperament proved
unable to realize. The anchor pull of reality in which Keats
gladdens is not nearly so constraining. It is a slack cable that
will allow him to continue to stray. Keats will not simply
settle, like Burns, for "things attainable" in order "not to go

mad after things which are not." He will continue to quest for those symbolic sources of poetry and vision, the mountains and the birthplace of poets, but without forgetting what Endymion calls "the tie / Of mortals each to each" (IV, 640–41). I would not say that Keats has resolved the problem of the relation of the imagination to reality that has been tormenting him since his work on the fourth book of *Endymion*. His use of "Brother's eyes" and "Sister's brow" to embody actuality shows that he has not, for they but represent the ordinary world as it preexists imagination. They do not imply any mode by which the imagination can work creatively on actuality; they merely assert the constraint of the workaday world upon excessive imaginative flight. But the poem shows that Keats is willing to recall himself to the resolution of the *Lear* sonnet, to remember his "mortal way" by groping with the painful complexities of a "sweet and bitter world."

The clearest evidence that Keats had yet to resolve his crisis is the poem that occupied him all fall. A full critical account of *Hyperion* would be out of place here, but that poem—or at least the first two books of it, for the fragmentary third book is a later and different thing—must be seen as the aftermath of the agonies over self-consciousness and actuality that Keats was suffering. Long ago Middleton Murry, without trying to diminish the beauties of *Hyperion,* brilliantly combined biography with criticism to show that the poem was something of a detour in Keats' development. Keats returned from Scotland in August to find that Tom had just taken a turn for the worse, and for four months he had to watch the boy "with an exquisite love of Life" die. "I wish I could say Tom was any better," writes Keats to Dilke near the end of September. "His identity presses upon me so all day that I am obliged to go out—and although I intended to have given some time to study alone I am obliged to write, and plunge into abstract images to ease myself of his countenance, his

voice and feebleness" (1:369). The actuality and misery of
Burns has been replaced by a more immediate and pressing
pain. "He was seeking," says Murry, "an asylum of refuge
from the pains of life in a world of abstract poetic creation."[40]
This, along with a genuine nostalgia for the largeness and
objectivity of epic, are at the root of the poem's famous impersonality, which Keats would boldly seek to eliminate in
the revised version by transposing the whole poem into the
first person.

But Murry did not appreciate the extent to which Keats'
motives in the first two books of *Hyperion* are mixed and
even contradictory. There is a tension between the abstract-
ness and impersonality of the form and the actuality of the
content. Keats is trying for the first time to deal on a large
scale with "the agonies, the strife / Of human hearts." The
fallen Titans have experienced a paradoxical humanization,
made all the more intense by novelty and heightened by the
grandness of Keats' technique. In the face of Saturn, Thea
sees

> direst strife; the supreme God
> At war with all the frailty of grief,
> Of rage, of fear, anxiety, revenge,
> Remorse, spleen, hope, but most of all despair.
> Against these plagues he strove in vain; for Fate
> Had pour'd a mortal oil upon his head,
> A disanointing poison.
>
> (II, 92–98)

Simply to name these emotions, however—and label them
baldly as "plagues"—is not to render them. Keats' narrative
distance leaves the action itself abstract. In most of *Hyperion*
Keats aims to present not emotions so much as the essence of
emotions, not the suffering of the Titans so much as the

40. *Keats and Shakespeare,* p. 83. See also pp. 70–71.

heightened essence of that suffering. This is consistent with Keats' theory, by which the "disagreeables evaporate" and "end in speculation," but it does not result in a rendering of reality. The opening scene of stillness and sadness is too much the epitome of stillness and sadness to allow "the true voice of feeling" to be heard.[41] The intensity which Keats seeks, by which he tries to unite epic largeness with the pains of real experience, too often devolves into something at once ineffectual and grotesquely excessive. Near the beginning of Book II we see the Titans

> pent in regions of laborious breath;
> Dungeon'd in opaque element, to keep
> Their clenched teeth still clench'd, and all their limbs
> Lock'd up like veins of metal, crampt and screw'd;
> Without a motion, save of their big hearts
> Heaving in pain, and horribly convuls'd
> With sanguine feverous boiling gurge of pulse.
>
> (II, 22–28)

What this verse has it owes to Milton; for what it lacks Keats alone is responsible. Despite Milton's transfiguring presence, there is much genuine Keats in the poem, to the point of anachronism. The Titans, for example, are repeatedly described as having fallen from the unmistakable old bower world of the early Keats. Hyperion asks,

> "Am I to leave this haven of my rest,
> This cradle of my glory, this soft clime,
> This calm luxuriance of blissful light,
> These crystalline pavilions, and pure fanes,
> Of all my lucent empire? . . ."
>
> (I, 235–39)

41. See Keats' own well-known explanation for abandoning the poem. *Letters*, 2:167.

Keats, like his Titans, has passed beyond the realm of Flora and old Pan, but he has yet to learn to deal with "the agonies, the strife / Of human hearts." That will require what he finds in Wordsworth but still hesitates to undertake on his own: genuine self-confrontation. As Shakespeare's Isabella tells Angelo, speaking the moral of *Measure for Measure,*

> Go to your bosom,
> Knock there, and ask your heart what it doth know....
> (II, ii, 136–37)

5

The Fierce Dispute:
The Odes

> Self-consciousness, that dæmon of
> the men of genius of our time, from
> Wordsworth to Byron, from Goethe
> to Chateaubriand, and to which this
> age owes so much both of its cheer-
> ful and its mournful wisdom. . . .
>
> John Stuart Mill, 1838

KEATS' own dissatisfaction with the sonorous and impersonal manner of the first two books of *Hyperion* becomes clear in the way he abandons it in the first few months of 1819— tentatively in the third book, wholeheartedly in the remarkable style, at once lush and quasi-ironic, of *The Eve of St. Agnes*. But only in the odes of that spring is Keats at last reconciled to the subject which history demanded of him and for which his maturing sensibility had prepared him. He turns inward like Wordsworth and writes of the growth of a poet's mind. This had emerged as his subject with Apollo in *Hyperion,* and had been the covert theme of *Endymion* as well; but the subjectivity of the quest romance of *Endymion* is different from the self-consciousness that defines the movement of the odes. For the early Keats, though prereflective wholeness and pastoral innocence cannot be permanently recaptured, though the fall into consciousness cannot be undone, the poet's quest is not so much inward as upward. The poet receives "shapes from the invisible world, unearthly singing / From out the middle air" and thereby seeks to "burst our mortal bars." Nothing could be more alien to such a quest than the real, the human self of the poet, which must be annihilated by rich entanglements and "self-destroying" enthralments, "till we shine, / Full alchemiz'd, and free of space."

The Keats of the odes is a different poet. These poems explore motifs of escape and transcendence ultimately to overcome them; they are built on a conception of the imagination which is dialectical and tragic rather than escapist. We have seen many anticipations of this change as far back as "Sleep and Poetry" and *Endymion*. The most important hints, in the months immediately preceding the odes, are the metamorphosis of Apollo in the third book of *Hyperion* and the dialectical patterns that qualify the romance action of *The Eve of St. Agnes*. The sensuous Apollo must die into life, must be convulsed by "knowledge enormous," as the "creations and destroyings" of human history are proved upon his pulses. Conversely, the lovers in *The Eve of St. Agnes*, surrounded by darkness and decay, by false music and false joy, their very motives hedged by the poet's near ironies, can only escape into myth and legend. They free themselves of those dark environs only by becoming the gliding "phantoms" of "ages long ago."

But both these poems, though tragic in some of their implications, though decisive in their abandonment of the pseudo-epic mode of the first two books of *Hyperion*, remain somehow tentative and impersonal even in their new subjectivity. After the odes Keats would recast them. In *The Fall of Hyperion* the poet himself would take the place of Apollo, to undergo a far more sombre ordeal of humanization rather than deification. And Keats would come to convict *The Eve of St. Agnes* of some of the sentimentality he also found in *Isabella* (*Letters*, 2:174). In *Lamia*, his last important romance, the lovers would not escape, and the ironies would be more blatant; Keats would make certain that his readers "would look to the reality."

All this happened later, in the summer and fall of 1819. The odes of April and May are the first poems in which Keats fully acts upon the mission to which he had consecrated himself in the sonnet on *Lear;* to put aside romance and "burn through" the "fierce dispute / Betwixt damnation and impassion'd clay." In these poems Keats manages for the first time to be both tragic and personal, though the personal content is mediated by symbolism and the tragic conflicts lead toward self-renewal rather than extinction. This too is in line with the *Lear* sonnet, which concludes with an image of the Phoenix:

> But when I am consumed in the fire,
> Give me new Phoenix wings to fly at my desire.

Tragedy is a purgatorial forge, a process of self-definition and self-creation—what Keats himself, shortly before undertaking the odes, calls "Soul-making."

The passage where Keats uses that term provides us with instructive evidence of the remarkable change that has taken place in the poet. It is also something of a prose prologue to the odes. Written on April 21 and included in a long journal-letter to George and Georgiana Keats, it begins with an attack on the idea of "perfectability":

> The nature of the world will not admit of it—the inhabitants of the world will correspond to itself—Let the fish philosophise the ice away from the Rivers in winter time and they shall be at continual play in the tepid delight of summer. (2:101)

We should not be too quick to identify the "philosophy" Keats jests at solely with Godwinism. The possibility of perpetual delight, an immortality of passion, had also been one of the mainsprings of the philosophy of *Endymion,* especially in the central passage on happiness. Keats here is renouncing his own notion of perfectability, which aims at a static "fellowship with essence" in "love's elysium." Nor will self-pity cause him to idealize and envy the natural process, which he now finds vulnerable to the ravages of mutability and circumstance, like human life:

> The point at which Man may arrive is as far as the paralel state in inanimate nature and no further—For instance suppose a rose to have sensation, it blooms on a beautiful morning it enjoys itself—but there comes a cold wind, a hot sun—it can not escape it, it cannot destroy its annoyances—they are as native to the world as itself: no more can man be happy in spite, the world[l]y elements will prey upon his nature. (2:101)

Keats does not therefore conclude that man and nature are fallen. His critique of "perfectability" is very different from the Christian one, as he immediately emphasizes. To the Christian this world "is 'a vale of tears' from which we are to be redeemed by a certain arbitrary interposition of God and taken to Heaven," but for Keats, as for the writer of tragedy, the process of salvation is an immanent one: "Call the world if you Please 'the vale of Soul-making'. . . . Do you not see how necessary a World of Pains and troubles is to school an Intelligence and make it a soul? A Place where the heart must feel and suffer in a thousand diverse ways!" These intelligences do not become souls "till they acquire identities, till each one is personally itself," which cannot occur "but in a world of Circumstances." The positive emphasis on personal identity is as crucial as the stern stress on the buffeting realities of the world. Keats is retracting the longing for self-annihilation that is central not only to the metaphysic of the early poems but to the aesthetic of his anti-Wordsworthian letter to Woodhouse on "the poetical Character" (27 October 1818).

Yet the odes themselves, for all their ultimate confirmation of this notion of soul-making, are far in mood from the assured, playfully dogmatic tone of this letter. The Keats of the poems is not out to make a "sketch of a system of Salvation." He is a living subject, full of contradictory desires, enacting rather than describing, risking his soul without any assurance of saving it. The "World of Pains and troubles," seen from within, looks gratuitous rather than necessary, a world "where youth grows pale, and spectre-thin, and dies." Similarly, though the final burden of the odes is to confirm Keats' commitment to a widening of consciousness, the poems do so only through a dialectical process that gives full expression to the pains of consciousness and his resistance to its claims. The poet of the "Ode to a Nightingale" has not ceased to long for the "sweet forgetting" of nature or the "forgetfulness divine," only recently invoked, of sleep. To him this remains a world "where but to think is to be full of sorrow / And leaden-eyed despairs." The nightingale and the Grecian urn are powerful new incarnations of the "material sublime" by which Keats, in the "Epistle to Reynolds," had hoped that consciousness might be kept within "its proper bound." Each of these symbols is "a friend to man" partly out of its ability to "tease us out of thought." Harold Bloom has written that "all Romantic horrors are diseases of excessive consciousness, of the self unable to bear the self." But the Romantics, unlike many later writers, did not rest in the evocation of this distinctively modern crisis. Part of the distance between them and our own writers is the counterblow which they struck against the paralyzing self-consciousness to which they were victim and witness. Bloom formulates it in this way: "A Romantic poet fought against self-consciousness through the strength of what he called imagination, a more than rational energy, by which thought could seek to heal itself."[1] Yet for the best of

1. Harold Bloom, "Frankenstein, or the New Prometheus," *Partisan Review* 32 (Fall 1965): 617.

the Romantics there was usually another step, a finer subjectivity, a proving of imagination by a scrupulous standard
of personal authenticity, and a respect for the sheer resistance
of reality to human will. The imagination could be a balm
that would too readily assuage the pains of thought, a deceiving anodyne that would anaesthetize the wound without
healing it. The first stanza of the "Ode on Melancholy" is a
warning against narcosis,

> For shade to shade will come too drowsily,
> And drown the wakeful anguish of the soul.

Yet this possibility of a heightened consciousness is a function
of the importance of imagination in the Romantic period.
Through imagination the poet becomes a creator, a lawgiver,
a god; yet by virtue of that largeness of vision he sees all the
more acutely that he is a mortal man.² Like Shakespeare's
Troilus he learns "that the will is infinite and the execution
confined, that the desire is boundless and the act a slave to
limit."³ The self-consciousness of the Romantic poet is an
inescapably double consciousness, although this assumes
many different forms. In Wordsworth this double consciousness is most often expressed through temporal juxtapositions.
His retrospective imagination is pervaded by a sense of loss,
yet it resists nostalgia, refuses to surrender itself to the past.
Instead it confronts the past from the pointed perspective of
the present, thus asserting the reality of growth and change
while keeping touch, movingly yet ambiguously, with its

2. Against Erich Heller, who accuses the Romantics of the sin of
intellectual pride and willful self-assertion, Paul de Man aptly stresses
"the great negative themes of the Romantics—the forces beyond our
power that threaten the self, . . . the themes of mutability, of time, and
of death." Review of Erich Heller, *The Artist's Journey into the Interior and Other Essays* (New York, 1965), in *The New York Review
of Books,* 23 June 1966, p. 19.

3. *Troilus and Cressida,* III, ii, 88–90.

own vital prereflective sources. In the odes Keats created a perfect form to express the doubleness of his own consciousness.

The most prominent structural feature of the odes, aside from the new stanza Keats developed, is the central symbol, which speaks for a part of the poet and provokes him dramatically into dialogue with himself. Some critics have, I think rightly, detected a certain willfulness in the manipulation of these symbols and the meanings attributed to them. Bridges' literal-minded quibble about the mortality of nightingales is well known. Allen Tate, though more responsive to Keats' symbolic intention, feels a similar uneasiness: "the bird, as bird, shares the mortality of the world; as symbol it purports to transcend it. . . . Keats merely *asserts:* song equals immortality; and I feel there is some disparity between the symbol and what it is expected to convey."[4] In a different vein D. H. Lawrence—in one of those revealing encounters in which one artist, intent on a comprehensive vision of his own, remains brilliantly insensitive to the work of another—even accuses Keats of misrepresenting the song of the bird. (Lawrence had an exact precedent in Coleridge, who, in "The Nightingale," had playfully attacked Milton for describing the bird as melancholy, hence spoiling nature with his own moods.)[5] "The nightingale," says Lawrence, "never made any man in love with easeful death, except by contrast." Yet contrast is precisely the point, as Lawrence himself goes on to indicate when he compares "the bright flame of positive pure self-aliveness, in the bird, and the uneasy flickering of yearn-

4. Robert Bridges, "A Critical Introduction to Keats," in *Collected Essays,* vol. 4 (London, 1929), p. 130. Allen Tate, "A Reading of Keats," in *On the Limits of Poetry: Selected Essays, 1928–1948* (New York, 1948), p. 172.

5. See Finney's useful summary of poetic representations of the nightingale from the medieval period to the Romantics. *The Evolution of Keats's Poetry,* 2:621–23.

ing selflessness, for ever yearning for something outside of himself, which is Keats."[6] Clearly Lawrence is intent not so much on restoring the "real" bird as in turning it (and turning the poet as well) from a Keatsian to a Laurentian symbol. Lawrence would have the poet emulate and be content with "the bright flame of positive pure self-aliveness" of the bird, but Keats' poem is built not on a singleness but on a division of purpose. Though Keats did write, as Brown tells us, in response to the singing of an actual bird, the poem can hardly be said to offer merely "his poetic feelings on the song of our nightingale."[7] The nightingale is manipulated willfully because it is a symbolic projection of his own mind, an externalization against which another part of his mind can locate itself. This is as true of the "Ode on a Grecian Urn" as of the "Ode to a Nightingale." The critical distinction which terms the former "objective" and "classical" and the latter "subjective" and "romantic" reveals an impoverished sense of Romanticism, and is inaccurate.[8] The movement of the Urn ode, despite the apparent absence of a first-person narrator, is, as Professor Wasserman has shown, not intelligible as description but only as a series of movements within a single (though divided) consciousness.[9]

The main weakness of the "Ode to Psyche," the first of the spring odes, is that it has only a rudimentary version of such a structure. It offers neither a significantly developed symbol nor a complex evolving consciousness and therefore lacks the genuine dialectical movement of the later poems. It is won-

---

6. D. H. Lawrence, "The Nightingale," in *Phoenix: The Posthumous Papers of D. H. Lawrence,* ed. Edward D. McDonald (London, 1936), p. 43.

7. Brown's words. Rollins, *The Keats Circle,* 2:65.

8. Surprisingly, such a distinction survives as late as D. G. James, *Three Odes of Keats,* The W. D. Thomas Memorial Lecture (Cardiff, 1959), pp. 14–15.

9. *The Finer Tone,* chap. 2, pp. 13–62.

derful in many ways, and Keats worked hard at it—he described the poem as "the first and the only one with which I
have taken even moderate pains" (2:105)—but much of his
work undoubtedly went into the new stanzaic form. Psyche,
though formally borrowed from traditional myth, is too thor-
oughly a creation of Keats' own mind to provide much resistance to that mind. The figure of Psyche lacks concreteness,
for Keats borrows separate elements from the myth without
quite fusing them. The girl passionately loved by Cupid; the
goddess who "was never worshipped or sacrificed to with any
of the ancient fervour—and perhaps never thought of in the
old religion" (2:106); the personification of mind or soul—
all these remain somewhat discrete in the poem. The opening
scene of the two lovers on the grass,

> Their arms embraced, and their pinions too;
> Their lips touch'd not, but had not bid adieu,
> As if disjoined by soft-handed slumber,
> And ready still past kisses to outnumber. . . .
>
> (15–18)

seems but tenuously related to the rest of the poem. Moreover,
because this passage has an inner tension that foreshadows
the later odes, it paradoxically serves to emphasize how different the rest of the poem is. "Psyche" is written, as Douglas
Bush recently indicated, more in the mode of the early poems
than that of the other odes.[10] I refer not primarily to the lapses
in diction, such as "at tender eye-dawn of aurorean love,"
which take us back to the Huntian excesses of the early Keats.
The poem has a much deeper connection to Keats' past,
though not as deep as the "Ode to a Nightingale," which can
be said to reenact the whole of Keats' development. One way
that the "Ode to Psyche" provides a prologue to the odes is
by summing up and refining an earlier vision, at once making

10. Bush, *John Keats: Life and Writings,* pp. 131–32.

it a more serious view of life and, by subsuming it in a new whole, bidding it farewell. "Psyche," like many of the early poems, is a poem of assertion and celebration, a hymn to imagination, free of the darker moods of skepticism and doubt that enter the other odes. But it celebrates an imagination much transformed from the early poems, and is in fact about that transformation.

It is significant that the scene of Cupid and Psyche on the grass, though linking the poem with the other odes, also takes us back to one of Keats' oldest *topoi,* the bower. We first see the lovers

> couched side by side
> In deepest grass, beneath the whisp'ring roof
> Of leaves and trembled blossoms, where there ran
> A brooklet, scarce espied.
>
> (9–12)

This bower owes something to the love nest of Adam and Eve in Book IV of *Paradise Lost,* but owes more to those of *Endymion.* We recall the importance for the earlier Keats not only of the *locus amoenus* but of love, both in itself and as a metaphor for imaginative activity. It seems possible then that the first twenty-three lines of the poem, which Bate dismisses as "little more than filler,"[11] are a deliberate evocation of the world of early Keats, especially since Psyche is later described as

> Fairer than Phoebe's sapphire-region'd star,
> Or Vesper, amorous glow-worm of the sky;
>
> (26–27)

fairer, that is, than Cynthia or Venus, the two love goddesses who figure most significantly in the early poems, especially *Endymion.* (We recall that the mainspring of the story in Apuleius is Venus' jealousy of Psyche, whose beauty is so

11. *John Keats,* p. 491.

great that the worship of Venus has fallen into decay.) Keats' description of Psyche comes after he has only belatedly succeeded in identifying her. At first, wandering "in a forest thoughtlessly," the poet recognizes only Cupid:

> The winged boy I knew;
> But who wast thou, O happy, happy dove?

Only in the twenty-third line comes the recognition: "His Psyche true!" Partly responsible for this failure, we gather, is the lateness of Psyche's own deification, and her consequent neglect, which the poem sets out to redress. She is the "latest born" but yet the "loveliest vision far / Of all Olympus' faded hierarchy" (24–25). But we should not ignore the personal resonance here. Keats' recognition of Cupid dramatizes, somewhat schematically, his earlier and simpler commitment to love, to the "worship" of Cynthia and Venus. Their place is now to be taken by Psyche, or rather by a Psyche linked with Cupid in a new synthesis. Here the allegorical meaning of Psyche becomes significant, for the wonderful last stanza of the poem depends more on Psyche as mind or soul than as beautiful girl. In that stanza Keats, no longer thoughtless, promises to build an altar for Psyche "in some untrodden region of my mind," and to adorn it with "the wreath'd trellis of a working brain." The worship will be achieved through his "branched thoughts" or "shadowy thought," with the emphasis on "thought." The earlier, naively visionary conception of the imagination was antithetical to thought, an antidote to consciousness through which "the soul is lost in pleasant smotherings." But in the critical year of 1818 nothing had been more on Keats' mind than "the difference of high Sensations with and without knowledge," and the letters testify to his gradual conversion: "an extensive knowledge is needful to thinking people—it takes away the heat and fever; and helps, by widening speculation, to ease the Burden of the

Mystery" (1:277). Thus the "Ode to Psyche" can be seen as dramatizing the same crucial transformation that occurs in the first part of the Mansion of Life letter, which turns upon "the awakening of the thinking principle—within us" (1:281). But it is only the later odes that go on, as the letter proposes, to "explore" the "dark passages."

It may be objected that "the thinking principle," however crucial to the last stanza, has little place in the central part of the poem (lines 24–49) in which Keats actually takes upon himself the worship of Psyche. To this two answers may be offered. Like the other odes, though more hesitantly, "Psyche" is a poem of process which seeks not to proclaim its meaning but to enact it through a gradual progress of consciousness. Otherwise there would be little point in the poet's failure to recognize Psyche. Just as the Psyche of the myth begins only as a more beautiful though mortal version of Venus—only at the end of Apuleius' tale is she transformed into a goddess—so Keats moves from simple attraction to a thing of beauty toward a more complex and reflective metaphor for the imagination. Also, we must remember that Keats is converted not to "thought" but to a notion of the imagination which, as Bloom says, comes from thought but is larger. Just as "knowledge" is not to replace "high Sensations" but is rather to be joined with them, Keats is converted not from his earlier goddesses to Psyche but to a union of Psyche with Cupid:

> And there shall be for thee all soft delight
> That shadowy thought can win,
> A bright torch, and a casement ope at night,
> To let the warm Love in!
>
> (64–67)

"Soft delight" will not be left behind in this new reign of "shadowy thought" ("shadowy" perhaps to distinguish its awareness of "light and shade" from "consequitive reasoning," or to indicate the "dark passages" that lie before it, cf. the "dark-cluster'd trees"). Keats goes even further than the myth, for in Apuleius Cupid and Psyche must make love in the dark, furtively; Keats provides Psyche with a bright torch with which to welcome him. It is not simply out of serio-comic exuberance that Keats eroticizes his catalogue of the forms of worship. His worship of Psyche, that is, his poetic imagination, will be sensuous as well as reflective. The world of early Keats is not eliminated but in the Hegelian sense *aufgehoben,* reborn in a new synthesis.

Keats' earlier sense of nature undergoes a similar transformation. The remarkable internalized landscape of the last stanza dramatizes a shift from nature to inwardness, in which nature nevertheless preserves an important place:

> Yes, I will be thy priest, and build a fane
>   In some untrodden region of my mind,
> Where branched thoughts, new grown with pleasant pain,
>   Instead of pines shall murmur in the wind:
> Far, far around shall those dark-cluster'd trees
>   Fledge the wild-ridged mountains steep by steep;
> And there by zephyrs, streams, and birds, and bees,
>   The moss-lain Dryads shall be lull'd to sleep.
>
> (50–57)

As Bloom says of the last four lines, "it takes an effort to recollect that these mountains and other phenomena are all within the mind."[12] Nature, though reduced to the condition of metaphor, achieves a greater complexity and integrity than many real natural scenes in earlier Keats. Nature is no longer a refuge, an antidote to consciousness and to the sense of mortality. Keats' "branched thoughts" are not to be confused with his earlier attempts to assimilate poetic creation to the

12. *The Visionary Company,* p. 423.

natural process. In the "Ode to Psyche" the analogy works in just the opposite way: rather than submerging mind in nature it keeps the two distinct. If anything, nature waits upon mind. It is as if this strange mental landscape, the peculiar geography of this "working brain," were the last and the only possible natural scene. This transformation is underlined by the circularity of the poem. Just as the last stanza reimagines, with new significance, the opening love scene of Cupid and Psyche, so too this mental "fane" that Keats builds is a transfigured version of the purely natural bower with which the poem had begun. Nature is not abolished, but rather absorbed and recreated within.

This spirit of reconciliation, though falling short of synthesis at times, pervades the last stanza, so that the very diction approaches paradox: "pleasant pain"; "soft delight" and "shadowy thought"; "wide quietness" and the murmuring pines of the "working brain." Nature itself, reconciled to mind and inwardness, is seen as a complex of opposing principles. No longer a locus of delight alone, it contains "dark-cluster'd trees" that "fledge the wild-ridged mountains steep by steep." These precipices, which appertain to both mind and nature, are suggestive enough to remind us of the more overtly terrifying scene of Hopkins:

> O the mind, mind has mountains; cliffs of fall
> Frightful, sheer, no-man-fathomed. Hold them cheap
> May who ne'er hung there.[13]

But beside them in Keats is a landscape that could not be more benign, where "by zephyrs, streams, and birds, and bees, / The moss-lain Dryads shall be lull'd to sleep." In the last stanza of the ode the sharpest antinomies are reconciled

---

13. "No worst, there is none," lines 9–11. *Poems of Gerard Manley Hopkins,* ed. Robert Bridges and W. H. Gardner, 3d ed. (London, 1948), p. 107.

within a new concept of the imagination. This is now the faculty that must proceed by both sensation and reflection, by wise passiveness and by strenuous activity, that must explore the dark passages as well as the bright. To Keats this complex terrain is yet an "untrodden region," but he affirms once more, and most beautifully, his determination to inhabit it.

What makes the "Ode to Psyche" so different from the other odes, however, is its refusal to describe this commitment as a tragic one that will involve the pains of self-consciousness and inner division. To the Keats of the "Ode to Psyche" the widening of consciousness involves only "*pleasant* pain," not the awareness of death crucial to the "Ode to a Nightingale" or "the wakeful anguish of the soul" that he demands in the "Ode on Melancholy." Douglas Bush puts the case against the poem forcefully: "The idea of the poet-priest, however richly developed, does not reach a plane of inclusive complexity or set up anything of the central tension that is the strength of the greater odes." Yet Bush goes wrong when he calls the poem "a sophisticated continuation of, or reversion to, the simple blend of nature, myth, and poetry of the youthful Keats" and when he insists that the conception of the imagination in the last stanza "does not rise above lush reverie."[14] The metamorphosis of the world of the youthful Keats may not be as complete as in the "Ode to a Nightingale" but it is the very point of the poem. What Bush seeks is that tension between imagination and actuality so central to the other odes, but he fails to see that the tensions of the poem are located within imagination itself, tensions brought into only unstable balance in the last stanza.

It would be excessive to claim that the last stanza, dense and original as it is, makes the poem a fully realized one. The movement of consciousness that culminates in that stanza is

14. Bush, *John Keats: Life and Writings,* pp. 131–32.

sketched rather than dramatized, and its progressive stages are less than inevitable. The fine middle section of the poem—with its great assertion "I see, and sing, by my own eyes inspir'd" (43)—is more a prolegomenon to the odes than a part of them. Its details will not bear close scrutiny, and it tells us little about the nature of imagination. Instead it makes that prior assertion of the *right* to imagination without which Romantic poetry cannot begin to exist. Its retrospection is cultural, not personal. Since Arnold it has been critical commonplace that the modern poet has assumed functions once arrogated to religion. But for the Romantic poet, whatever his professed religious belief, the authenticity of vision and the creative autonomy of the self had still to be claimed and defended. Not long before Keats wrote the odes Coleridge had likened the "primary Imagination" to that power by which God had created the universe ("a repetition in the finite mind of the eternal act of creation in the infinite I AM").[15] Now Keats, with what Bate describes as "mock nostalgia,"[16] but with more than a twinge of real nostalgia as well, tells his Psyche of that Golden Age of religious worship for which she had been born too late,

> When holy were the haunted forest boughs,
>   Holy the air, the water, and the fire.
>
>   (38–39)

She must content herself with the priestly attentions of a poet, whose vision perceives her even in a world no longer numinous and alive with meaning; she must content herself with a *mental* fane and a merely symbolic deification.

It is only in the last stanza, in describing that fane, that Keats, his creative right assured, goes on to define a new con-

15. Coleridge, *Biographia Literaria,* chap. 13. *The Portable Coleridge,* ed. I. A. Richards (New York, 1950), p. 516.
16. *John Keats,* p. 492.

ception of the imagination. Yet it is too much a mere concept; it involves too little expense of self, too little of that "fierce dispute" through which the self achieves what Keats calls identity. This is not to denigrate the remarkable synthesis that Keats achieved in the last stanza of the "Ode to Psyche," but only to understand why that synthesis proved unstable, why Keats had to forego it when he sat down to write the "Ode to a Nightingale."

We enter a different world when we move from the playful and celebratory atmosphere of the "Ode to Psyche" to the tormented opening stanzas of the "Ode to a Nightingale."

> My heart aches, and a drowsy numbness pains
>   My sense, as though of hemlock I had drunk,
> Or emptied some dull opiate to the drains
>   One minute past, and Lethe-wards had sunk.
>
>   (1–4)

Without introduction we are propelled to the center of Keats' anguished meditation on consciousness. We meet Keats in a drugged stupor, the archetypal state of numbness and unconsciousness which has dogged him since the early "Fill for me a brimming bowl," through the many versions of "the feel of not to feel it." Every variant of that experience is here, and the effect is one of reinforcement and accretion. (Compare the even more explicit though more literary catalogue of what Keats wishes away at the beginning of the "Ode on Melancholy.") "Drowsy numbness" suggests not only affectlessness but sleep, once benign but now paradoxically painful to his "sense" (i.e., mind as well as feeling). The mention of Lethe brings in the old motif of "sweet forgetting," and the metaphorical hemlock adds overtones of death, foreshadowing its later appearances in the poem.

In the fifth line Keats addresses the nightingale directly; in such a state talk is therapy, a way of not going under. It is also an apology, for as in the "Epistle to Reynolds" Keats' mood "spoils the singing of the Nightingale."

> 'Tis not through envy of thy happy lot,
>   But being too happy in thine happiness,—
>   That thou, light-winged Dryad of the trees,
>   In some melodious plot
>   Of beechen green, and shadows numberless,
>   Singest of summer in full-throated ease.
>
> (5–10)

The location of the nightingale (*pace* Brown) remains indeterminate, though as tree-dweller the bird seems for the moment close by. Still, between the poet and the nightingale there is a distance he had never experienced with the less resistant Psyche. Even so, Keats disclaims envious longing. He boasts of self-abnegating rather than covetous feelings; he suffers from excessive empathy, from being too happy for the bird. Immediately, ever so subtly, the happiness of the nightingale becomes ambiguous, associated as it is with the poet's painful numbness, and subject to self-destroying excess. It is happiness nonetheless, and it tells Keats of a summer world not yet present in nature, but the bird's visionary power leaves it in turn invisible (and inaccessible) among the "shadows numberless," disembodied into a "melodious plot" and into the "full-throated ease" of pure song.

In all this—including the qualifications, which we do not forget, even when Keats gives full sway to a desire to be united with the bird—the first stanza deftly introduces the various symbolic meanings of the bird. As a singer she suggests art, and as bird and Dryad she represents an aspect of nature. Yet it is an art already associated with airy uncertainty, distance and disembodiment—and by the second stanza, where wine becomes the true fountain of the Muses, with intoxication. Above all, as the poem goes on, the bird comes to signify an art free of self-consciousness and a nature free of tragic necessity, a nature that pits sensation and process *against* consciousness. From the perspective of our survey of Keats' development, his longing to join the nightingale, which becomes so intense in the second, third, and fourth stanzas, can only be seen retrospectively. The poet's desire to "fade far away, dissolve" and "leave the world unseen" powerfully sums up and reenacts the impulses toward self-annihilation and luxurious transcendence that played so predominant a part in his earlier poetry. "The viewless wings of Poesy" of the fourth stanza, like the intoxicating Hippocrene of the second, can only refer to the poesy of *Endymion* and the early poems, not to that newer conception of the imagination painstakingly developed in the *King Lear* sonnet, the letters, the third book of *Hyperion,* and the last stanza of the "Ode to Psyche." It is poetry as a visionary bower for the spirit, a refuge from the pains of selfhood and actuality, rather than a tragic poetry of self-knowledge and the widening of consciousness. Keats returns to these earlier impulses because they still move him, still represent a real idea of happiness and imagination for him. Where he has failed to exorcise them by simply setting them aside or transmuting them, he may succeed by giving them full expression, by bringing them into the light of consciousness and freshly exploring them. The synthesis of "Psyche" proves to have been too easily achieved; the self must undergo a new polarization, a new interior dialogue.

The stages of the dialectic in the first part of the poem are not difficult to distinguish. Keats describes a series of wavelike gestures toward self-dissolution and union with the bird. The first, for a moment all too successful, has taken place just before the poem begins. It has resulted, as Keats tells in the opening lines, not in the genuine extinction of self-consciousness but in what he elsewhere calls an "unpleasant numbness" t "does not take away the pain of existence" (1:287). Yet each wave sets in motion a counter-current, as Keats' mind moves from bird to self and self to bird. From "being too happy in thine happiness" he sinks into the paralyzing condition described in the opening lines; in anatomizing that condition he draws his mind upward again toward the happy song of the nightingale. This leads to the second wave, as Keats imagines joining the bird through Bacchus. The terms of the dialectic now broaden and deepen; the song's "full-throated ease" becomes a foretaste of the completion and wholeness of summer. This leads Keats to dream of a delicious summer world of "Dance, and Provencal song, and sunburnt mirth," an ideal "warm South" of sensation without pain and imagination without consciousness. But the large gesture of the second stanza leads to the counter-movement of the third. The attempt to flee to an idyllic world suddenly makes Keats all the more poignantly aware of the world of actuality which he is trying to escape. It is a world "where men sit and hear each other groan," that is, where the only community is one of pain, the exact opposite of the world of dance and song and mirth. It is a world in which suffering is magnified by the desperate consciousness of suffering:

> Where youth grows pale, and spectre-thin, and dies;
>> Where but to think is to be full of sorrow
>>> And leaden-eyed despairs.

> (26–28)

It is a world of temporality in which all is perishable, all must change:

> Where beauty cannot keep her lustrous eyes,
>> Or new Love pine at them beyond to-morrow.[17]
>> (29–30)

17. In spite of these two good concluding lines, in spite of the im-

Clearly this second fantasy of union with the happy song of the bird has failed Keats even more dismally than the first. But out of his complete despair comes an equally powerful though strained new gesture of escape:

> Away! away! for I will fly to thee,
>   Not charioted by Bacchus and his pards,
> But on the viewless wings of Poesy,
>   Though the dull brain perplexes and retards.
>
> (31–34)

What follows is perhaps the most lovely yet surely the most variously interpreted section of the poem. Some things are clear, however. No matter how we read "Already with thee!" —whether we follow Bate and others in assuming the poet to have achieved sudden though perhaps illusory union with the bird or agree with Wasserman that "such a reading can lead only to inconsistencies, if not to nonsense"[18]—by the next line ("haply") and thereafter ("But here there is no light") the poet is separate from the bird. Keats for the moment settles for a lower paradise than that suggested by the song of the nightingale. He returns, as he had done in the "Ode to Psyche," to the favorite *topos* of the early poems, the bower. The poet's spirit has been sorely tried, and now the Poesy of *Endymion,* to which he has at last appealed at the beginning of the fourth stanza, responds with the bower vision that is its only cure, its best treasure. One key to the passage is the "embalmed darkness" which envelops the scene as Keats writes. "Balm" is a significant word in some of the bower

---

portance of the whole passage in the poem's structure, I share Allen Tate's dissatisfaction with the rhetoric of the third stanza: *"Keats has no language of his own for this realm of experience,"* that is, for dealing with actuality. *On the Limits of Poetry,* p. 174. Yet in the light of the second half of the poem, especially the seventh stanza (see discussion below), the failure here has a measure of appropriateness.

18. Bate, *John Keats,* p. 505. Wasserman, *The Finer Tone,* p. 198.

scenes of *Endymion* as well. We are told that after the death
of Adonis the love-sick Venus

> Heal'd up to the wound, and, with a balmy power,
> Medicined death to a lengthened drowsiness:
> The which she fills with visions, and doth dress
> In all this quiet luxury.

> (II, 483–86)

Similarly, in the "golden clime" of Circe's den ("this arbitrary queen of sense"),

> every eve, nay every spendthrift hour
> Shed balmy consciousness within that bower.
> (III, 465–66)

"Balmy consciousness" as opposed to a consciousness of pain;
a balm which can heal death and yet, as "lengthened
drowsiness," is a kind of death itself, the death of the mind
for the sake of "visions" and sensuous "luxury." It is this
death of the mind which Keats prays for when he addresses
Sleep as the "soft embalmer of the still midnight" ("To
Sleep").

In spite of its ancestry, this bower, like the one in the "Ode
to Psyche," is fundamentally different from those in *Endymion.* In *Endymion* there is a simple polarity between the
bower and the world, between vision and actuality, sensation
and consciousness. In the "Ode to Psyche" Keats had sought
to reconcile these antinomies, to refine and transform the
bower by altering its regressive and infantile character. In
the first four stanzas of the Nightingale ode the polarities are
restated, definitively, one might say. In the fifth stanza, the
closest in spirit to the "Ode to Psyche," Keats comes to rest for
a moment on a middle ground, a lower paradise, in Geoffrey
Hartman's words, "the middle-ground of imaginative activity, not reaching to vision, not falling into blankness."[19]

19. *Wordsworth's Poetry,* p. 11.

It is also a middle ground between "balmy consciousness" and thought, enjoyment and awareness. It is instructive to observe the effects of the darkness on this scene.

> I cannot see what flowers are at my feet,
>   Nor what soft incense hangs upon the boughs,
> But, in embalmed darkness, guess each sweet. . . .
>   (41–43)

The failure of sight seems to set Keats' other senses going more vividly, as such synaesthetic phrases as "soft incense" make clear. Yet also it sets the *mind's* eye functioning more intensely, for the mind, bereft of vision, must construct the whole scene from sheer *knowledge* of the natural world. (The timeless and symbolic Nature represented by the nightingale will not do here.) But this, like other dualities in the stanza, is only a germ, a suggestion that is important insofar as it is taken up in the next stanza, which is the real turning point of the poem. The fifth stanza, like the conclusion of the "Ode to Psyche," proves an unstable compound. The reflective mental activity in the stanza anticipates the new self-consciousness that appears in the sixth, just as the passive sensuousness of the "embalmed darkness" foreshadows the desire for "easeful Death." The polarities reassert themselves, for the purpose of confrontation rather than reconciliation.

The sixth stanza of the "Ode to a Nightingale" is perhaps the most significant moment in Keats' poetry, and one of the most important in all Romantic literature. It is foreshadowed as early as "Sleep and Poetry," when Keats sees the visionary car of the imagination, only to have it displaced by "a sense of real things" (157). It is the culminating moment of Keats' lifelong struggle against consciousness, his quest for self-annihilation made all the more complicated by his strong commitment to "the thinking principle" and to the painful extension of self-knowledge. The logical conclusion of that desire for self-annihilation is the desire for death, the wish to be wholly free of the burdens of selfhood, a longing to which so many of the Romantics were willing prey.

> Darkling I listen; and, for many a time
>   I have been half in love with easeful Death,
> Call'd him soft names in many a mused rhyme,
>   To take into the air my quiet breath;
> Now more than ever seems it rich to die,
>   To cease upon the midnight with no pain,
>   While thou art pouring forth thy soul abroad
>   In such an ecstasy!
>
>   (51–58)

The darkness of the bower leads to the thought of death, and death suddenly seems to be the only road by which Keats can make his last attempt to join the nightingale. Now the retrospective meaning of the whole poem becomes for the first time explicit. Keats is caught up not only in the desire to die but in a sudden brilliant awareness of the importance of that wish to the whole history of his imagination. At this point criticism, having long since rescued Keats from decadence and convinced itself of the essential "health" and "vitality" of his imagination, clears its throat uneasily and cites the convenient but enigmatic sonnet "Why did I laugh?" of which a verbal echo occurs in this stanza. Convenient too is Keats' own assurance to his brother and sister-in-law of his health and sanity in composing that sonnet: "it was written with no Agony but that of ignorance. . . . I went to bed, and enjoyed an uninterrupted sleep—Sane I went to bed and sane I arose" (2:81–82). The very need for such assurance, and his hesitation in sending them the poem, shows us how much Keats felt his balance threatened by the death wish. But that sonnet does not readily fit the specifications of this stanza. Keats insists, for one thing, on the recurrence and frequency of his longing ("many a time . . . in many a mused rhyme"). Furthermore, he describes it in erotic terms, which bring to mind not "Why did I Laugh?" but the oft-repeated desire of the early Keats to "die a death / Of luxury," to experience "richer entanglements, enthralments far / More self-destroying," when the self is entirely sloughed off and "our state / Is like a floating spirit's."

Keats had already, in the third stanza, enviously praised the nightingale for its ignorance of the harsh world of actuality. He had longed to

> Fade far away, dissolve, and quite forget
>   What thou among the leaves hast never known,
> The weariness, the fever, and the fret. . . .
>
> (21–23)

He had felt himself trapped by self-consciousness, in a world "where but to think is to be full of sorrow / And leaden-eyed despairs." Now Keats restates the innocence of the nightingale in positive terms, as an experience of perpetual self-transcendence. It is "pouring forth [its] soul abroad / In such an ecstasy!"—literally, in separation from itself. This desire for self-transcendence is the basis of Keats' death wish: the nightingale exists wholly within the terms of his own inner conflict.

At this point the poem turns. His association of the thought of death with the song of the now transcendent nightingale suddenly seems an incongruity;

> Still thou wouldst sing, and I have ears in vain—
>   To thy high requiem become a sod.
>
> (59–60)

The thought of real death intervenes, not "easeful Death . . . To cease upon the midnight with no pain," but to "become a sod," a clod, a piece of earth. The song of the nightingale, no longer happy, now becomes a "high requiem" sung over the oblivious corpse of the all-too-human poet. Death is not a fulfillment, a luxury or a transcendent passage, but simply the end. At this recognition an unbridgeable abyss opens up between the poet and the nightingale.

> Thou wast not born for death, immortal Bird!
>   No hungry generations tread thee down.
>   (61–62)

The tone of this seventh stanza is different from that of the third, which had made a similar statement. The description of man's condition is comparable, and the bird remains blissfully free of it, but there is now no sickly pathos in Keats' tone and no envy in his view of the nightingale. The spell of the bird's song has begun to relax its hold on him; he is becoming, quite literally, dis-enchanted.

In the third stanza, most of the images of suffering were unconvincing ("Here, where men sit and hear each other groan; / Where palsy shakes a few, sad, last gray hairs"). Keats seemed to be glancing at everyday reality over his shoulder, in the act of fleeing from it, with no will to confront it or even observe it concretely. Something decisive has intervened between those images and that of the "hungry generations" or Ruth, "sick for home," standing "in tears amid the alien corn." The palsied old men and spectre-thin youths of the third stanza are just victims, and pathetic ones. The "hungry generations" are both victims and agents: they do the treading too, though they themselves are eventually trod upon.

We are reminded, in spite of the difference of emphasis, of the message of Oceanus to his fellow Titans:

> "So on our heels a fresh perfection treads,
>   A power more strong in beauty, born of us
>   And fated to excel us. . . ."
>   (*Hyperion*, II, 212–14)

The message of Oceanus, which is central to *Hyperion,* has a special relevance to the concluding idea of the "Ode to a Nightingale," especially in this seventh stanza. His speech is usually read as an expression of cosmic optimism, and indeed it does assert a belief in progress. Yet the central doctrine of the speech is almost tragic. Oceanus informs the shattered Saturn of the law of mutability and transience: "Thou art not the beginning nor the end" (II, 190). Though he uses sometimes cosmic and sometimes natural terms, his message is no more or less than a philosophy of history—history rather than accident, history rather than myth: "We fall by course of Nature's law, not force / Of thunder, or of Jove" (II, 181–82). Saturn, however, being king of the gods, has been "blind from sheer supremacy" (II, 185). A figure of myth, he had ruled over a world of apparent mythic permanence. What Oceanus explains to him is the action of the first two books of the poem: his fall from myth into history (a fall whose effect, as we have seen, is one of humanization). He tells Saturn of the simultaneous "creations and destroyings" of history, and calls for a tragic acceptance free of self-delusion:

> ". . . to bear all naked truths,
> And to envision circumstance, all calm,
> That is the top of sovereignty."
>   (II, 203–5)

In the sixth stanza of the ode Keats suddenly confronts the "naked truth" about death, which separates the human self of the poet from the visionary song of the nightingale. As a result a vast distance begins to open out between the poet and the bird. In his disenchantment with the bird Keats moves from myth to history. He situates himself firmly on "this passing night," in the endless procession of the "hungry generations." The nightingale's song, which a moment earlier he had envied as a sign of ecstatic self-transcendence, now becomes merely "self-same," which suggests that it is not only identical at all periods of history but also, unlike the poet, self-less. For Keats the recognition of this difference is not depressing, as in the third stanza, but challenging. The difference between the third and seventh stanzas is akin to the difference between Saturn and Oceanus, the one stunned, bereft of his mythic "identity" and therefore of the will to live, the other announcing to Saturn "the pain of truth, to whom 'tis pain" (II, 202), by which the individual may hope to endure. Endurance is the subject of the seventh stanza, as death was of the sixth, but it is not only the immortal nightingale that endures. Beyond the transhistorical permanence of the nightingale is the more tenuous but relevant seizure of life of the human agent within tragedy: that of the "hungry generations," or that of the poet who can choose at last to fall out of love with death, or that of the bereaved and exiled Ruth, who is taught by her mother-in-law to begin life anew, and is rewarded by becoming the mother of a dynasty.

Readers who ignore the implicit but growing disenchantment of the poet with the nightingale, who see it merely, if at all, as an increasing distance, are likely to be unpleasantly jarred by the conclusion of the seventh stanza and by the final stanza that follows. Keats describes the song as

> The same that oft-times hath
> Charm'd magic casements, opening on the foam
> Of perilous seas, in faery lands forlorn.
>
> (68–70)

To E. C. Pettet the word "forlorn," even if "taken with the minimum of emotional tone . . . is certainly a strange one to be attached to a dream and a sort of poetry that Keats had always regarded with such unqualified imaginative delight." He even wonders whether "the word slipped in without much consideration as an easy, sound-pleasing, alliterative rhyme to finish the stanza."[20] This disregards the pointed

20. Pettet, *On the Poetry of Keats,* p. 278. It is all the more remark-

emphasis that Keats puts on the word when he uses it as a bridge to the concluding stanza. It ignores the rejection of romance that had been foreshadowed as early as the last two books of *Endymion,* and announced programmatically in the sonnet on *Lear.* Now, in his most completely retrospective poem, a genuine poem of conversion and self-definition, Keats associates the song of the nightingale with the poetry of romance, with the "poesy" perhaps of his own long "Poetic Romance." For the nightingale has already been identified with that aspect of romance which Keats had always singled out over all others, escape, and in the end it is escape that Keats mainly wishes to reject.

Among professional critics there are two broad groups that have usually chosen to ignore or deemphasize this rejection. The older critics, still attached to the nineteenth-century image of an aesthete cultivating beauty and sensation for their own sake, could hardly have been responsive to Keats' final disenchantment with the nightingale. Thus Bridges and Garrod single out for censure the description of the song in the last stanza as a "plaintive anthem."[21] More recently some writers, heirs in a special way of the doctrine of *l'art pour l'art,* have stressed the visionary side of Romantic poetry, the creation of autonomous imaginative worlds free of the inhibiting immediacies of self-consciousness and actuality.[22] No poem is a more purposeful refutation of such an emphasis than the

able that he can say this after correctly observing the reversal in the sixth stanza.

21. Bridges, *Collected Essays,* 4:130. H. W. Garrod, *Keats* (Oxford, 1926), p. 116.

22. Harold Bloom says that the "creative mode" of the Romantics is "the heterocosm, or the poem as an alternative world to that of nature." "Yeats and the Romantics," in *Modern Poetry: Essays in Criticism,* ed. John Hollander (New York, 1968), p. 501. The debt to Frye's baneful theory of archetypes is clear. Elsewhere Bloom recoils unchivalrously from "the compromising arms of the ugliest of Muses, the reality principle." "The Internalization of Quest Romance," *Yale Review* 58 (1969): 533.

"Ode to a Nightingale," which is among other things an account of how immediate experience and radical self-awareness intervene in a Romantic poem to challenge and alter its mythicizing direction. Professor Wasserman, who reifies the visionary and self-annihilating impulses of the early Keats into doctrine, which he then applies to the greater poems, writes a long and revealing chapter on this ode. He reads the poem closely, but only to quarrel with it at every turn, to wish it different. Professor McLuhan, in his interesting essay on the odes, refuses to impute escapism to the early part of the poem, or even to the death wish of the sixth stanza. He speaks of "the paradox that ideal or disembodied beauty is richer in ontological content than actual life with its defeats and deprivations and 'leaden-eyed despairs.'" It is for this reason, he says, that "the stark negation of death is viewed as a positive good ('rich to die'), not so much as an evasion of difficulties as a seemingly easy means of transmuting the leaden stuff of life into glorious beauty."[23] Professor Bloom, reading backward from the work of Wallace Stevens, praises the poem for

> giving the sense of the human making the choice of a human self, aware of its deathly nature, and yet having the will to celebrate the imaginative richness of mortality. The *Ode to a Nightingale* is the first poem to know and declare, wholeheartedly, that death is the mother of beauty.[24]

Each of these interpretations contains some truth but all must come to grief on the last twenty-two lines of the poem. The "Ode to a Nightingale" is a tragic poem rather than a

23. Herbert Marshall McLuhan, "Aesthetic Pattern in Keats's Odes," *University of Toronto Quarterly* 12 (1943): 168.

24. Harold Bloom, "Keats and the Embarrassments of Poetic Tradition," in *From Sensibility to Romanticism: Essays Presented to Frederick A. Pottle,* ed. Frederick W. Hilles and Harold Bloom (New York, 1965), p. 520.

visionary one, founded like so many of the best Romantic poems not on imaginative flight but rather on the dialectical tension of the poet's divided self. But Keats, who could so readily luxuriate in his own inner tensions, here drives onward towards a tentative resolution. The seventh stanza ends on a note of surprise and paradox, "faery lands forlorn," but Keats concludes with a stanza of epilogue that explicitly reverses his longing for the nightingale and for all the deceptions of fancy that the nightingale has come to represent.

> Forlorn! the very word is like a bell
>   To toll me back from thee to my sole self!
> Adieu! the fancy cannot cheat so well
>   As she is fam'd to do, deceiving elf.
> Adieu! adieu! thy plaintive anthem fades
>   Past the near meadows, over the still stream,
>   Up the hill-side; and now 'tis buried deep
>   In the next valley-glades:
>   Was it a vision, or a waking dream?
>   Fled is that music:—Do I wake or sleep?

Nothing could be more decisive than the characterization of the nightingale as a "deceiving elf," not even the phrase at the parallel point in the "Ode on a Grecian Urn": "Cold Pastoral!" Keats at last takes up residence, as he has repeatedly promised, in the difficult domain of the "sole self." There is a note of loss here, for as McLuhan points out there is something funereal in the tolling bell of the opening lines.[25] But surely the primary meaning is of an awakening to life; "forlorn" serves as the bell that brings us back from the dreamworld of the nightingale and from the faery lands. It is rather the immortal nightingale who paradoxically dies, whose now "plaintive" song "fades" away and is "buried deep" in the

25. "There is something utterly paradoxical in 'toll me back,' as though returning to life were actually death" (McLuhan, p. 177). Pettet makes a similar point (*On the Poetry of Keats,* p. 280).

next valley. (The song of course does not really change: it is the poet's response that turns it from a happy song of summer to a "high requiem" and finally to a "plaintive anthem," as if the bird were in the end aware of the poet's desertion.)

Yet for all the decisiveness of this epilogue, the poem ends on a knife-edge of uncertainty. In the last two lines Keats asks himself whether the departure of the nightingale represents a fall from vision into blankness—as in "Sleep and Poetry," where the "sense of real things . . . like a muddy stream, would bear along / My soul to nothingness" (157–59)—or whether it constitutes the emergence from a dreamworld into the reality of actual life? In the final line, much more distinctly than in the two opening lines of the stanza, we hear a genuine note of regret: "Fled is that music." A few months later, referring to another music which he had left behind, that of *Paradise Lost,* Keats would say that "I have but lately stood on my guard against Milton. Life to him would be death to me" (2:212). Like his tutelage to Milton, Keats' enchantment with the song of the nightingale had in the end turned into a struggle for survival. The bird, which would have presided over the poet's "easeful Death," has itself died; Keats is recalled to life, yet bids the bird farewell with a sense of bereavement.

Keats' final judgment is a balanced one, but the whole last part of the poem contains an emphasis opposite from that of "Sleep and Poetry" and *Endymion.* It is simply not true that for Keats, as Paul de Man asserts, "the condition of the 'sole self' is one of intolerable barrenness, the opposite of all that imagination, poetry and love can achieve. The experience of being 'tolled back to one's sole self' is always profoundly negative."[26] This is the case in *Endymion,* where "the journey

26. *John Keats: Selected Poetry,* ed. Paul de Man (New York, 1966), p. xxiii.

homeward to habitual self" (II, 276) is always painful,
though, significantly, even there a journey Keats always insists on making. De Man feels that even the "Ode to a Nightingale" gives evidence of Keats' continued fear of self-
confrontation. "The 'I' of the Nightingale Ode," he says,
"... is always seen in a movement that takes it away from its
own center."[27] But that describes only the movement of the
first part of the poem. The poem as a whole moves toward
the final exorcising of that fear. Yet it is an exorcism which,
given Keats' temperament, must be perpetually reenacted:
only thus can we explain the history of his poetry from the
Lear sonnet to the odes, and even the relation of the odes to
each other.

The "Ode on a Grecian Urn" covers in its special way the
same ground as the Nightingale ode and thus it is superfluous
for me to undertake a full-scale reading. But the poet learns
from the conclusion of the Nightingale ode as he found it
expedient *not* to learn from the "Ode to Psyche." The "Ode
to a Nightingale" is a poem of discovery and self-definition,
and could not but be in the first-person. The "Ode on a
Grecian Urn" is rather a reaffirmation of discoveries already
made, discoveries that can now be dramatized without the
device of the narrative "I." The limitations of the nightingale
are discovered only in the course of the poem. The limitations
of the urn are built into the poem from the start; they are
inextricably linked with its attractions:

> Fair youth, beneath the trees, thou canst not leave
>   Thy song, nor ever can those trees be bare;
>   Bold Lover, never, never canst thou kiss,
>   Though winning near the goal—yet, do not grieve;
>   She cannot fade, though thou hast not thy bliss,
>   For ever wilt thou love, and she be fair!
>
> (15–20)

27. Ibid., p. xxiv.

We must not ignore the negative strain here. As Cleanth Brooks has emphasized,[28] the figures on the urn, though fixed in their intensity, are also dead in their fixity. Furthermore, Keats goes out of his way to underline the absence of fulfillment that is the price of this permanence. The repetition of "never" is significant: the lovers will not consummate their love, will come no more than "near the goal." There is no grief on the face of the marble lover: it is Keats who grieves for him and is moved to console him. (In earlier versions this is even more of an emotional interjection: "O do not grieve!")

In reading the poem we feel no sense of inappropriateness in the interjection, for far from being an "objective" or descriptive poem, its action, like that of the Nightingale ode, takes place entirely within the consciousness of the poet. Yet there is a difference. In the Nightingale ode we see consciousness turning upon itself, seeking its own annihilation in fusion with the bird, in flight. Here Keats accepts the activity of consciousness from the start. The poet always remains an observer of the urn, a creator of myths about it. He preserves the integrity of self that is inherent in the act of contemplation. Keats still comes to the urn with a need to be "teased out of thought"—otherwise there would be no poem—but most of his thoughts about the "legend" of the urn show us how much he remains in the world. This is made especially clear by the interrogative mode of the first stanza.

The urn is introduced as an artifact of the Golden Age, a version of pastoral:

> Thou still unravish'd bride of quietness,
>   Thou foster-child of silence and slow time,
> Sylvan historian, who canst thus express
>   A flowery tale more sweetly than our rhyme:

28. Cleanth Brooks, "Keats's Sylvan Historian: History Without Footnotes," in *The Well Wrought Urn: Studies in the Structure of Poetry* (New York: Harcourt, Harvest Brooks, 1956), pp. 156–59.

What leaf-fring'd legend haunts about thy shape
Of deities, or mortals, or of both,
In Tempe or the dales of Arcady?

(1–7)

We are back in the world of the first book of *Endymion*, the Arcadian world of pastoral romance, of the Latmians whose

fair living forms swam heavenly
To tunes forgotten . . .
not yet dead,
But in old marbles ever beautiful.
High genitors, unconscious did they cull
Time's sweet first-fruits.

(*Endymion*, I, 315–16, 318–21)

The urn is "unravish'd" because it has not been subjected to the assault of real history rather than "sylvan" history, language and time rather than "silence and slow time." Language, Keats seems to say both here and again in the next stanza, is too involved in the flux of time and consciousness to be able to render this static and utopian "flowery tale" and "leaf-fring'd legend" of the Golden Age. Only the ancient sculptor can capture the sweetness—he does not say truth—of pastoral romance. But even in *Endymion* Keats cannot resist seeing the "fair living forms" not simply as mythic but as pre-historical, as "high genitors" "whose young children's children bred / Thermopylae its heroes" (I, 317–18). So too in the "Ode on a Grecian Urn" Keats cannot resist assaulting the silent urn with questions that it cannot answer, questions that are the product of a historical consciousness and of a will-to-knowledge that only living language could satisfy:

What men or gods are these? What maidens loth?
What mad pursuit? What struggle to escape?
What pipes and timbrels? What wild ecstasy?

(8–10)

The silence of the urn, its integrity and inviolability, suddenly seem to frustrate the speaker into blank uncertainty, into frenetic interrogation.

A moment later Keats accepts this silence and praises it, but he persists in trying to bring the scene to life, to project emotions and reactions upon the characters. He seeks to unfreeze the figures on the frieze, to thaw what he already unconsciously knows to be a cold pastoral. Keats' purpose is divided: he wants to bring the figures to life and yet to keep them free of existential impurities, to use them as alternatives to the life he knows. This division leads in the third stanza to the strained repetition of the word "happy," and at the midpoint of the poem his identification with the urn and his revulsion against himself and against the actual world make him almost inarticulate: "More happy love! more happy, happy love!" No metaphysical exposition of the concept of happiness in other poems of Keats can alter the fact that in attempting to identify with the ecstasy that he has projected upon the lovers (as he had projected it upon the nightingale) he almost falls into a speechlessness like that of the urn, a silence alien to poetry.

Now, however, the poem turns. There is little that Keats can say about this happy love. He has evoked a world of static perfection, beyond time, yet only valuable in a context of time and change, only meaningful in dialectical relation to the world Keats knows he inhabits. Like the nightingale, like the "happy, happy tree" and the "happy, happy Brook" of "In drear-nighted December," the scene on the urn is purely the creation of the mind of the poet in dialogue with itself. It is not enough for Keats to dwell in his vision of happy love, "For ever warm and still to be enjoy'd / For ever panting, and for ever young." He must go on to assert its superiority to love in the actual world, where pleasure is mingled with pain and regret, where satisfaction, he tells us, is cloying and transient; it is

> All breathing human passion far above,
>> That leaves a heart high-sorrowful and cloy'd,
>>> A burning forehead, and a parching tongue.
>>>> (28–30)

Keats grasps for a pejorative, but at first his mind betrays him. "Breathing," engendered probably by the "panting" of the previous line, is an exceptionally rich word, both in sound and sense. "Breathing human passion" seems more unambiguously desirable than the eternal panting of the lovers on the urn. "Far above" now comes as something of a shock, wrenching us back to what must have been Keats' original pejorative intention, but, as Wasserman says, "the damage has been done," and out of it, in the next two lines, "comes an unexpected attention to merely human passions."[29] As in the third and sixth stanzas of the Nightingale ode, the flight from the actual, even the explicit attack upon it, leads to a paradoxical engagement with actuality.

This involvement does not diminish in the fourth stanza, though Keats turns his attention back to the frieze. The sacri-

29. *The Finer Tone,* p. 41. "Damage" indeed, from Wasserman's point of view, for whom such attention to "merely" human passions is a great falling off (though insufficient evidence for a different reading of the poem). Wasserman's analysis of the poem's movement is valuable, and I am indebted to it, but one must stand it on its head, because of the pervasive, un-Keatsian animus toward the phenomenal world. To Wasserman all Keats' poetry moves toward some visionary country at "heaven's bourne." Thus the rest of the "Ode on a Grecian Urn" from this point, and indeed all of the Nightingale ode, marks a decline. In the fourth stanza of the Urn ode, Wasserman laments, Keats is impelled "to make a commentary upon the mortal world, not the realm of pure spirit. Yet," he admits, "Keats does not hate the world for not being a heaven. To him, it is a source of rich beauty . . ." (p. 43). Not, alas, to this critic.

ficial procession that Keats describes seems, like the scenes of the first stanza, to frustrate his desire for meaning, in particular when he directly questions the "mysterious priest." Like the panting lovers of the two previous stanzas, the procession is arrested before its consummation, though in an earlier version of the scene (in the "Epistle to Reynolds") Keats had beautifully described the moment of sacrifice. The lovers, albeit constrained, were yet granted an "eternal present" (to use Kenneth Burke's well-known phrase),[30] but now Keats resists the arrest that art imposes on the action. Just as he had projected grief upon the lover in the second stanza, now Keats endows the action with a future (the green altar) and a past (the little town), a goal which the figures can never reach and a home to which they can never return. Keats historicizes the action; he imagines a fluid interchange between art and reality which is alien to art, which resists its immutability and timelessness. The point becomes inescapably clear in the last three lines:

> And, little town, thy streets for evermore
> Will silent be; and not a soul to tell
> Why thou art desolate, can e'er return.
>
> (38–40)

Fixity impoverishes, bereaves, literally de-humanizes: the town is desolate because all its inhabitants have been trapped on the urn, fixed in the permanence yet immobility of art. The poignant silence of the streets is like the sinister underside of the earlier silence of the urn. As in the Nightingale ode art turns out to be dangerous in its enchantment; Keats discovers that it can despoil reality as well as enrich it.

With this recognition the spell of the action on the urn, like the spell of the nightingale's song, is broken. The urn becomes

30. Kenneth Burke, "Symbolic Action in a Poem by Keats," in *A Grammar of Motives* (New York, 1945), p. 449.

an object again, belonging not only to the ages but to a historical moment; it becomes a Greek vase, an "Attic shape," a
"silent form," and the lovers become "marble men and
maidens" (yet with a suddenly tangible tread):

> O Attic shape! Fair attitude! with brede
>   Of marble men and maidens overwrought,
> With forest branches and the trodden weed;
>   Thou, silent form, dost tease us out of thought
> As doth eternity: Cold Pastoral!
>   When old age shall this generation waste,
>   Thou shalt remain, in midst of other woe
> Than ours, a friend to man, to whom thou say'st,
>   Beauty is truth, truth beauty,—that is all
>   Ye know on earth, and all ye need to know.

Like the details of the last stanza of the Nightingale ode, the
ejaculation "Cold Pastoral!" will distress us only if we have
been inattentive to the final movement of the poem, the dis-
engagement of the poet from the thing of beauty that he himself has created. The silent urn, like the idea of eternity that
it partly represents, would tease us out of language and consciousness, but Keats chooses in the end to dwell not in
eternity but in history. The urn remains "a friend to man,"
but only as a consolation for man's condition, not as an alternative to it or an escape from it. "We have *Art,*" as Nietzsche
said, "in order *not to perish of Truth,*"[31] an aphorism very
different from the concluding message of the urn (though
much in the spirit of Keats' own proem to *Endymion*). The
sense of history in this last stanza is resolutely tragic and
echoes the "hungry generations" of the Nightingale ode. It
is only in the context of this tragic conclusion that the last two
lines of the poem are to be read, whatever the punctuation.
Keats has already made clear the limitations of the urn as "a

31. Quoted by Erich Heller, *The Disinherited Mind* (Harmonds-
worth: Penguin, 1961), p. 153.

friend to man." Both of the great odes tell us in the end that a friend that teases us out of thought can be a dangerous friend indeed! "Old age shall this generation waste": this is a truth that is not beautiful. We may thank the "thing of beauty" for distracting us from such a thought, but at the same time we know that we are being consoled more than enlightened.[32]

Yet the tragic conception that underlies the odes is affirmative rather than bleak. In the "Ode to a Nightingale" Keats moves beyond despair, and all the odes finally resist that flight from consciousness which is only another form of despair. "No, No, go not to Lethe," begins the "Ode on Melancholy,"

> For shade to shade will come too drowsily,
> And drown the wakeful anguish of the soul.

"The wakeful anguish of the soul": there is perhaps no better description of tragedy in English literature. Tragedy is the dialectic between anguish and wakefulness, suffering and consciousness—"the fierce dispute / Betwixt damnation and impassion'd clay"—from which the soul emerges new born, even in the face of its destruction. We may recall again the letter on "Soul-making" in which Keats, after insisting, as in the odes, on the inevitability of decay, suffering, and death, takes pains to distinguish his insistence from the Christian one. To the Christian, he says, suffering is an argument against world, against "a vale of tears." To Keats, however, this is "the vale of Soul-making," for suffering is the fire

32. This is not to say that Keats "rejects" the urn, only that he places it—leaves it poised at a distance, indicates its partial perspective through an extreme dramatic utterance. Keats means the sweeping generality of the urn's statement to be self-limiting, a piece of dramatic irony, and the final tableau—Keats and urn (whether we think Keats answers the urn or not)—like the questions in the last two lines of the Nightingale ode, expresses Keats' residual ambivalence, his residual nostalgia for the kind of art he has left behind, the kind represented by the nightingale and the urn, which has now in effect been superseded by the dialectical and tragic art of the odes themselves.

through which the self forges its "identity" (2:100–104). A strikingly similar conception of tragedy was later developed by Nietzsche:

> ... Dionysus versus "the Crucified One": there you have the contrast. It is not martyrdom that constitutes the difference—only here it has two different senses. Life itself, its eternal fruitfulness and recurrence, involves agony, destruction, the will to annihilation. In the other case, suffering—"the Crucified One as the Innocent One"—is considered an objection to this life, as the formula of its condemnation. Clearly, the problem is that of the meaning of suffering: whether a Christian meaning or a tragic meaning. In the first case, it is supposed to be the path to a sacred existence; in the second case, *existence is considered sacred enough* to justify even a tremendous amount of suffering. The tragic man affirms even the harshest suffering: he is sufficiently strong, rich, and deifying for this; the Christian negates even the happiest life on earth: he is sufficiently weak, poor, and disinherited to suffer from life in any form. The God on the cross is a curse on life, a pointer to seek redemption from it; Dionysus cut to pieces is a *promise* of life: it is eternally reborn and comes back from destruction.[33]

We need not give Nietzsche the final word, for Keats himself wrote the poetic counterpart to this text.[34] The great last stanza of the "Ode on Melancholy" turns the wisdom of the two long odes into a credo of direct tragic affirmation.

> She dwells with Beauty—Beauty that must die;
>   And Joy, whose hand is ever at his lips
> Bidding adieu; and aching Pleasure nigh,
>   Turning to poison while the bee-mouth sips:
> Ay, in the very temple of Delight

33. *The Portable Nietzsche,* ed. and trans. Walter Kaufmann (New York, 1954), p. 459.

34. Perhaps two, for Apollo's "dying into life" and into his godhead at the end of *Hyperion* may be based, as the late Andrew Chiappe once suggested to me, on the death and rebirth of Dionysus.

Veil'd Melancholy has her sovran shrine,
    Though seen of none save him whose strenuous tongue
Can burst Joy's grape against his palate fine;
 His soul shall taste the sadness of her might,
    And be among her cloudy trophies hung.

When Douglas Bush, with much qualification and hesitation, calls this statement "decadent," or when Dr. Leavis asserts that here "the besetting fret of transience" is itself "turned into a luxury," they surely mistake Keats' emphasis.[35] The temple of Delight and the shrine of Melancholy are bowers again but bowers transformed, linked opposites turning into one another, forms of passage. "Je ne peinds pas l'estre, je peinds le passage."[36] Most critics write as if Keats were proposing some abstract doctrine about pleasure and pain, or writing a recipe for mixing melancholy and joy, death and sensuality, a recipe of which some approve but which others find decadent. Actually, as Karl Kroeber writes, these contraries "are represented by Keats not as states of mind but as processes by which the mind passes from one condition to another."[37] This is what links the "Ode on Melancholy" to the *via negativa,* the eccentric path, of the other odes, where perverse longings signify so much more than decadence or nostalgia.

We ought not to misread the bittersweet ending of the "Ode on Melancholy." This is not the "easeful Death" which tempts Keats in the "Ode to a Nightingale," "to cease upon the midnight with no pain." Neither is transience merely a "besetting fret." This is real death, an ineluctable fate, involving real pain and real destruction, but also involving the pleasures and

35. "*Melancholy* is the only poem of Keats that might be said, not altogether unjustly, to approach the 'decadent'" (Bush, *John Keats: Life and Writings,* p. 148). Leavis, *Revaluation,* p. 260.

36. Montaigne, "Of Repentance."

37. Karl Kroeber, *The Artifice of Reality: Poetic Style in Wordsworth, Foscolo, Keats, and Leopardi* (Madison, Wisc., 1964), pp. 77–78.

pains of heightened awareness, lucid anguish, and momentary sensory intensity. The permanence that the nightingale
and the Grecian urn seemed to offer is forgotten here. Keats
no longer seeks passive dissolution, freedom from the flux
and tension of actuality; he dismisses that wish, demands
passionate, active assault on the world of experience, with all
its contrary sensations, with all its intimations of mortality.
He whose strenuous tongue bursts Joy's grape both pene-
trates to the heart of Joy and shatters Joy. He who cherishes
beauty finds not "a joy for ever" but becomes infinitely vulnerable to the transience and death of beauty. He who com-
mits himself to "breathing human passion" must also accept
"a heart high sorrowful and cloy'd, / A burning forehead,
and a parching tongue." The odes tell the story of that commitment and acceptance, of the finitude that is not "a curse
on life" but rather "a promise of life."

6
New Thresholds,
New Anatomies

No VERSION of the Keats story can end happily: not a biography certainly, but not even a history of his creative life. The poems that follow the odes provide a melancholy legacy to posterity, a painful suggestion of what might have been. This is particularly true of the greatest of them, *The Fall of Hyperion—A Dream,* which is a fragment intermittently punctuated by perplexity, despair, and retreat. The odes themselves, though an extraordinary and achieved body of work, are more a manifesto for a new stage of consciousness than a complete representation of that consciousness. Just as Keats a year earlier had described "Tintern Abbey" as a transitional poem and a necessary prologue to Wordsworth's explorations of the "dark passages" of "the heart and nature of Man" (1:281), so the odes look both before and after. They look back to the Chamber of Maiden Thought, still very much a part of Keats' mind, yet forward to a widening of consciousness, to a poetry of actuality and self-definition. But Keats' "Tintern Abbey" is followed by no *Prelude*. We have only the new induction to the revised *Hyperion* to tell us what his *Prelude* might have been like.

It may be that Keats was mistaken, that he did not have it in him to make poetry out of the "sole self" and "the agonies, the strife / Of human hearts." Both *Lamia* and *The Fall of Hyperion* contain new versions of the Chamber of Maiden Thought, new symbols of the bower-world which Keats had so many times bidden farewell. Perhaps the luxuriant dream-world of the early poems ran too deep to be uprooted, much as he wished to do so. Poets can sometimes will themselves into commitments which go against the grain of their genius, as Wordsworth did in "Peele Castle" in dedicating himself to a new sense of tragedy, and as Keats did in trying to write Shakespearean plays. Perhaps this inner resistance to change was the only agony and strife that Keats really knew; perhaps Keats' only subject was the process of transformation itself, which he could never consummate and yet would never abandon. Such a supposition is belied in the end by the verse itself. The language of *Lamia,* though awkward at times, is notably disintoxicated and consciously avoids the sensuous extravagance of *The Eve of St. Agnes*.[1] But this pales when compared to the new idiom of *The Fall of Hyperion,* which is at once weighty and unadorned, full of direct tragic seriousness, without a touch of Spenserian lushness or a capitulation to Miltonic grandeur and sonority. Such verse suggests a transformation not merely intended but achieved.[2]

Lamia need not detain us long since, like Keats' earlier narrative romances, it is more an offshoot of the poet's inner

1. On the other hand, the language of *The Eve of St. Agnes* is full of comic exaggeration, especially in its combinations of lush delicacy or religiose solemnity with marvelously restrained irony. The result, though unique in tone, is more than a little Byronic (as Jerome McGann has argued in an unpublished essay), and foreshadows the more disintoxicated language of *Lamia*.

2. See Dr. Leavis' sensitive discussion of the verse of *The Fall of Hyperion* (*Revaluation,* pp. 268–73).

..opment than a distinctive stage. Romance was a "refuge" for Keats, as he himself had admitted in the "Epistle to Reynolds." Neither *Isabella* nor *The Eve of St. Agnes* offer much access to the rich turbulence of Keats' interior life and speculative growth. *Lamia,* however, is something of a mutant. Critics have universally recognized it to be an enigmatic and ambivalent poem. For the first time Keats manages to embody some of his deepest conflicts in the narrative itself rather than in a verbal radiance that bathes the narrative in a glow of "significance," as in *The Eve of St. Agnes.* "I have been hovering for some time," Keats had written the previous year, "between an exquisite sense of the luxurious and a love for Philosophy" (1:271). Yet the story of *Lamia* is not a wholly adequate vehicle for such conflicts. We are often told that *Lamia* portrays the conflict between poetry and philosophy, or between sensation and reflection, or, in modern terms, between the pleasure principle and the reality principle. All these terms are relevant, and some were suggested by Keats himself: the poem is rich with implication. But we betray both Keats and our best selves if we consider Lamia an adequate embodiment of poetry or Apollonius of philosophy. Moreover, such schematic emphasis tends to ignore the pivotal figure of Lycius, Lamia's lover, to see him as doubly victimized, when in fact he is more responsible for the final catastrophe than Lamia or Apollonius.[3] In one respect it's understandable that we tend to ignore him, for in a psychological schema Lycius would represent the weak ego unable to achieve overall integration, unable to mediate between the absolutely demanding id and a harshly repressive superego. Such integration Keats himself had tried to imagine in the odes, particularly the "Ode to Psyche," which ends with the union of Cupid and Psyche, of "soft delight" and "shadowy

3. See Wasserman, *The Finer Tone,* pp. 169–70.

thought." In *Lamia* the polarities reassert themselves with disastrous consequences. To Lamia (and perhaps to Keats in this darker time) thought and sensuality, public life and love life, cannot be reconciled. She fears to allow Lycius even a moment of distraction, for "but a moment's thought is passion's passing bell" (II, 39). To Apollonius, the philosopher and "realist," Lamia is no more than a threat and an illusion; he sees nothing of her beauty. He easily sees through the illusions of Lycius and the deceptions of Lamia but is himself deluded. The poet shows this to us not only by direct comment (II, 221–38), but by concluding the story differently from his source, which makes no mention of the death of Lycius. Here the young man dies a moment after the philosopher claims to be protecting him "from every ill / Of life" (II, 296–97). The dramatic irony is blatant: Apollonius preserves him from life as well. Only the philosopher survives, evidently with the self-satisfaction of having solved a "knotty problem" (II, 160).

Lamia and Apollonius are intransigent opposites, as both recognize better than Lycius. Lamia embodies only one side of Keats' poetic ideal, as evidenced by her ability "to unperplex bliss from its neighbour pain" (I, 192), which Keats himself had sought to do in his early poems, but had renounced in the odes, particularly the "Ode on Melancholy." Similarly in *The Fall of Hyperion* Moneta tells Keats that the poet cannot experience "the pain alone; the joy alone; distinct" (I, 174). If Lamia does represent poetry it is only Keats' earlier poetry of the love nest and the bower, of sensation and dream and "faery lands forlorn." Once again Keats is bidding these joys farewell, but now he may fear that his imagination cannot survive the transition. How else shall we interpret the concluding lines of the poem, in which Keats emphasizes how much the life of Lycius had been bound up with his passion for Lamia?

> And Lycius' arms were empty of delight,
> As were his limbs of life, from that same night.
> On the high couch he lay!—his friends came round—
> Supported him—no pulse, or breath they found,
> And, in its marriage robe, the heavy body wound.
>
> (II, 307–11)

There is perhaps a stronger note of personal regret when Keats berates Lycius directly for having betrayed the bower of his love:

> O senseless Lycius! Madman! wherefore flout
> The silent-blessing fate, warm cloister'd hours,
> And show to common eyes those secret bowers?
>
> (II, 147–49)

Yet Lycius' betrayal is different from Keats' own. Lycius betrays them not to "pass them for a nobler life" but only out of vanity and self-will; he makes them public, turning his love for Lamia into mere display. His insistence on a public wedding feast, to which Lamia weakly accedes, is the mainspring of the final catastrophe. The scene in which this is decided is something quite new in Keats. It has a realistic complexity and psychological insight which we have not previously encountered in his work, and which may indicate that he was indeed moving toward a poetry of actuality, not only in intention but in ability. Keats himself preferred *Lamia* to his two earlier romances for its realism. With his remarkable powers of self-criticism, he steadfastly rebuffed his friends' desire that he publish the sentimental *Isabella:*

> There is too much inexperience of live [*for* life], and simplicity of knowledge in it. . . . There are very few would look to the reality. . . . There is no objection of this kind to Lamia —A good deal to St. Agnes Eve—only not so glaring. (2:174)

What is the "reality" that Keats finds even below the mawkish surface of *Isabella?* It may be the direct incursion of the author into the poem, which in *Lamia* takes the form of witty Byronic asides sometimes directed against sentiment itself, and which in *Isabella* startles us in stanzas 14–16 with an account of the economic infrastructure of the romantic situation.

There is another possibility however. The elusive "reality" of *Isabella* may be a psychological dimension, which foreshadows the more trenchant psychological insight of *Lamia*. *Isabella's* mad attachment to the Basil-pot which contains the head of her murdered lover is more than grotesque pathos. Isabella loses her reason but survives the death of her lover by becoming fixated on the Basil; when that is taken she pines away and dies lamenting not Lorenzo but the pot: "O cruelty, / To steal my Basil-pot away from me" (stanza 63). Geoffrey Hartman has defined similar characterizations in the *Lyrical Ballads,* where we see "people clinging to one thing or idea with a tenaciousness both pathetic and frightening." This clinging, he says, results from loss or separation and saves the survivors "from a still deeper sense of separation."[4] In the case of *Isabella* the apparent pathos of the conclusion is thereby tinged with a kind of irony, and the extreme grotesquerie serves to alienate rather than engage our sympathies, just as Keats frequently fends off our emotional involvement in *Lamia*. Keats himself did not hesitate in a letter to attribute to *Isabella* "an amusing sober-sadness" (1:174). His correspondent Woodhouse, who liked the poem and had urged publication, was probably not amused.[5]

4. Hartman, *Wordsworth's Poetry,* p. 143.

5. Since writing this I have come upon Jack Stillinger's very original exploration of the "reality" of *Isabella* in "Keats and Romance," *Studies in English Literature, 1500–1900* 8 (1968): 593–605. He marshals much evidence for an anti-romantic side to the poem, too much I think. Only by reducing romance to "naive romance" (what the poem calls "The simple plaining of a minstrel's song") can he treat every grotesque and gothic detail, as well as every realistic one, as (in his words)

The "reality" of *Lamia* is also a psychological one, though of a different order. There is a real man and woman in the poem, and they exhibit feelings different from the conventional romance emotions which, despite various ironic and realistic touches, still dominate the lovers in *Isabella* and *The Eve of St. Agnes.* At the beginning of Part II we see the lovers on their couch of pleasance. Lycius is distracted by a sound of trumpets—a call from the active, masculine world that he has abandoned. Lamia is distressed, for she wishes to possess him totally:

> His spirit pass'd beyond its golden bourn
> Into the noisy world almost forsworn.
> The lady, ever watchful, penetrant,
> Saw this with pain, so arguing a want
> Of something more, more than her empery
> Of joys.
>
> (II, 32–37)

Lycius replies that far from deserting her he wishes to possess her even more completely,

> ". . . to entangle, trammel up and snare
>   Your soul in mine, and labyrinth you there
>   Like the hid scent in an unbudded rose."
>
> (II, 52–54)

He will accomplish this, he says, by asserting his title publicly, by sending his "prize" to "pace abroad majestical," in order "that other men / May be confounded and abashed withal" (57–59). Foreseeing the "keen, cruel, perceant, stinging" gaze of the real world (II, 301), Lamia objects, weeps:

"*anti*-romance." The Gothic novel was after all one of Keats' earliest "romantic" interests. Stillinger rightly emphasizes Keats' turn from romance during the winter and spring of 1818 (see chap. 4 above), and valuably relates *Isabella* to this context, but the second half of the poem is not quite the piece of tragic realism that he makes it.

> at last with pain
> Beseeching him, the while his hand she wrung,
> To change his purpose. He thereat was stung,
> Perverse, with stronger fancy to reclaim
> Her wild and timid nature to his aim:
> Besides, for all his love, in self despite
> Against his better self, he took delight
> Luxurious in her sorrows, soft and new.
> His passion, cruel grown, took on a hue
> Fierce and sanguineous. . . .
>
> (II, 67–76)

Love, possession, and sadistic desire for domination inter-
mingle here, under the significant banner of Keats' old ideal
of "luxury." The lover's passion turns imperceptibly into
cruelty and aggression, and soon the die is cast, but not without the masochistic collaboration of the all-too-human lady:

> She burnt, she lov'd the tyranny,
> And, all subdued, consented to the hour
> When to the bridal he should lead his paramour.
>
> (II, 81–83)

It is for this public display that Lamia must build the faery
palace, which, in the words of Keats' source, is "no substance
but mere illusions."[6] There is nothing insubstantial about her
love, but in its public form it is no longer love: the philosophic
eye of Apollonius merely confirms that it has already been
destroyed from within.

As if for emphasis, Keats has presented us at the beginning
of the poem with a seriocomic parallel, the love of the "ever-
smitten" Hermes for the nymph. Lamia, we recall, plays a
double role in that affair, as if to point up the ambiguity of
her character. She assumes protection of the nymph and gen-
erously shields her from sexual demands, from "the love-

6. Garrod (1958), p. 214 n. The source is a passage in Burton's
Anatomy of Melancholy.

glances of unlovely eyes, / Of Satyrs, Fauns, and blear'd Silenus' sighs" (I, 102–3). She does so by making the nymph invisible, thus protecting not only her chastity but, as she stresses, her privacy as well. Yet she plays the madam and sells the nymph to the flighty Hermes to gratify her own sexual longing.

The invisibility of the nymph is but another version of a familiar Keatsian motif: the prolonged preadolescent paradise, here again portrayed as an idyllic contentment and an immersion in nature (I, 94–99). Keats had described this prelapsarian happiness in several of the parallel stories of *Endymion,* and the language here echoes that of Arethusa (*End.,* II, 965–68), whom this nymph resembles. As in *Endymion* Keats stresses the inevitability of the fall; both nymphs experience a harsh but necessary sexual awakening. But Alpheus is really in love while the mercurial Hermes is on a fling, momentarily smitten by desire. The love scene that follows is something of a rape, though a beautiful and ambiguous one, and Keats puts touching emphasis on the nymph's unwillingness, her sense of violation. This inevitably reflects back on Lamia herself, who has just been likened to Circe (I, 115):

> Upon the nymph his eyes he bent
> Full of adoring tears and blandishment,
> And towards her stept: she, like a moon in wane,
> Faded before him, cower'd, nor could restrain
> Her fearful sobs, self-folding like a flower
> That faints into itself at evening hour.
>
> (I, 134–39)

The imagery reminds us of another seduction that borders on violation, what one critic has called "the hoodwinking of Madeline."[7] In *The Eve of St. Agnes* the moon signifies

7. Jack Stillinger, "The Hoodwinking of Madeline: Scepticism in *The Eve of St. Agnes,*" in *Keats: A Collection of Critical Essays,* ed. W. J. Bate (Englewood Cliffs, N.J., 1964), pp. 71–90.

sexual consummation ("St. Agnes' moon hath set
36), and the closing flower describes the tantalizing
born innocence that precedes the fall (stanza 27): Madeline
falls asleep, "Blissfully haven'd both from joy and pain; . . .
As though a rose should shut, and be a bud again." It is not in
the rose's nature to become a bud again. On the verge of
passage both Madeline and the nymph feel impelled to fall
back like Blake's Thel toward an unspoiled innocence. But
to Keats, the flower which folds at evening must open in the
morning, to give and receive "a fair guerdon from the Bee":

> But the God fostering her chilled hand,
> She felt the warmth, her eyelids open'd bland,
> And, like new flowers at morning song of bees,
> Bloom'd, and gave up her honey to the lees.
>
> (I, 140–43)

The ambiguity of this initiation is summed up in the last line.
The nymph flowers as never before, but she is also drained
to the dregs by the hungry Hermes. A lovely harmony is for
the moment established, but one that still includes violation;
in this case it seems unlikely "that we should rather be the
flower than the Bee." But this is a story of gods. Here domination and aggression, though explicit enough, have no consequences. The story ends happily.

> Into the green-recessed woods they flew;
> Nor grew they pale as mortal lovers do.
>
> (I, 144–45)

We hear no more of Hermes and the nymph, and we recall
their fate only by contrast. In the human world to which we
now turn things end differently.

Human world? Yes, the serpent and Circe of the prologue
becomes the most human figure in the poem. She first must
undergo a transformation akin to the nymph's passage from

innocence to experience. But the metamorphosis of Lamia is more significant, because it involves explicit humanization, which makes it a direct link between the metamorphosis of Apollo at the end of *Hyperion* and the initiation of the poet in the revised version. The odes have interceded, with their emphasis on tragic self-definition and identity: deification now gives way to humanization. It is Lamia's turn to be ravished and violated.

> The colours all inflam'd throughout her train,
> She writh'd about, convuls'd with scarlet pain:
> A deep volcanian yellow took the place
> Of all her milder-mooned body's grace;
> And, as the lava ravishes the mead,
> Spoilt all her silver mail, and golden brede,
> Made gloom of all her frecklings, streaks and bars,
> Eclips'd her crescents, and lick'd up her stars:
> So that, in moments few, she was undrest
> Of all her sapphires, greens, and amethyst,
> And rubious-argent: of all these bereft,
> Nothing but pain and ugliness were left.
>
> (I, 153–64)

Here Keats is retracting detail by detail his earlier description of the beauty of the snake (I, 47 ff.). Lamia must go beyond artificial beauty, must pass through pain and ugliness in order to be humanized.[8] The celestial ornaments, the silver moons and stars that represent her supernatural powers, must give way to a deep volcanic eruption from within the earth; something akin to a "lava" must ravish the field of her beauty and her immortality. Like Cynthia in Book IV of *Endymion* she must "throw the goddess off" (I, 336) in order to win her human lover.

The Fall of Hyperion is even more centrally a poem of

8. I am indebted to Geoffrey Hartman for first making me aware of the importance of this passage.

passage in which the poet must undergo a radical humanization in order to gain access to the sources of vision. The realism of the poem is not psychological, nor does it involve unmediated self-confrontation, as we might expect after the odes. This is not Keats' *Prelude,* though he significantly recast the poem in the first person. This is not a poem about the "sole self," but rather an attempt to embody the transformation that takes place in the odes in a new myth. Despite this mediation of myth and allegory, and the fact that Keats is a witness to the tragedy rather than its central subject, there is a peculiar new nakedness in the poem, which reminds us of Keats' model, Dante, or of Wordsworth in his most exposed and sombre moments.

> Without stay or prop
> But my own weak mortality, I bore
> The load of this eternal quietude,
> The unchanging gloom. . . .
>
> (I, 388–91)

In earlier Keats such moments of nakedness would have been evidence of failure, experiences inimical to poetic creation. But in the *Fall* Keats seeks to "purge off" his "mind's film" (I, 145–46), to find words which will express vision by demystifying it, for words "alone can save / Imagination from the sable charm / And dumb enchantment" (I, 9–11). Art is no longer to be identified with an ideal and timeless silence, like the "ditties of no tone" and "silent form" of the Grecian urn, but with language that can express both our joys and pains, our "guesses at Heaven" (I, 4) and the "high tragedy" of "some old man of the earth / Bewailing earthly loss" (I, 277, 440–41). Such art may lack epic dignity or classical grace and harmony, may keep our eyes and ears from acting "with that pleasant unison of sense / Which marries sweet sound with the grace of form" (I, 442–43), but we can hope it will compensate in truth for what it lacks in exterior beauty.

Yet *The Fall of Hyperion* is beautiful enough in its harsh
and uncompromising modern way. What it entirely abjures is
Beauty, the sensuous self-indulgence and visionary "phantasms" of the early poems, as well as their real luxurious
exuberance and opulence. As in the odes the poet must reenact
his whole development, but there is hardly a trace of nostalgia
in the retrospection of the *Fall*. For the first time Keats can
look back to his Edenic bower-world without being betrayed
back (as Lawrence is "betrayed back" to his childhood in his
wonderfully ambivalent poem about nostalgia, "Piano"). In
the garden in which he finds himself at the beginning of the
poem he sees

> a feast of summer fruits,
> Which, nearer seen, seem'd refuse of a meal
> By Angel tasted or our Mother Eve;
> For empty shells were scattered on the grass,
> And grape stalks but half bare. . . .
>
> (I, 29–33)

This is not simply a garden world of mythical fruitfulness,
like Endymion's Latmos. Though Keats will soon invoke the
fabled horn of plenty, the scene is already partly despoiled, a
paradise in which others have already eaten. We see what
looks like the "refuse" of an interrupted meal in an Eden
from which our mother Eve was suddenly expelled. Even
darker undertones qualify the mysterious draught that Keats,
overcome by his appetite and by the sensuous surroundings,
drinks in this garden:

> No Asian poppy, nor Elixir fine
> Of the soon fading jealous Caliphat;
> No poison gender'd in close monkish cell
> To thin the scarlet conclave of old men,
> Could so have rapt unwilling life away.
>
> (I, 47–51)

He struggles hard against "the domineering potion" but finally sinks down in a "cloudy swoon." This drink, though delicious, does not resemble "the pure wine / Of happiness" that we encountered in *Endymion* (III, 801–2), or the "draught of vintage" of the second stanza of the "Ode to a Nightingale," or even its own original, Apollo's "bright elixir" in the first *Hyperion* ("as if some blithe wine / Or bright elixir peerless I had drunk / And so become immortal," III, 118–20). Here, just as appetite has unforeseen consequences, intoxication and sleep prove more sinister than gratifying; loss of consciousness is deathlike and terrible, and Keats fiercely resists it.

The poet's transformation, though clearly a reworking of the metamorphosis of Apollo, is not as easily accomplished. The earlier metamorphosis came to Keats, as it comes to Apollo, in an inspired fit, like "something given to him."[9] The initiation of the poet requires a more extended and intense effort, a more human effort of *self*-transformation. Unlike Apollo the poet must "die into life" more than once: the potion is insufficient; he must undergo the ordeal of the stairs, and raise himself up consciously by his own powers. It is only then, having "felt / What 'tis to die and live again before / [His] fated hour" (I, 141–43), that he can be granted the vision of Moneta and the knowledge that she bears, which in a sense is his final ordeal, the ordeal of consciousness.

The poet awakens from his unwilling sleep, to find the garden replaced by a temple, identified, he later discovers, with Saturn's reign.

> I look'd around upon the carved sides
> Of an old sanctuary with roof august,
> Builded so high, it seem'd that filmed clouds

9. According to Woodhouse, the whole passage "seemed to come by chance or magic—to be as it were something given to him." Rollins, *The Keats Circle*, 1:129.

> Might spread beneath, as o'er the stars of heaven;
> So old the place was, I remembered none
> The like upon the earth: what I had seen
> Of grey Cathedrals, buttress'd walls, rent towers,
> The superannuations of sunk realms,
> Or Nature's Rocks toil'd hard in waves and winds,
> Seem'd but a faulture of decrepit things
> To that eternal domed monument.
>
> (I, 61–71)

The temple stretches out towards the eternal and the infinite, with a dome that seems as high as the stars, with a "massy" range of columns "ending in mist / Of nothing" (I, 84–85). There is "none / The like upon the earth"; yet, perhaps because of the Miltonic problem of "making comparisons of earthly things" (II, 3), the awesome temple takes on the sense of all the metaphoric things that but poorly suggest it. Though apparently intact, the temple seems more battered than any natural rock, more ruined than any earthly ruin, more sunken than any earthly realm. It is lonely and bleak in the very grandeur of its survival, in its simultaneous massiveness and nothingness. It is a relic of the sunken kingdom of Saturn, the realm of myth and pre-history: a paradoxical relic of the infinite. It is a religious monument, not because Keats feels any sudden attraction to what he elsewhere calls "the pious frauds of Religion" (2:80), but rather to convey a sense of the remote and archaic. The sacred instruments of lapsed rituals lie before the poet "in a mingled heap confus'd" (I, 78). Once again, as in the "Ode to Psyche," Keats is enveloping an account of his own growth and transformation in a sketch of the history of culture—from myth to human history, from nature to hieratic ritual, and then to imaginative consciousness and consciousness of self. For Keats the true temple remains where this temple will turn out to be: "In some untrodden region of my mind" ("Psyche," 51).

He approaches the altar and is overcome for a moment by the delicious odor of the incense which, in a beautiful simile (I, 97–101), he likens to a fragrant, renovating mid-May breeze.[10] Its effect on Keats, however, is not renewal but a relapse into happy unconsciousness: "Forgetfulness of everything but bliss" (I, 104). It is the sort of reversion that takes place in the Chamber of Maiden Thought. Though we have been impelled out of the "infant or thoughtless Chamber" by "the awakening of the thinking principle," in the second chamber we nevertheless "become intoxicated with the light and the atmosphere, we see nothing but pleasant wonders, and think of delaying there for ever in delight" (1:280–81). This sensuous delay is what calls forth Moneta's threat and challenge to ascend the stairs. Invaded by a "palsied chill," numb with impending death, he finally achieves the ascent, but only by dint of enormous effort, overcoming surreal and dreamlike difficulties. Only then does Moneta explain the meaning of his trial:

> "None can usurp this height," returned that shade,
> "But those to whom the miseries of the world
> Are misery, and will not let them rest.
> All else who find a haven in the world,
> Where they may thoughtless sleep away their days,
> If by a chance into this fane they come,
> Rot on the pavement where thou rotted'st half.—"
>
> (I, 147–53)

Here at the culmination of his career Keats returns to his first important poem, "Sleep and Poetry," perhaps to measure the distance he has covered between 1816 and 1819. The *Fall* is a final renunciation of sleep, thoughtlessness, and the sensuous self-sufficiency of the realm of Flora and old Pan. "And can

10. The origin of the simile is Cary's translation of the *Purgatorio* (canto 24, lines 142–47), but there are anticipations in several early poems of Keats.

I ever bid these joys farewell?" Keats had asked himself with genuine uncertainty.

> Yes, I must pass them for a nobler life,
> Where I may find the agonies, the strife
> Of human hearts.

(122–25)

The *Fall* is a massive attempt to take these lines seriously, as Keats' imagination could not in "Sleep and Poetry."

Keats' problem in the *Fall* is not an inability to take human suffering seriously enough; if anything, he takes "the giant agony of the world" almost too seriously, so that his humanist commitment to alleviate it calls into question the value of poetry. "I am convinced more and more day by day," Keats wrote to Reynolds, "that fine writing is next to fine doing the top thing in the world" (2:146). But Moneta, "the admonisher," becomes so fierce a spokesman for "fine doing" *against* "fine writing" that Keats, after an uncertain gesture of self-defense, falls into a lacerating, petulant diatribe against himself and some of his fellow poets. The passage recalls the unfortunate outbursts against various poets in "Sleep and Poetry." Keats, perhaps realizing that the poem was falling into self-contradiction, ungracious personal animosity and stifling despair, wisely decided to cancel the whole exchange (I, 187–210).[11] But the passage remains a valuable testimony

11. Another link with "Sleep and Poetry," and another reason Keats may have wished to cancel these lines, is the way they fall back upon the earlier conception of poetry as a soothing "balm" for the pains of humanity: the poet "pours out a balm upon the world" while the dreamer (including Keats himself, in this dejected and uncertain moment) merely "vexes it" (I, 198–202).

In the *Fall* as a whole Keats rejects this notion of poetry, just as he passes far beyond his fruitless feelings of personal unworthiness. The most thorough discussion of this problem and the most impassioned argument for cancellation of these lines is by Middleton Murry, "The Poet and the Dreamer," in *Keats,* pp. 238–49. For another view see Brian Wicker, "The Disputed Lines in *The Fall of Hyperion,*" *Essays in Criticism* 7 (1957): 28–41.

to the anguish and self-doubt that Keats at times felt while composing the poem.

Even if we ignore the personal digression of this disputed passage, a deeper anguish remains in the text, particularly in the exchange with Moneta that directly precedes it. Keats begins by asking why he alone seems to have undergone the ordeal of the stairs. "Are there not thousands in the world," he asks,

> "Who love their fellows even to the death;
> Who feel the giant agony of the world;
> And more, like slaves to poor humanity,
> Labour for mortal good?"
>
> (I, 154, 156–59)

One is reminded of the dying words of the man in Kafka's parable who has for so many years vainly sought admission to the Law. "Everyone strives to attain the Law," he says; "how does it come about, then, that in all these years no one has come seeking admittance but me?" "No one but you could gain admittance through this door," the doorkeeper replies, "since this door was intended only for you. I am now going to shut it."[12] Moneta, whose "sooth voice" had encouraged the poet to speak freely, will eventually admit the poet, but here she answers with a similar combination of solicitude and brutal sternness, in terms that devalue poetry and seem to exalt not only the active life but the complacent, unreflective one:

> "They whom thou spak'st of are no vision'ries,"
> Rejoin'd that voice—"they are no dreamers weak,
> They seek no wonder but the human face;
> No music but a happy-noted voice—
> They come not here, they have no thought to come—
> And thou art here, for thou art less than they—

12. Franz Kafka, "Before the Law," trans. Willa and Edwin Muir, *Parables and Paradoxes* (New York, 1961), pp. 64, 65.

What benefit canst thou do, or all thy tribe,
To the great world? Thou art a dreaming thing;
A fever of thyself—think of the Earth;
What bliss even in hope is there for thee?
What haven? every creature hath its home;
Every sole man hath days of joy and pain,
Whether his labours be sublime or low—
The pain alone; the joy alone; distinct:
Only the dreamer venoms all his days,
Bearing more woe than all his sins deserve.
Therefore, that happiness be somewhat shar'd
Such things as thou art are admitted oft
Into like gardens thou didst pass erewhile,
And suffer'd in these Temples; for that cause
Thou standest safe beneath this statue's knees."

(I, 161–81)

I quote the speech in its entirety because, along with the vision of Moneta's face, it is at the moral and imaginative center of the poem. Nevertheless, like the disputed passage that follows, it does not have a completely coherent relation to its context. When Moneta asks "what haven" there is for such as the poet, we have a right to feel puzzled. A moment earlier she had denounced those "who find a haven in the world / Where they may thoughtless sleep away their days." He had ascended the stairs on the strength of his difference from them; now Moneta says that he is "less than they."

Middleton Murry, with persuasive ingenuity, has argued that Keats is introducing a new distinction here: "The first division was between unimaginative men and the imaginative, 'those to whom the miseries of the world are misery'. In this division Keats belongs to the imaginative men. But the imaginative men are divided into those like Keats, who dream, and those who act for immediate human good. These latter imaginative men are one with the common, unimaginative men in that they both—'whether their labours be sublime' (the imaginative active man) 'or low' (the unimaginative active man)—experience their pain and their joy distinct. Only the dreamer (the imaginative, inactive man) venoms *all* his days, that is, experiences pain in all his joys. Therefore such as he are admitted often into the garden, and into the temple, in order that they may taste some pure happiness."[13] But if Keats was so much the inactive dreamer, why was his ordeal, through which he had passed successfully, described so much in terms of an active exertion? Why was he given the impression that he had been saved, only to be cruelly rebuffed a moment later? Why should Moneta, who has just reviled the "unimaginative men" and condemned them to rot on the pavement, suddenly praise them for not coming to the temple at all? Why should she bracket these ordinary souls with the true (and active) humanitarians, those "who love their fellows even to the death" and actively "labour for mortal good"? These questions become especially vexing if, as Murry insists, we cancel the disputed passage. There Keats makes at least an eloquent attempt to defend the poet:

> sure not all
> Those melodies sung into the world's ear
> Are useless: sure a poet is a sage;
> A humanist, Physician to all men.
>   (I, 187–90)

In the light of these lines, and in view of the undeniable fact that Moneta soon assumes a more benign attitude toward Keats, to what extent can the author be said to endorse her charges?

Moneta's speech is part of an ongoing dialogue whose contraries embody Keats' own enormous ambivalence toward poetry and life. A few months earlier Keats himself had expressed feelings comparable to those of Moneta. Finding

13. Murry, *Keats,* p. 245.

himself rather detached at the news of the impending death of his friend Haslam's father, Keats is led to reflect on how far he is "from any humble standard of disinterestedness." It is a failing, he says, that he shares with most of mankind.

> Very few men have ever arrived at a complete disinterested-
> ness of Mind: very few have been influenced by a pure desire
> of the benefit of others. . . . The greater part of Men make
> their way with the same instinctiveness, the same unwander-
> ing eye from their purposes, the same animal eagerness as the
> Hawk. . . . The noble animal Man for his amusement smokes
> his pipe—the Hawk balances about the Clouds—that is the
> only difference of their leisures. This it is that makes the
> Amusement of Life—to a speculative Mind. I go among the
> Feilds and catch a glimpse of a stoat or a fieldmouse peeping
> out of the withered grass—the creature hath a purpose and
> its eyes are bright with it—I go amongst the buildings of a
> city and I see a Man hurrying along—to what? The Creature
> has a purpose and his eyes are bright with it. (2:79–80)

It is not difficult to translate the poem into these terms. Only "those to whom the miseries of the world / Are misery" would be capable of a really "disinterested" sympathy for Haslam. Most men live with animal instinctiveness; they have their home, their haven, "an unwandering eye from their purposes." They are by nature unconscious and self-interested, and would not come to the temple of Saturn to learn of "the giant agony of the world." In the letter there is a third type, the "speculative Mind," the negatively capable poet, who can marvel at bright and instinctive animal energies and yet feel humble before the heroic and disinterested altruism of men like Jesus and Socrates, the moralists and philosophers. As he says shortly afterward,

> Though a quarrel in the streets is a thing to be hated, the
> energies displayed in it are fine; the commonest Man shows
> a grace in his quarrel—By a superior being our reasoning[s]
> may take the same tone—though erroneous they may be fine

—This is the very thing in which consists poetry; and if so
it is not so fine a thing as philosophy—For the same reason
that an eagle is not so fine a thing as a truth. (2:80–81)

In the poem all these categories recur, but in a new relation
to each other, and in a drastically altered tone. To Keats, in
the bleak moment when he composed Moneta's speech, poetry
is not only less fine than philosophy but the poet is also "less
than" the instinctive *homme moyen sensuel,* whose "purpose"
and activity can now be bracketed with the purposeful activism of those "influenced by a pure desire of the benefit of
others." Behind this shift is the meditation on consciousness
that is at the heart of the poem. In *The Fall of Hyperion* Keats
storms directly (though at moments uncertainly) the citadel
around which he had so long been maneuvering. The temple
of Saturn, as Murry insists, is the temple of consciousness
itself,[14] particularly the consciousness of suffering and pain
that Keats had frequently sought to repress. In ascending the
stairs and witnessing the unveiling of Moneta and the tragic
vision of Saturn, Keats accepts this consciousness as his own
fate and endowment. In Moneta's speech he makes a dialectical counter-statement that expresses the torment and anguish, the doubt and despair, the final impulse of resistance,
which afflict him because of this painful project.

This dialectic is at the root of much Romantic and modern
literature, and Moneta's speech is full of prophetic anticipations that foreshadow some of the best and worst in the modern literary sensibility. Here, fully elaborated, we find the idea
of the artist's alienation from the ordinary life of society, with
the artist confirmed in his isolation but envying the rooted-
ness of the "natural" man who is content with the immediate
world around him. Here we confront the modern sense of
self-consciousness as diseased and solipsistic ("Thou art a
dreaming thing; / A fever of thyself—think of the Earth").

14. *Keats and Shakespeare,* p. 182.

By this self-consciousness the poet is said to add to the inevitable suffering attendant upon mortality, to compound ordinary human trials and bear "more woe than all his sins deserve." Wordsworth too, in "Resolution and Independence," had asked what haven and what home there could be for such as him, "who for himself will take no heed at all?" (42); he too had foreseen that the free consciousness, the source of his power, could turn on him and venom all his days:

> By our own spirits are we deified:
> We poets in our youth begin in gladness;
> But thereof come in the end despondency and madness.
>
> (47–49)

Here too in the *Fall* we come upon the characteristically modern envy of the political activist, of the mind not inhibited by too exquisite a sensibility or too scrupulous a sense of nuance. We can relate this easily to the fascination with energy that Keats' letter reveals. Nothing is more fraught with anticipations of modern literature than the association of poetry with grace and energy ("though erroneous they may be fine") and the relegation of truth and morality to the abstract thinker. For the modern writer this dissociation has led not only to extraordinary literary adventure, but also, unfortunately, to the most dubious political associations, when he seeks a politics of energy to complement the poetics of energy. It was evidently Hazlitt who alerted Keats to this dissociation and, with remarkable acuity, to its political consequences as well. Six days earlier, in the same letter, Keats had copied a long extract from Hazlitt's polemical *Letter to Gifford,* in which the critic quoted from and defended his view of *Coriolanus* against the editor of the *Quarterly Review:* "The cause of the people," Hazlitt had written, "is but

little calculated for a subject for Poetry; . . . the language of
Poetry naturally falls in with the language of power."

> I affi[r]m, Sir, that Poetry, that the imagination, generally
> speaking, delights in power, in strong excitement, as well as
> in truth, in good, in right, whereas pure reason and the moral
> sense approve only of the true and good. I proceed to show
> that this general love or tendency to immediate excitement or
> theatrical effect, no matter how produced, gives a Bias to the
> imagination often [in]consistent with the greatest good,
> that in Poetry it triumphs over Principle, and bribes the pas-
> sions to make a sacrifice of common humanity. (2:74–75)

This conception of poetry[15] very much influences Keats, and
in *The Fall of Hyperion* he sets out to create an alternative to
it. Within ten years it would triumph, for Carlyle would
complain of a new sensibility, a new mode of judgment, by
which "we praise a work, not as 'true,' but as 'strong;' our
highest praise is that it has 'affected' us. . . ."[16] In the *Fall*
Keats renounces the poetry of energy and grace for the poetry
of truth; he refuses "to make a sacrifice of common humanity," and argues that the poet can become "a sage; / A humanist, Physician to all men."[17] But Keats harbors a lingering and
agonizing doubt about this, and he expresses his doubt in the
words of Moneta's condemnation. "What benefit canst thou
do," he asks himself, "or all thy tribe, / To the great world."

15. And of politics and morality: later in the same journal-letter, in
questioning the altruistic purity of many supposed benefactors of humanity, he says that "some meretricious motive has sullied their greatness—some melodramatic scenery has fascinated them" (2:79). In
other words, they gave way, consciously or not, to the selfish temptations of art and public illusion, what Hazlitt calls "immediate excitement or theatrical effect."

16. Thomas Carlyle, "Signs of the Times" (1829), in *Scottish and
Other Miscellanies,* Everyman's Library (London, 1915), p. 242.

17. See Jerome Hamilton Buckley, *The Victorian Temper: A Study
in Literary Culture* (New York, 1964), p. 20.

But Moneta's speech is not the last word; the anguish of
Keats that animates it is genuine but momentary. After the
even sharper self-condemnation of the cancelled lines the poet
proceeds in a different vein, earnestly questioning the fierce
figure. Then, for reasons not adequately explained, Moneta
turns mild and generous toward him and finally grants him
her knowledge and unveils her face. The passage that describes her unveiling is a direct rebuttal to Moneta's speech.
No one could be further from those "who seek no wonder
but the human face; / No music but the happy-noted voice"
than the man who gazes at Moneta's face and listens to her
voice. Though she promises him an experience "free from
all pain" (I, 248), the vision of the fallen Saturn is as painful
as the sight of her face is frightening; she makes no attempt
"to unperplex bliss from its neighbor pain." Her appearance
is a locus of bizarre contraries, of a mother's softness and an
oracle's distance and mysteriousness, of the human and the
inhuman, of knowledge and blankness, suffering and serenity, death and immortality.

> As near as an immortal's sphered words
> Could to a mother's soften, were these last:
> But yet I had a terror of her robes,
> And chiefly of her veils, that from her brow
> Hung pale, and curtain'd her in mysteries,
> That made my heart too small to hold its blood.
> This saw that Goddess, and with sacred hand
> Parted the veils. Then saw I a wan face,
> Not pin'd by human sorrows, but bright blanch'd
> By an immortal sickness which kills not;
> It works a constant change, which happy death
> Can put no end to; deathwards progressing
> To no death was that visage; it had pass'd
> The lily and the snow; and beyond these

I must not think now, though I saw that face—
But for her eyes I should have fled away.
They held me back, with a benignant light,
Soft-mitigated by divinest lids
Half-closed, and visionless entire they seem'd
Of all external things—they saw me not,
But in blank splendor beam'd like the mild moon,
Who comforts those she sees not, who knows not
What eyes are upward cast.

(I, 249–71)

One is reminded of the revitalizing desolation of the Cave of Quietude. There too the most extreme antitheses coexist and are transcended; it is "the proper home / Of every ill" in which ultimately "anguish does not sting." The final effect differs. In the Cave of Quietude we pass beyond pain to a Centre of Indifference. In that sense it is a psychological adaptation of the bower. In being initiated into Moneta's mysteries the poet passes, in the manner of tragedy, through suffering to knowledge, from the sorrows of her wan face to the "high tragedy / In the dark secret Chambers of her skull."

There is a center of indifference here too, but only for Moneta, not for the poet. Her eyes seem "visionless entire . . . Of all external things." They have a "blank splendor," which Keats compares to that of "the mild moon, / Who comforts those she sees not, who knows not / What eyes are upward cast." The reference to the moon is revealing, for what we have here is half a parody and half an astonishing transformation of the imaginative reciprocity which the early Keats had embodied in the figure of Cynthia. From the beginning, the description of Moneta "curtain'd . . . in mysteries" is oddly reminiscent of the quest for mystery so important in the early poetry. We think of Pan, "dread opener of the mysterious

doors / Leading to universal knowledge" (*End.,* I, 288–89);
of the sea, with

> Its voice mysterious, which whoso hears
> Must think on what will be, and what has been;

and of the image that follows immediately in the same poem:

> Cynthia is from her silken curtains peeping
> So scantly, that it seems her bridal night,
> And she her half-discover'd revels keeping.
> ("To My Brother George," 7–8, 10–12)

In "I stood tip-toe" this curtained mystery still attracts and
eludes Keats, though now it turns from a metaphoric to an
actual bridal night ("O for three words of honey, that I
might / Tell but one wonder of thy bridal night!"). From
here it is but a short step to the "long love dream" of *Endymion,* which is also a poet's quest for the sources of vision.
By the time of the *Fall,* however, such a quest has greatly
changed. Cynthia offers "an immortality of passion" (II,
808), but Moneta, who embodies an immortality of pain and
suffering, offers a different kind of knowledge.[18] Her mysteries are terrible, and even when we pass beyond this, to a
kind of grace, she becomes more subtly terrifying, chillingly
blank and impersonal in her very generosity.[19] The scene is
closer to the ambiguous reciprocity of Coleridge's late poem
"Limbo" than to *Endymion;* there we see a blind old man
"with moon-like countenance" who is transfigured when by
chance he sets his face toward the moon. Coleridge describes
an interchange that is —to use Keats' words—"visionless en-

18. The connecting link is the goddess Melancholy, whose for-
bidding shrine offers us access to our "sorrow's mysteries," but who
also embodies a tragic version of Cynthia's large sensual appeal. But in
the *Fall* the emphasis on sensuality and self-annihilation is entirely replaced by the language of witness, "wonder," and knowledge.

19. "The face is alive only in a chill and inhuman way." Frank
Kermode, *Romantic Image* (London, 1961), p. 10.

tire," a reciprocity of blindness: "He seems to gaze at that which seems to gaze on him!"[20]

In the *Fall* only Moneta seems visionless. The poet sees all too well, and the difference is crucial to the passage and the poem. "My power," she says, "which to me is still a curse, / Shall be to thee a wonder" (I, 243–44). This is the secret of the initiation. In *Endymion* Glaucus is condemned by Circe to age and wither a thousand years, until Endymion comes to undo the curse. Moneta's curse cannot be undone, but the poet can transcend her "electral changing misery," can turn it into wonder, into art. Moneta can part the veils, but it takes the poet to describe her face, to turn her sufferings into knowledge. Moneta is but the "Sole priestess of [Saturn's] desolation" (I, 227); her function is no more than sacramental; she is "the pale Omega of a wither'd race" (I, 288). Keats can do more than keep the sacrifice and tend the fire. With the power she grants him, and with the power he himself displayed in ascending the stairs, he can institute a more meaningful and lasting sacrifice. As in the "Ode to Psyche" he can replace the devotions of religion with the devotions of the imagination; he can build a new altar, in the mind and with words on the page.

There remains one remarkable detail in Keats' quest for knowledge and his initiation into the mysteries of Moneta and Saturn. It comes in his immediate reaction to the vision of her face:

> As I had found
> A grain of gold upon a mountain's side,
> And twing'd with avarice strain'd out my eyes
> To search its sullen entrails rich with ore,
> So at the view of sad Moneta's brow,
> I ached to see what things the hollow brain
> Behind enwombed: what high tragedy

20. Richards, *The Portable Coleridge,* pp. 205–6.

In the dark secret Chambers of her skull
Was acting. . . .

(I, 271–77)

The desire to know takes a peculiar form here. What Keats describes as avarice actually indicates the desire to violate, to search the sullen entrails, to penetrate the womb of Moneta's consciousness; yet he had likened her voice to the soft voice of a mother (I, 250). As in *Endymion* consciousness involves not harmony but the violation of an original harmony. As in *Oedipus Rex,* a work that plays with innumerable variations on the verbs to know and to see, knowledge of self can only be achieved both by a return to one's origin and a violation of that origin. This is no regression, as happens frequently in *Endymion,* to the infantile position at the breast, as a refuge from consciousness. On the contrary, this is an independence and selfhood, achieved through destructive appropriation. Moneta is not destroyed, but not because she is an immortal. "The dark secret Chambers of her skull," which suggests the forbidden sexual lure of her knowledge, also reminds us how deathly she already is; she is beyond destruction.

In the first *Hyperion* one cannot imagine a further role for Mnemosyne after Apollo is deified. While he listens "In fearless yet in aching ignorance" (III, 107) she still has something to offer him. But once he reads "a wondrous lesson" in her "silent face," once "knowledge enormous makes a God" and a poet of him, she may continue to serve but can have nothing to offer him, for he is now himself. In the equivalent moment of the *Fall* the deification is only metaphorical. Becoming a God means learning to exercise what Blake called the "inward Eye."[21] Once the poet learns that, then Moneta,

21.   For double the vision my eyes do see,
               And a double vision is always with me.
               With my inward Eye 'tis an old Man grey;
               With my outward a Thistle across my way.
       Blake, letter to Butts, in Keynes, *Poetry and Prose,* p. 860.

who had guided his passage and initiation, can be of little additional use.

> Whereon there grew
> A power within me of enormous ken,
> To see as a God sees, and take the depth
> Of things as nimbly as the outward eye
> Can size and shape pervade. . . .

> I set myself
> Upon an Eagle's watch, that I might see,
> And seeing ne'er forget.
>
> (I, 302–6, 308–10)

Keats becomes at last the true poet, the eagle which he had earlier despaired of being (I, 191–92). Moneta's attack on poetry is reversed, but her identification of poetry with consciousness is accepted and ennobled. A new humanistic conception of poetry emerges, one foreshadowed as early as "I stood tip-toe" and "Sleep and Poetry," but which does not receive Keats' full allegiance until the *Fall*. Keats' final humanism does not lead him in the end to abandon poetry for political activism and "fine doing": the poet, he realizes, is a humanist not by abjuring consciousness but by exploring new forms of consciousness. Neither is his commitment to knowledge based upon a narrow rationalist conception of human nature. He plans both to fly as high as an eagle and to "take the depth / Of things." He must both ascend the stairs and "search" the "sullen entrails" of the earth, the "dark secret Chambers" of Moneta's brow. This poetry will be humanistic yet still in touch with the dark, chthonic sources of knowledge. In the end the poet's knowledge must be both visual and visionary; he must be at once a detached witness and an initiate into sacraments and mysteries.

The story of the fall of Saturn and Hyperion soon proves irrelevant to such meanings. The early gods, though humanized by their fall, are not adequate embodiments of the sufferings of humanity. The mythic largeness and impersonality of both the characters and style of the first *Hyperion* carry over: the epic grandeur of the earlier poem is maimed and softened without being transformed. Keats does not go far with the revision. The following year it is the first version that he will allow to be published.

The main story of Keats' literary life ends here. He goes on immediately to write "To Autumn," but that is no more than a flawless and seemingly effortless footnote to the odes of April and May. It should not be used to prove that his poetic career culminates in impersonal serenity and naturalistic harmony, any more than the final version of "Bright Star" should show that it concludes in an apotheosis of sexual desire. Nor can I agree with Paul de Man that the strange, broken, sometimes haunting poems to Fanny represent a significant new stage of Keats' development, towards which *Lamia* and *The Fall of Hyperion* are merely "works of transition."[22] Besides overvaluing these last poems, de Man brings to bear an extreme standard of self-consciousness ("an acute sense of threatened selfhood") which, however relevant to such continental crisis poets as Hölderlin and Nerval, should not be used to cast Keats' whole preceding *oeuvre* into inauthenticity. Whether Keats could ever have made great poetry out of so contingent and existential a sense of selfhood,

22. *John Keats: Selected Poetry*, pp. xxvii–xxxiv. "To ———" ("What can I do to drive away") is the only one of these poems that is even intermittently successful. Their diction often takes us back to the awkward love scenes of *Endymion*. Their attitude toward self-consciousness, which de Man considers a breakthrough, seems rather a reversion to the sense of crisis of such 1818 poems as the "Epistle to Reynolds." What Keats is repeatedly asking is "Where shall I learn to get my peace again?" ("To ———," line 30). He longs to return to philosophical impersonality and negative capability; he feels again that his consciousness has been "brought/Beyond its proper bound," that he has seen "too far into the sea" of actuality and spoiled his happiness.

which he often invokes and approaches, is an unanswerable question, but the forms of passage that he explored—in the dialectical patterns of flight and return of the odes, in the purgatorial quest-vision of *The Fall of Hyperion*—were their own authentic mode of self-discovery. This cannot be said of "To Autumn" which, even more so than the "Ode on Melancholy" (with which it was placed in the 1820 volume), is not a poem of quest and discovery so much as a concluding emblem of the tragic wisdom of the odes, the tragic knowledge that is also the subject of *The Fall of Hyperion*. That Keats in his last year of life had to prove that knowledge upon his pulses provides the story not with a new chapter but with an unbearably poignant epilogue, whose language cruelly echoes and renews the discoveries of the later poems:

> I wish for death every day and night to deliver me from these pains, and then I wish death away, for death would destroy even those pains which are better than nothing. Land and Sea, weakness and decline are great seperators, but death is the great divorcer for ever. When the pang of this thought has passed through my mind, I may say the bitterness of death is passed. (30 September 1820, 2:345)

Index

Wherever possible, a literary work is listed under the name of its author.